CW00801341

Churches of Herefordshire & their Treasures

Churches of Herefordshire & their Treasures

by
John Leonard

Logaston Press

LOGASTON PRESS
Little Logaston, Logaston,
Woonton, Almeley, Herefordshire HR3 6QH

First published by Logaston Press 2000
Copyright © text John Leonard 2000
Copyright © recent photographs John Leonard 2000

All rights reserved. No part of this publication
may be reproduced, stored in a retrieval system,
or transmitted, in any form or by any means,
electronic, mechanical, photocopying, recording
or otherwise, without the prior permission,
in writing of the publisher

ISBN 1 873827 91 1

Set in Times by Logaston Press
and printed in Great Britain by
Redwood Books, Trowbridge

Front cover illustrations:
Clockwise from top left: St. James, Cradley; St. Michael, Croft;
St. Catherine, Hoarwithy; St. Mary, Pembridge with detached bell-tower;
St. Lawrence, Stretton Grandison

For Marjorie

Those stately Structures which on Earth I view
To God erected, whether Old or New;
His Sacred Temples which the world adorn,
Much more than Mines of Ore or Fields of Corn,
My soul delight: How do they please mine Ey
When they are filled with Christian Family! . . .

The Arches built (like Hev'n) wide and high
Shew his Magnificence and Majesty
Whose House it is: With so much Art and Cost
The Pile is fram'd, the curious Knobs emboss'd
Set off with Gold, that me it more doth pleas
Than Princes Courts or Royal Palaces;
Great Stones pil'd up by costly Labors there
Like mountains carv'd by human skill appear;
Where Towers, Pillars, Pinnacles, and Spires
Do all concur to match my great Desires,
Whose Joy it is to see such Structures rais'd
To th'end my God and Father should be prais'd.

Thomas Traherne (1637-1674)
Rector of Credenhill

Contents

Acknowledgments

Once more I must sincerely thank Mrs. June Morgan of Photoworld Altrincham for her skill and patience in developing and printing the black-and-white photographs. I am also most indebted to Christopher Train CB and Professor Malcolm Thurlby for reading sections of the text, and for their helpful comments and advice. Many of the incumbents, wardens and parishioners of the churches visited have given generously of their time and knowledge, often providing insight into matters which would otherwise have escaped me. I am most grateful to Herr H. Wagner of REHAU for permission to visit the former church at Hom Green. I also thank Mr. Paul Mason, County Archivist at the Record Office, Hawarden, Flintshire, for giving me access to the notebooks of Sir Stephen Glynne; Dr. D.J. Craig, research Fellow for the British Academy Corpus of Anglo-Saxon Stone Sculpture, for help and advice concerning the sculpture at Llanveynoe; Mr. and Mrs. I. Ruell for permission to view and photograph the corbels at Peytoe Hall; Ken Hoverd for providing photographs of the old images reproduced; the staff of Hereford City Library for their help in locating many references. Andy Johnson and Ron Shoesmith of Logaston Press have made many helpful and constructive comments, for which I am very grateful. Above all, I thank my wife Marjorie, who accompanied me on many of my journeys to Herefordshire, and to whom the book is dedicated, for her never-failing love and encouragement.

All royalties from the sale of this book will be donated to the Herefordshire Historic Churches Trust.

Foreword

This is a wonderful book and very many people will be indebted to Dr. John Leonard for his clear, informative and affectionate work. He introduces us to the churches of Herefordshire, of all periods from a few fragmentary remains of Saxon craftsmanship to some distinguished 20th-century work. The historical introduction is masterly and clear, and most helpful in forming an understanding of the context in which these churches were built in this glorious and immensely varied landscape, from the bleak uplands of the Black Mountains to the rich pastures of the Wye Valley.

I have known Herefordshire for nearly forty years, and have been privileged to minister here since 1990, but I have found in this book much that has added to my knowledge, enlightened my understanding and increased my sense of wonder at the churches of this county. The treatment here is less academic than in the standard work of Pevsner, but equally learned. The descriptions of the churches, together with an excellent range of photographs and a user-friendly glossary of architectural terms, provide us with a most attractive guide, and will, I hope, inspire many to explore the churches of Herefordshire in greater detail, and with a better informed appreciation. Dr. Leonard encourages us by showing how many of the churches have been splendidly restored in recent years, a few by the Churches' Conservation Trust, but most by the love and care of parishioners. The churches of Herefordshire are now better looked after than ever before in their history, but they are, above all, holy places, places where parishioners and visitors alike encounter the presence of God, and respond to his love in worship and prayer before going out into the world to live to his praise and glory.

+ John

Outline map of Herefordshire, showing the areas into which the gazetteer of churches is divided, showing the location of 56 three- and two-starred churches (see p.xii)

Introduction

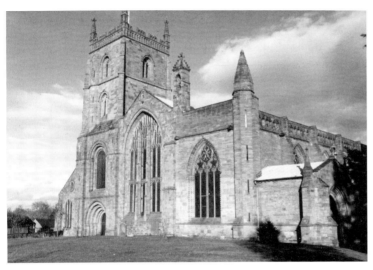

Fig. 1 The Priory of St. Peter and St. Paul, Leominster

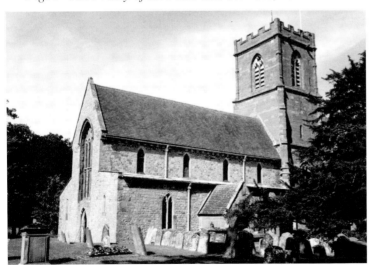

Fig. 2 St. Bartholomew, Much Marcle

With few exceptions, the churches of Herefordshire are not well-known outside the county: only Kilpeck and Shobdon are famous and are included in almost every book about English parish churches. In addition, the fine town churches of All Saints, Hereford, Ledbury, Leominster (Fig. 1), and Ross-on-Wye are much visited. The rest are ignored, except by enthusiasts. And even within the county, it is probably safe to say that only half a dozen or so are widely known outside their own parishes.

Why is this? It is true that for the most part the churches are not architecturally distinguished: there are no Norman churches to compare with Tewkesbury, no Perpendicular to compare with Lavenham. Yet the county possesses an abundance of attractive medieval village churches, and many of the villages are, of course, celebrated in their own right—Abbey Dore, Dilwyn, Eardisland, Eardisley, Madley, Much Marcle (Fig. 2), Pembridge, Weobley— all have excellent churches and attract increasing numbers of visitors. But for some, and I confess for me, it is the isolated churches of Herefordshire that constitute the greatest attraction, even more than the town or village churches.

Craswall (Fig. 3), Hentland, Llancillo, Llanrothal, Llanveynoe, Michaelchurch, Pixley, Richard's Castle, Sarnesfield, Stretford, Yatton—all these are situated on their own, with scarcely a cottage for company. They are oases of beauty and tranquillity, and are completely ignored by the standard books on English churches. And it is not only medieval churches which are excellent: Shobdon, (Fig. 4; 1752-56), Hoarwithy (Fig. 5; *c*.1885) and Brockhampton-by-Ross (1901-02) are renowned, for each in their time broke new ground in architectural development.

This book also draws attention to the treasures of the churches, and here Herefordshire comes into its own. The works of the so-called Herefordshire School of Norman carving, which extend far beyond the limits of the county, are the finest of their kind in English parish churches. Kilpeck (Fig. 6), Shobdon before its 'destruction', Eardisley and Castle Frome are the pinnacles of achievement. On a similarly exalted plane are the stained glass at Eaton Bishop, the screen at Aymestrey, the rood-loft at St. Margaret's (Fig. 7), the effigies at Much Marcle (Fig. 8). And few of the humblest churches are without lesser treasures to evoke wonder and delight.

After an historical survey of the origins of the church in Herefordshire, the first part of the book presents a summary of the treasures, dealing in turn with sculptures, fonts, memorials and monuments, stained glass etc. The second part is a gazetteer of medieval churches arranged in the various regions of the county, and of the post-Reformation churches arranged more or less chronologically. In compiling this book, I have visited virtually all the 158 medieval churches, all 12 churches from the 17th and 18th centuries, and most of the 69 Victorian ones. I have indicated by a starring system those churches which seem most rewarding to visit; as in the old Michelin guides, *** indicates a church worth a special journey; ** a church worth a detour; and * a church worth a visit *en passant*.

Specific sources of information about the churches are listed in the bibliography and

Fig. 3 St. Mary, Craswall

Fig. 4 St. John the Evangelist, Shobdon.
The north transept, pulpit and part of the sanctuary

Fig. 5 (left) St. Catherine, Hoarwithy   Fig. 6 (right) St. Mary and St David, Kilpeck. The south doorway

references at the end of the book; these exclude the many church guides which have often proved useful, and one or two booklets. General sources are few, for no books have been written confined to Herefordshire churches; but I have found the following to be extremely helpful. The oldest account is in the pages of Sir Stephen Glynne's notebooks; these are in the County Record Office at Hawarden, Flintshire, and have not yet been published. Glynne (1807-74) visited 139 churches in Herefordshire, and his records constitute an invaluable description of churches in Victorian times. The Royal Commission on Historical Monuments, England (RCHM) published in 1931-34 three large volumes describing architectural structures and furnishings and fittings prior to the end of the reign of Queen Anne (1714). Sir Nicolaus Pevsner's *Hereford-shire* in *The Buildings of England* series published in 1963 includes all the parish churches and is rightly regarded as the

Fig. 7 St. Margaret, St. Margaret's. The rood-loft

standard work on the subject. Finally, the *Transactions of the Woolhope Naturalists' Field Club* (TWNFC) are a mine of information on almost every topic related to Herefordshire churches; in particular, George Marshall wrote widely on the subject, and made many original observations. The *Transactions* may be inspected in the City of Hereford library.

I hope that this book will encourage both the residents of Herefordshire, and those who visit the county, to explore the treasures in our midst, and at the beginning of the third millennium, to appreciate anew the wonders of our Christian heritage.

Fig. 8 St. Bartholomew, Much Marcle.
The monument to Blanche Mortimer, Lady Grandison

The Origins of the Church in Herefordshire

Herefordshire presents a smiling, peaceful aspect, as befits one of England's most rural counties. Yet this masks a discordant past arising from its situation between England and Wales. Even during the early years of the Roman conquest of Britain, this was frontier territory: the Romans fought to subdue the Silures, the British tribe of southern Wales, conquering the whole area covered by the present county, and establishing a number of settlements, notably at Leintwardine (*Bravonium*), Kenchester (*Magnis*) and Weston-under-Penyard (*Ariconium*). Roman roads criss-crossed the county—Watling Street West, running northwards from Kenchester to Wroxeter (via Leintwardine and Church Stretton); a road south-east from Stretton Grandison towards Gloucester; and a road north of Hereford from Stretton Grandison westwards to Kenchester and on into mid-Wales. Stretches of all these roads are incorporated in present-day roads in the county.

But even in respect of its frontier position, Herefordshire is different from the other border counties—Cheshire and Shropshire—shires that are basically English, with Welsh influence largely confined to the western fringes. Herefordshire, on the other hand, bestrode the frontier: Offa's Dyke represented the western limit of Mercian power in the 8th century. Entering Herefordshire in the north-west and crossing the county diagonally to leave it at the extreme south-eastern corner near Welsh Bicknor, it bisected the county, roughly dividing it into English and Welsh zones. To the east of the dyke is English Herefordshire, to the west, Welsh; and south and west of the Wye—between the Wye and the Monnow— the Welsh language was predominant until well into the Middle Ages. This area was known by the English as Archenfield, by the Welsh as Erging, and it is here that there are the oldest references to Christianity. To the west of Erging, in the valleys of the Dore and upper Monnow, is the wild hilly country of Ewyas, bordering the Black Mountains.

The Welsh Heritage

The two hundred years following the Roman withdrawal (*c*.400)—the 5th and 6th centuries—are the most impenetrable for historical study. These two centuries witnessed the emergence of the Welsh language and the gradual spread of Christianity. The Romano-British population survived, and among them there was probably some Christian worship amidst a sea of paganism. It was in Erging that the first firm evidence of Christianity became established. Erging in these centuries was a petty Welsh kingdom; originally it probably extended east of the Wye in the region of Ross, for it takes its name from *Ariconium* (Weston-under-Penyard) which was, presumably, contained within the kingdom.[1] It appears that Erging had an extraordinary concentration of Christian foundations.[2] Much of the evidence for this derives from the *Book of Llandaff*, compiled in the 12th century, which pretends to consist of ancient records of the previous six hundred years. In fact, it is a baffling mixture of genuine records and forgeries designed to buttress the claims of the see of Llandaff. The Llandaff charters refer to 36 monasteries and a further 38 'churches' in the south-east of Wales (i.e. Erging and Gwent); west of Gwent there were only 11 foundations in the whole of Glamorgan. Included in the Llandaff charters is evidence that Welsh Bicknor and Llandinabo were founded in the late 6th century, and Garway c.615.

Fig. 9 St. Dubricius, Hentland

Some writers have presented evidence that Erging in the 6th century was a diocese presided over by St. Dubricius (sometimes known as St. Devereux). Dedications to him remain at parish churches in Ballingham, Hentland, Llanwarne, St. Devereux, and Whitchurch, all within Erging, the area particularly associated with the saint.[3] He is said to have been born in Madley, the son of Pepiau of the family of Brychan who ruled over Erging; the *Book of Llandaff* records that St. Dubricius 'retained two thousand clergy for seven successive years at Hentland (Fig. 9) ... in the study of divine and human wisdom'. He appointed St. Samson abbot of the monastery at Caldey Island, and he died on the Isle of Bardsey, c.545.[4] Other dedications in Archenfield to obscure Welsh saints include Llandinabo (St. Dinabo), Llangarron (St. Deinst), Sellack (St. Tysilio) and St. Weonard's (Welsh St. Gwenarth). Foy was originally the church of St. Moi.[5] Erging had its own bishop, possibly located at Welsh Bicknor or near Kenderchurch,[6] and this bishopric apparently persisted long after Erging had been absorbed into the Saxon kingdom of Mercia. Thus Archenfield still had its own (Welsh) bishop in 914 when he was captured by marauding Vikings.[7]

It is perhaps paradoxical that the other Welsh area of Herefordshire, Ewyas, is less obviously 'Welsh'. The Saxons settled here, as indicated in the Golden Valley names of Bacton, Turnastone and Vowchurch. The Normans arrived here even before the Conquest, and built a major stronghold at Ewyas Harold. Another Norman castle (though post-Conquest) was at Ewyas Lacy (now called Longtown) in the upper Monnow valley; here also are English place-names—Craswall, Walterstone—though there is also the church at Clodock (just south of Longtown) dedicated to St. Clydog. Like Pembrokeshire, and probably for the same reason (the influence of the Normans), this area is a 'little England beyond Wales'. Further north, major Norman castles at Clifford, Wigmore and Ludlow commanded the main river routes (the Wye, Lugg and Teme respectively) leading from Wales into England.

The Welsh legacy to the church in Herefordshire is rather tenuous, but nevertheless still present. The unusual dedications, the frequency of Welsh place-names (now sometimes anglicised), the isolation of some of the churches—all these factors combine to give an atmosphere different to that of 'English' Herefordshire. Indeed, the seclusion of some parish churches still presents a challenge to the visitor and inconvenience for the worshipper. Churches such as Garway, Hentland, Llancillo, Llanrothal, Llanveynoe and Welsh Bicknor are difficult to find—'Llanrothal (Fig. 10) occupies a site whose inaccessibility is typical of so many foundations of the Celtic church. It stands alone amid the meadows by the banks of the Monnow and can only be reached by a footpath'.[8] It may be that some of these isolated churches served villages which have since disappeared.

Fig. 10 St. John the Baptist, Llanthrothal

The Anglo-Saxon Heritage

The origins of the Church in 'English' Herefordshire had to await the conversion of the kingdom of Mercia. It was probably early in the 7th century that the Mercians began to push westwards into the area covered by the present counties of Shropshire and Herefordshire. North Shropshire was at that time part of the petty kingdom of the Wreocensaetan, while the southern part, and most of Herefordshire, constituted the kingdom of the Magonsaetan. It is said that the boundary between the Wreocensaetan and the Magonsaetan still demarcates the limits of the dioceses of Lichfield and Hereford in Shropshire. To the east lay the kingdom of the Hwicce (later centred on Worcester). The Magonsaetan appear to have been conquered by Penda, the pagan king of Mercia, in 628, and in 641 he defeated and slew the Christian King Oswald of Northumbria at the battle of Maserfelt, which some believe to have been where Oswestry (St. Oswald's Tree) now stands. In 655, Penda was slain in battle by Oswald's brother Oswy, his son and heir Peada was converted to Christianity, and the formal conversion of Mercia rapidly followed—Mercia was the last of the Anglo-Saxon kingdoms to embrace the faith.

The reign of King Peada was short, and he was succeeded as king of Mercia by his brother Wulfhere (659-675), and then by a second brother, Aethelred (675-704). A third brother, Merewalh, ruled only over the Magonsaetan, but he was a pivotal figure, for he was converted c.660 by Eadfrith, a missionary from the Celtic church of Northumbria. Merewalh then founded the first Christian church in 'English' Herefordshire at Leominster, placing Eadfrith in charge. Thus Leominster is an older Christian site than both Hereford and Wenlock, the latter being the oldest foundation in Shropshire, dating from 680, and where Merewalh's daughter, Mildburg, became the first abbess. Following the conversion of Merewalh, four missionary priests were sent from Northumbria to evangelise the pagan kingdom: Chad (Ceadda), Adda, Betti and Diuma. Chad, the first bishop of Mercia, was appointed in 669 by Wulfhere, and fixed his see at Lichfield.

The diocese of Lichfield initially covered an enormous area, but it appears that within 20 years of its foundation, the dioceses of Lindsey, Leicester, Worcester and Hereford were created out of it. It has traditionally been accepted that the first bishop of Hereford was Putta. He had been consecrated bishop of Rochester in 669, but when, seven years later, Kent was ravaged by the forces of Aethelred, it was believed that Putta fled and established his episcopal seat on the banks of the Wye at Hereford, and remained as bishop until his death in 688, when he was succeeded by Tyrhthel. However, in a scholarly review, Joe Hillaby persuasively demolished this scenario, and concluded that in fact Tyrhthel was the first authenticated bishop of Hereford, c.693, and that Putta sought sanctuary with Seaxwulf (who had succeeded Chad as bishop of Lichfield). Chad, according to Bede, 'granted him a church and a small estate, where he ended his life in peace'.[9]

Merewalh died in 685, and was succeeded as king of the Magonsaetan by his elder son Merchelm (685-690) and then by his younger son Mildfrith. Hillaby suggested that Mildfrith presided over the move

3

from Leominster to Hereford, thus establishing a diocese in the Roman tradition, based on Canterbury, rather than the Celtic church of Romano-British origin. This is not certain, however, and the move to Hereford may have come later.[10] But well before the reign of king Offa, (757-796), the kingdom of the Magonsaetan had been fully absorbed into Mercia, and the cathedral was certainly at Hereford. Hereford is a Saxon word meaning 'army ford', and in the 7th and early 8th centuries it was a frontier settlement, the area south of the Wye being Erging amd not in Mercian hands. It remained a frontier city, but Welsh annals record a battle of Hereford in 760 after which Erging seems to have come under Offa's control, becoming Archenfield.

Fig. 11 St. Mary, Marden

Yet although the Anglo-Saxons became dominant in Archenfield, the area remained culturally Welsh until the Norman Conquest or even after. Evidence for this is found in the very high frequency of Welsh place-names (in contrast to the rest of Herefordshire). 'Llangarron and Llanwarne are obvious Welsh medieval formations of a type which was once widespread in south Herefordshire. A number of parishes now bearing only a saint's name, such as Foy, St. Weonard's, Sellack and Clodock are Lanntiuoi, Lann Santguainerth, Lann Suluc, Merthirclitauc and the like in the charters preserved in the Book of Llandaff. In Kentchurch, Dewchurch, Kenderchurch and Michaelchurch, English -church has clearly replaced Welsh Llan-'.[11]

Towards the end of Offa's reign, in 794, Ethelbert, king of East Anglia, was treacherously murdered at Marden (Fig. 11), a few miles north of Hereford; he was said to have come there to seek the hand of the king's daughter in marriage. Offa was full of remorse and built a stone church at Hereford, dedicating it to Ethelbert, who after his death had been canonised. Thus Ethelbert became the patron saint of the cathedral of Hereford. The usual claims in those days for miraculous events led to a flourishing cult, which reached its apogee in the 12th century.

In the 8th century there were two minster churches in Hereford—the cathedral of St. Ethelbert and St. Guthlac's. Gelling has summarised evidence that the latter may have been an earlier foundation than the cathedral.[12] Indeed, archaeological excavations have suggested that St. Guthlac's may have been founded as early as the late 7th century—and perhaps this was the reason for the choice of Hereford as the bishop's seat.

One of the strange facts concerning Offa's Dyke is its disappearance between Bridge Sollers and the south-eastern corner of the county at Welsh Bicknor. It may well be that the river Wye took the place of the dyke between these two places; and that Archenfield, as a sort of client-state of the Mercian kings acted as a buffer-zone, preventing marauding Welsh tribesmen from invading Mercian territory.

In the 9th century, following the reign of Offa, Mercia was in decline, and Wessex finally emerged as the greatest kingdom of Anglo-Saxon times. Herefordshire was peripheral to the prolonged campaigns waged by Alfred the Great (871-899) against the Danes. Edward the Elder (899-924), Alfred's son and successor, formally annexed Mercia to the kingdom of Wessex by being proclaimed King of the Anglo-

Saxons. He re-organised Mercia into defensive counties, each with a *burh* as its administrative centre.[13] As a result of this, Hereford lost the northern half of the territory of the Magonsaetan to Shrewsbury, leaving the county rather small, with a very substantial area in which Welsh was culturally dominant. However, the *diocese* of Hereford remained unchanged, and to this day includes south Shropshire almost as far north as Shrewsbury; thus it largely retains the geographical area of the original Magonsaetan.

For the next 150 years, until 1066, the struggles for the mastery of England between the Anglo-Saxons and the Danes lay largely outside Herefordshire and have little to do with this story. During the Anglo-Saxon centuries, however, it is now apparent that many more churches were founded than was previously believed. Those that have survived (none in Herefordshire) are only a minuscule proportion of the total. The churches were nearly all built of wood, and so have perished without trace. Stone was used only for cathedrals and monasteries until *c*.950, but thereafter was used increasingly for some parish churches. But it was not until a hundred years later that large-scale building of local churches in stone was undertaken.

The organisation of the church in Saxon times was relatively loose. Originally, a number of minsters arose, usually serving a very wide area, and staffed by a variable number of canons. In Herefordshire, Bromyard, Ledbury and Leominster are examples of such minster churches, and so is the little-known church of Stoke Edith (see p.181). In the later Saxon centuries, many village churches were founded by laymen, with perhaps only a tenuous relationship with the local bishop. These churches were often regarded by the local thane as part of his personal property, almost as a capital investment; for ownership of a church increasingly brought in revenue in the form of tithes.

What is the Anglo-Saxon legacy to the church in Herefordshire? In terms of buildings, there is virtually nothing; no Saxon churches survive, though some suspect that part of the fabric of various churches may retain some Saxon work. It is generally accepted that the north-east corner of the nave at Kilpeck antedates the Norman conquest (though Thurlby has recently cast doubt on this) and there is evidence of Saxon building at Peterstow (p.164).[14] A recent writer in the *Herefordshire Archaeological News* suggested that several churches in the Ewyas Lacy (Longtown) lordship may conceal Saxon remains, mentioning particularly Walterstone, Rowlstone, Llancillo and Clodock; this, however, is speculation. At the present time, apart from the vestiges at Kilpeck and Peterstow, the sole *material* legacy of the Anglo-Saxons is the sculptural remnants described in the next chapter. But of course the religious and political legacy is huge, for the cathedral, the city, the diocese and the county are all of Anglo-Saxon origin.

Romanesque Carving

Herefordshire is unrivalled amongst English counties for the quality of the Romanesque sculpture in its parish churches. This is because of the output of the so-called Herefordshire School which flourished for about 30 years from *c*.1130. But the work of the School was preceded by a number of works of varying quality; and it is increasingly recognised that the products of the Herefordshire School are not confined to the county but can be found over a wide area of adjacent shires, from mid-Wales in the west to Warwickshire in the east.

Fig. 12 St. Beuno and St. Peter, Llanveynoe. Anglo-Saxon carving of the Crucifixion

Anglo-Saxon and early Norman carving (to *c*.1140)

The oldest work of Christian sculpture in Herefordshire is the four-feet-tall Crucifixion stone at Llanveynoe (Fig. 12). It is worth visiting this remote, beautifully situated little church in the Olchon valley, close to the Welsh border, to see this elementary yet moving work. The stone, now reset in the south wall of the nave, portrays Christ with the arms outstretched at the level of the shoulders and the palms outwards; the legs are extended side by side, with the knees slightly bent and the feet turned to the right.[1] Its age is uncertain: an 11th-century origin was suggested by the Royal Commission on Historical Monuments, but it may well be older than that.[2] The style is rude and primitive, and such work in so isolated an area might have been produced at any time from the 9th century onwards. Nash-Williams thought it was from the 9th or 10th centuries. Also in the south wall of the church is a smaller slab carved with the lower part of a cross and inscribed 'Haerdur fecit crucem' (Haerdur made this cross). This was dug up by quarrymen in 1899 just outside the churchyard and is thought to date from the same period.[3]

Several churches have pieces of Saxon or early Norman carving now embedded in their structure. The finest is at Acton Beauchamp where a lintel over the doorway into the tower is probably fashioned from the shaft of an Anglo-Saxon cross (Fig. 13). It shows scrollwork inhabited with a bird and beasts, and is believed to date from the 9th century. At Cradley in the north wall of the

Fig. 13 St. Giles, Acton Beauchamp.
Fragment of Anglo-Saxon cross-shaft used as a lintel

tower is a section of an Anglo-Saxon frieze with crockets.

More sophisticated, though not necessarily much later, is the carving of St. Peter with his key above the south doorway at Bromyard (Fig. 14). To the right of the figure is a cross carved in relief, very similar to the cross above the Saxon north doorway at Stanton Lacy, Shropshire. This has been dated to the last decade of the 11th century by Gethyn-Jones.[4]

Above a Saxon or Norman doorway is placed a horizontal stone, the lintel, and the space between this and the rounded arch above is known as the tympanum. Both lintel and tympanum were commonly enriched with carving, at first simple geometric patterns, but later involving increasingly complex representations until the peak of artistry is seen in the work of the mid-12th-century Herefordshire School. The lintel is commonly composed of a single stone, but at Chepstow Castle (built as early as 1067-70) a lintel over the entrance to the tower is composed of three pieces joggled together; the tympanum above is made of rectangular blocks set lozenge-wise, and already carved with a sunken-star pattern.[5] These features are later found in several churches in Herefordshire. At Hatfield (Fig. 15) and Much Dewchurch, the lintel is constructed of three stones articulated together to form a 'T' pattern; this may indicate a date before 1100. Above the lintel, the tympanum is composed of stones set either diagonally as at Chepstow (Hatfield) or horizontally (Much Dewchurch, Hampton Bishop). The lintel at Hampton Bishop is carved with a shell pattern above and a sunken star or saltire cross pattern below.

At Byton in the north-west of the county the tympanum (Fig. 16) has been reset into the south wall of the Victorian church; it depicts in shallow relief a lamb with a cross (the Agnus Dei) in a circle, and on either side two large knot motifs; the latter is common in Celtic art — in Herefordshire it is found on a re-used stone built into a buttress at Llangarron.[6] The Byton tympanum is thought to date from *c.*1080-90.

Fig. 14 St. Peter, Bromyard.
Figure of St. Peter above the
south doorway, probably
Anglo-Saxon

Fig. 15 St. Leonard, Hatfield.
Early Norman lintel comprised of three stones joggled together

Fig. 16 St. Mary, Byton. The Norman tympanum

Fig. 17 St. Andrew, Bredwardine. Lintel over the north doorway

Fig. 18 (above) St. Andrew, Bredwardine. Lintel over the south doorway and Fig. 19 (below) as drawn in 1850

Further early Romanesque carving in Herefordshire is seen in a set of six capitals removed from the east presbytery of the cathedral, and now displayed there. Each capital is carved on two faces with narrative scenes, one of which represents the Harrowing of Hell. Most of these capitals are carved in a robust Anglo-Saxon style, but two display bulky and solid figures and are more Romanesque, thought to derive from continental sources.[7] It had been thought that these capitals dated from the late 11th century, but as they were an integral part of the building of the cathedral, Thurlby has argued that they should be dated to *c*.1115.[8]

In a small area in the Wye valley in the west of the county are three churches with carved sandstone lintels—Bredwardine, Letton and Willersley. Letton is about 1½ miles east of Willersley, and about the same distance north of Bredwardine. The three lintels show striking similarities, and are almost certainly the work of the same local craftsman.[9]

There are two lintels at Bredwardine: above the south doorway (Figs. 18 and 19) the lintel shows a central rosette, flanked by sunken stars and variants. Carving extends to the underside of the lintel and to the cushion capitals on each side. The lintel of the north doorway (Fig. 17) has a symmetrical pattern: a pillar at each side, within which are two large rosettes, and in the centre two primitive figures under arches. One of these figures appears to be human, the other animal, but there has been much inconclusive debate about their identity.

At Letton (Fig. 20) the lintel has a central large rosette; to the left are two stars in circles, and to the right a more complex pattern of smaller circles and crosses. In two of these circles are very small figures of heads (above) and animals (below). The lintel at Willersley (Fig. 21) shows variations on the same theme: a large rosette, stars and circles, concentric squares and a fish-scale pattern.

Both Bredwardine and Letton churches include herringbone masonry and extensive use of tufa, signs accepted of early Norman work (late 11th or early 12th century—p.75). Willersley church, now a private dwelling, does not show these features, and may be a little later. It is thought that the lintels at Bredwardine and Letton were inserted after the main structure had been built, and it may be that the date of the lintels is the date of the foundation of the church at Willersley. Gethyn-Jones suggests 1100-1115.

Chevron, or zigzag, decoration is everywhere the hallmark of Norman carving, and is seen from about 1100 onwards. It is found in external and internal arches, or above windows, and at Letton it runs vertically in the lintel, extending to the shaft below. At Letton also the sunken star ornament is present in the outer order of the arch above the tympanum. Chevron decoration is frequently found above Norman doorways, as at Peterchurch (Fig. 22), Thornbury and Upper Sapey; at Middleton-on-the-Hill, the lintel is made of three stones articulated together to form a 'T' pattern, as at Hatfield; the sunken star pattern is found on the imposts. At Wolferlow the arch has an outer band of the sunken star pattern.

Finally, at Yatton there is a tympanum exhibiting the Tree of Life motif (Fig. 23). The doorway at Yatton has three orders of shafts; the inner one has corbels supporting the tympanum, carved with the chevron pattern

Fig. 20 St. John the Baptist, Letton.
Lintel over the south doorway

Fig. 21 St. Mary Magdalene, Willersley.
Lintel over the south doorway

Fig. 22 (left) St. Peter, Peterchurch. The Norman south doorway
Fig. 23 (right) Yatton chapel. The south doorway

running vertically (as at Kilpeck and Letton). The two outer orders have nook-shafts—the inner one on the east side has a spiral pattern running downwards. The capitals of the outer orders are carved with volutes and semicircles. In the tympanum is a crude Tree of Life within a pelleted border; comparison with Kilpeck (Fig. 31) shows the tremendous leap forward which the sculptor(s) of the Herefordshire School made. Above the doorway is a round arch enriched with chevron decoration. The date of Yatton has been judged to be *c*.1135-40.

The Herefordshire School

Until the fourth decade of the 12th century, there is nothing specially striking about the quality of Romanesque sculpture in Herefordshire as compared with other counties; on the whole it is work of a pedestrian, if competent, character. But around 1130, a giant stride forward was made—nothing seen before then leads one to expect the great flowering of sculpture that followed.

Before considering the evolution of the style, an attempt should be made to summarise the influences and the motifs displayed in these carvings. The style is rooted in Anglo-Saxon art, especially that of the Winchester School which flourished in the 10th and 11th centuries.[10] In this style, human figures are usually slender and elongated, the height being accentuated by lines depicting fluttering folds of drapery.[11] There is much acanthus leaf decoration, and often plant-scrolls inhabited with birds. But Anglo-Saxon art itself was subject to Scandinavian influences, exemplified by flat interlacing motifs, human, animal and floral, often so stylised as to appear almost abstract.[12] The Ringerike was a Scandinavian style which evolved towards the end of the 10th century, often depicting an animal interwoven with bands of ribbon, and using foliage designs—such as a snake entangled in asymmetrical but well-balanced foliage. The Urnes, another Norse style, often displays an animal enmeshed in thin, rope-like strands of foliage ending in very small leaves; sometimes there may be a monster with a snake's body but with a foreleg and a second leg instead of a tail. Other influences which have been identified come from western France and Italy; where human figures are bulky and solid, the influence of Norman Romanesque may be dominant.

Certain themes recur regularly in the work of the school. Birds abound, especially birds of prey in the act of attacking their victim. Human figures are often clad with tightly-fitting garb, with segmental folds, and many show trousered figures, either saints or warriors.

It is apparent that multifactorial influences were at work—from England, France, Scandinavia and Italy—and that these were blended by the genius of the sculptors into a recognisable school. In his paper published as early as 1918, Marshall recognised the links not only between the lintels at Bredwardine, Letton and Willersley, but also the features common to the tympana at Shobdon, Rowlstone and St. Giles', Hereford; and between the tympana at Brinsop and Ruardean. He recognised similarities between the workman-

Fig. 24 St John the Evangelist, Shobdon. The Arches

ship at Kilpeck, Fownhope, Aston and Stretton Sugwas; and presciently concluded that 'many of them emanated from the same guild of masons, and in some instances were the handiwork of the same sculptor'. Zarnecki suggests that it was Sir Arthur Clapham in 1936 who first recognised the sculpture in Herefordshire as a 'definite local school'.[13] The elucidation of the probable course of events was first outlined by Zarnecki, in his unpublished PhD thesis for the University of London. In an excellent recent review of the work of the School, Thurlby linked the various sites with the patronage of great Norman families; thus the Mortimers, through the steward Oliver de Merlimond, appear to have been responsible for Shobdon, Aston, Brinsop, Rock, Ribbesford and Alveley; the de Lacys for Rowlstone, St. Giles Hospital, and Castle Frome; the de Baskervilles for Eardisley and Stretton Sugwas; Fitz Baderon for Ruardean and Monmouth.

At the time of the Domesday survey (1087), the manor of Shobdon, in north-west Herefordshire, was held by Ralph de Mortimer; and early in the 12th century, Ralph de Mortimer gave it to his steward Oliver de Merlimond, who built a castle, and founded an abbey and a church. Around 1125, de Merlimond went on a pilgrimage to Santiago de Compostela. Zarnecki has argued that in his pilgrimage to Spain, de Merlimond took a mason and a sculptor with him, and on their journey through France they were profoundly impressed by the Romanesque carving which they witnessed. Particularly impressive is the close resemblance between the tympanum at Parthenay-le-Vieux (Deux Sèvres) with those at Brinsop and Stretton Sugwas; the themes of a figure on horseback slaying the dragon and Samson struggling with the lion at Parthenay-le-Vieux are closely followed in the Herefordshire churches.

On the return of de Merlimond's party to England, Shobdon church was built, and was consecrated in 1131 by Robert de Bethune, bishop of Hereford. It was extensively decorated with an excellence never seen before in this area. It was probably a small church, but, like Kilpeck, it was adorned with the most astonishing sculpture, the first extensive work of what is now recognised as the Herefordshire School. Apart from the font, these carvings are now re-erected as a folly in the park, the so-called Shobdon Arches, being transferred there in 1751. The Arches comprise the original chancel arch, and the north and south doorways with their tympana (Fig. 24). Two hundred and fifty years of exposure to the weather have wreaked havoc, and to prevent further deterioration the group has recently been treated with a preservative.

Indeed, the carvings are now so worn that only a poor impression can be gained of their quality. Fortunately, G.R. Lewis published in 1852 *The Ancient Church of Shobdon* containing 19 lithographs of the ruins; these greatly help to recapture the splendour of the sculpture.

The chancel arch has three orders, the inner and outer with chevron ornament, the middle with a roll flanked by an 'arrow-head' motif.[14] The shafts are much enriched—on the right with rings connected by grotesque heads and enclosing doves or other birds and beasts, and with monsters in interlacing vine-ornament; and on the left with scrolls and birds and a series of trousered warriors. The capitals of the outer shafts are carved with spirals, leaves, dragons and vine-scroll.

The doorway on the east (the former south doorway) is semicircular and has three orders—the outer has a scrolled band terminating in a grotesque head, the middle a series of beasts and human figures, probably zodiacal signs, and the inner a series of animals and birds now almost weathered away. The outer jambs have chevron ornament, the inner shafts have varying interlace; the capitals are carved with beasts, standing figures, scrolls or volutes, and a winged dragon. The tympanum (now set over an adjoining opening) depicts Christ in Glory (Fig. 25) and is very similar to that at Rowlstone.

The doorway on the west (the former north doorway) is generally similar—the outer order has four intertwined snakes, the voussoirs of the middle order each show a beast, and the inner order has interlace. The outer jambs have chevron ornament, and the inner shafts have interlace on the east and trousered figures on the west. The capitals are carved with a dragon, three small figures, and scrolls. The tympanum

The Arches, Shobdon: Fig. 25 (left) Defaced tympanum showing Christ in Glory;
Fig. 26 (right) Defaced tympanum showing the Harrowing of Hell

(now set over an adjoining arch) is carved with a Harrowing of Hell, with Christ in the middle, souls in limbo on the right, and two standing figures on the left (Fig 26). The theme is treated very differently in the much later font at Eardisley.

The Shobdon font, now replaced in the church having been used as a garden ornament, is described on p.19.

From Shobdon, it is likely that the team moved to Leominster. In 1121, the priory there was refounded as a cell of Reading Abbey, which Henry I had just founded following the death of his son at sea in the Channel. The church was quickly rebuilt, and the decoration of the capitals at the west door was entrusted to the Shobdon team in *c*.1130; the most unusual feature of this doorway is that it is decorated both internally and externally.

The four interior capitals show (from south to north): a pattern of single interlaced strands; a bearded human mask, from whose mouth issue vine-scrolls with bunches of grapes; a rather similar animal mask, again with vine-scrolls and grapes; a pattern of intersecting circles becoming more complex on the east.[15]

External capitals on the west doorway of Leominster Priory:
Fig. 27 (left) A dove in interlaced foliage; Fig. 28 (right) A stooping man cutting foliage

External capitals on the west doorway of Leominster Priory:
Fig. 29 (left) A malevolent serpent; Fig. 30 (right) A pair of lions

Above this last capital, the abacus is carved with confronted volutes, and also a small (six inches long) carving of Samson slaying a lion—almost an exact miniature of the tympanum at Stretton Sugwas.

The outside capitals are more varied. There are three shafts on each side of the doorway, and each capital has two faces meeting at a right-angle. Looking at the doorway, from left to right they are as follows: a pair of doves (Fig. 27), in interlaced foliage; two low stooping human figures (Fig. 28) thought to be reapers cutting foliage; a pair of malevolent serpents (Fig. 29), mouths wide open; three rows of acanthus leaves and buds, as seen in Corinthian capitals; a pair of lions (Fig. 30); strands of foliage held together by bands at the waist. High up in the west window above the door are two more capitals depicting, on the left, a series of rings inhabited by doves and between two human masks, and on the right a bird of prey attacking a dove.

From Leominster, the team may have moved to Kilpeck, where in 1134 a Benedictine priory was established as a cell of St. Peter's Abbey, Gloucester. The extraordinary carving, on which Kilpeck's distinction rests, is displayed in four areas: externally, the south doorway (Fig. 6, p.xiii), the west window, and the corbel-table, and internally, the chancel arch.

Fig. 31 The west doorway at Kilpeck, showing the capitals
on the shafts, the lintel, the tympanum with a Tree of Life
and the arches above

Above the doorway, there is vertical zigzag on the lintel, and above this the tympanum (Fig. 31) is carved with a symmetrical Tree of Life, in the form of a vine-scroll with grapes. The tympanum is enclosed by an arch of three orders, the inner one of zigzag set at right-angles; the middle one of beakhead and fantastic animal designs, with an angel at the apex; and the outer

one in the form of a chain of nine rings, each ring containing a bird or monster or one of the signs of the zodiac; at each end of the outer order is an inverted dragon's head. Both jambs of the doorway are carved with intertwining serpents, but the adjacent shafts are treated differently: on the west are two elongated men with peaked caps and trousers (Fig. 32); on the east, complex foliage patterns, with a pair of doves at the base. The capitals of the shafts show, on the west a pair of dragons, and on the east a grotesque head.

The rather wide west window has nook-shafts on each side, decorated with interlace which is continued in varying forms all round the arch above the window; on the capitals of the shafts are strange heads (said to be 'green men'—pagan fertility symbols), and at the bases scrolls. At the centre of the west front, and from the angles of the nave, are dragons' heads, reminiscent of Scandinavian art.[16]

All round the church is the corbel-table, festooned with an amazing array of carvings, mostly home-spun and irreverent: indeed the only ones with a religious theme are two representations of the Agnus Dei. The carvings are lively, giving the impression of being direct observations from nature, not copied from books.[17] There are many human caricatures, two rams, a dog and a hare (Fig. 33), a fertility symbol, two wrestlers, serpents and many others. Thurlby points out that understanding of these sculptures is greatly enhanced by the *Bestiary* (the Book of Beasts); this work of Greek origin was translated into Latin in the 5th century, and the oldest extant manuscript dates from *c*.1120. It describes the nature and habits of many creatures, real or mythical.

From the humour of the corbel-table, one turns to the sanctity of the chancel-arch. On each side are three religious figures, usually identified as apostles, and indeed the middle figure on the left is clearly St. Peter with his key (Fig. 34). The figures, which are said to be the earliest pillar figures in England, are in some contrast with those elongated ones on the church doorway: these are much more solid and stocky, with rather heavy folds of drapery; in each figure, the left hand is holding a book, while the right holds a variety of objects, doubtless of symbolic significance. The arch itself is bedecked with zigzag, one order of which is at right-angles to the wall. Beyond, in the rib-vault of the apse, there is a central boss carved with four animals' heads.

Fig. 32 Elongated figure with peaked cap and trousers on the west jamb of the south doorway at Kilpeck

Shobdon (*c*.1125-30), Leominster (*c*.1130-35), Kilpeck (*c*.1135-40)—the stage was now prepared for an extensive series of works which extended far beyond the boundaries of Herefordshire. However, within the county, the sculptors of the school executed work on the tympana at Aston (which apparently antedated Shobdon),

Fig. 33 Dog and hare on a corbel table, Kilpeck

14

Fig. 34 The figure of
St. Peter on the
chancel arch at
Kilpeck

Fig. 35 St. Giles, Aston. The tympanum showing the Agnus Dei
flanked by a griffin and an ox

Rowlstone, St. Giles (Hereford), Stretton Sugwas, Brinsop and Fownhope, and
the fonts at Shobdon, Orleton, Castle Frome and Eardisley.

At Aston, the subject of the tympanum is the Agnus Dei, the Lamb of God
(Fig. 35)—said to be, next to the Cross, the most frequent subject of Norman
tympana in England.[18] The Lamb is shown supporting the cross on the right
forefoot, within a circular medallion carved with saltire crosses; on either side,
with paws resting on the circle, is a griffin on the left, and an ox on the right.
Around the central subject is an outer band of animals and foliage. The whole is
set under a Norman arch much enriched with chevron decoration. On either side
of the tympanum, the imposts are carved with dragons (on the left) and foliage
(on the right). The quality of the carving is not so sophisticated as at Kilpeck;
this is considered an early carving of the sculptor who later worked at Shobdon
and Kilpeck..[19]

Inside Aston church is a stoup carved with a lion pursued by a dragon; this
is now upside down, but is also thought
to be the work of the sculptor of the
tympanum.[20]

Fig. 36 St. Peter, Rowlstone.
The tympanum of Christ in Glory

At Rowlstone, the south doorway
has one order of shafts, and on the capitals and abaci are birds and intertwining
foliage. There is also the face of a green
man, with foliage emerging from his
mouth. Around the arch is a roll
moulding and a band of rosettes. The
tympanum (Figs. 36, 37) is outstanding,
and well preserved—in contrast to the
sadly weathered examples of the same
subject at Shobdon and St. Giles
Hospital, Hereford (Figs. 25, 39). All
three tympana represent Christ in Glory,

15

Fig. 37 Rowlstone: detail of the tympanum

and are very similar—the work, perhaps, of the same craftsman. Christ is portrayed seated, with a cruciform halo, the right hand raised in benediction, the left on a book resting on his left knee, the knees apart but the feet together. Around him is an oval mandorla supported by four flying angels with their heads downwards.

The capitals of the chancel arch at Rowlstone are richly adorned with carving. Facing each other across the entry into the chancel is a pair of birds enmeshed in foliage. Lateral to these birds, on the north is an angel and a bishop and on the south two figures which are upside down (Fig. 38); one of these is an angel, and the other may be St. Peter. It is not certain whether the inversion of the figures is deliberate or accidental; in a church dedicated to St. Peter, could this be a reference to the traditional story of Peter's crucifixion upside down? There is, however, no evidence of Peter's symbol, the key. Above the figures are a row of confronted volutes, and a further row of birds. These repeated representations of birds, on the doorway and the chancel arch, must be significant: some authorities have described them as doves, others as cocks—if they are the latter, they recall Peter's thrice-repeated denial of Jesus.

In the north wall of St. Giles Hospital, Hereford, in St. Owen Street, is reset a Norman tympanum from the former chapel; it is very weathered, but depicts Christ in Glory, supported by angels (Fig. 39), and is very similar to the tympana at Rowlstone and Shobdon.

The tympanum at Stretton Sugwas (Fig. 40) is one of the prime works of the Herefordshire School. It is now reset above a doorway in the north wall of the nave, and has been thought to be by the same carver as the tympanum at Brinsop nearby and the fonts at Eardisley and Castle Frome. The subject is Samson astride a lion, forcing open its jaws; the lion is powerfully

Fig. 38 One of capitals of the chancel arch at Rowlstone with a row of birds above, volutes in the middle and a dove and inverted figures below

constructed, and Samson's drapery and his mane are carved in rope-like coils;[21] beneath the animal is cable ornament. The hood-mould over the tympanum rests on two heads. Like the tympanum at Brinsop, this work is related to a similar production at Parthenay-le-Vieux, Deux-Sèvres;[22] and as already noted, a miniature version of this subject can be seen inside the west doorway at Leominster.

Set into the north wall at Brinsop is the magnificent tympanum (Fig. 41) of St. George on his charger, with the dragon below (*cf.* Ruardean). At both Brinsop and Ruardean, St. George is depicted as a mounted horseman with flying cloak — as noted above, the very animated composition is remarkably similar to one at Parthenay-le-Vieux. Above the tympanum a series of radiating voussoirs are carved with a variety of subjects, including lions, a bird, human figures, angels and two fish. Above the doorway leading into the vestry is further carving in the voussoirs of the archway consisting of an angel flying down, human figures, animals, etc. (*cf.* Shobdon) (Fig. 42); Zarnecki points out that this method of decorating arches was especially popular in western France.

There is further Romanesque carving at Brinsop: in the north chapel is a small section of an interlaced frieze; and near the south doorway is a panel built into the wall showing doves enclosed by rings, with the heads of beasts between.[23]

At Fownhope, the tympanum (Fig. 43), previously above a doorway, is now mounted inside, on the west wall of the nave. It used to be outside, and was so described in Methuen's *Little Guide* in 1917. It has been dated to *c*.1140. At first sight, it appears to represent the figures of the Virgin and Child seated frontally, the Virgin's feet rather far apart, with the hands of both mother and child raised in an act of benediction. On either side are a bird and a winged lion, presumably the

Fig. 41 (right) St. George, Brinsop.
The tympanum of St. George and the dragon

Fig. 39 St. Giles Hospital, Hereford. The defaced tympanum showing Christ in Glory

Fig. 40 St. Mary Magdalene, Stretton Sugwas. The tympanum of Samson astride a lion

Fig. 42 (right) Drawing made in 1850 of the voussoirs above the doorway into the vestry at Brinsop

symbols of St. John and St. Mark. The animals are enclosed by long stalks with a few leaves, and in the lower left corner is a bunch of grapes. There are several unusual features in the iconography here: the 'Virgin', most unusually, has a cruciform halo (normally reserved for Christ or God the Father) ; it is also most unusual for the Virgin to be depicted with her hand raised in blessing. It has been postulated that the seated figure represents not the Virgin, but God the Father, with the Son on his knee, and that the figure of a Dove representing the Holy Spirit, may have been carved above on a voussoir now lost—this would mean that the whole was a representation of the Trinity, a startling suggestion![24] [25] In fact this suggestion is not new; for in 1846 Sir Stephen Glynne (see p.xiii) visited Fownhope and wrote: 'In the tympanum is some curious

Fig. 43 St. Mary, Fownhope. The tympanum with St. Mary and Child, or is it a representation of the Trinity?

Fig. 44 (above) The font at Shobdon, with lions around the stem

Fig. 45 (right) St. George, Orleton. The font with figures of the apostles, each holding a book

The font at St. Mary Magdalene, Eardisley: Fig. 46 (left) shows the Harrowing of Hell;
Fig. 47 (right) two knights fighting

sculpture which appears to represent the Holy Trinity – also the figures of a bird amidst twining foliage and dragons'.

There are four fonts in Herefordshire attributed to the Herefordshire School—Shobdon, Orleton, Castle Frome and Eardisley. The first two are relatively inferior products, but the last two are outstanding, and can claim to be the finest Norman fonts in all England. At Shobdon (Fig. 44), the font has four lions around the stem, said by Boase to be larger versions of the beasts on the capital at Leominster. At Orleton the limestone font is bucket-shaped and sculpted with the figures of nine bearded apostles separated by a Norman arcade. It is not known why there are only nine apostles: the inferior font at Hereford Cathedral has all 12. Of the nine apostles, only St. Peter is identified by his symbol—a key. All the figures hold a book in their left hand (Fig. 45), and some also hold a short sword or staff.[26] Also in Orleton is a fragment of a carved shaft displaying a dragon which appears to be about to bite a serpent or another dragon.

At Eardisley, the font, although of outstanding quality, has posed problems of interpretation. Between the knot patterns on the stem and the plaiting around the rim of the bowl are a series of figures and scenes. Many different explanations have been offered, but there is now a consensus that the main theme is the Harrowing of Hell. This is a well-known motif in Romanesque art but Eardisley is the only font in England depicting the subject. Christ is shown rescuing a small figure from hell (Fig. 46); on his right is another figure holding a book, which is thought to represent God the Father; on Christ's shoulder is a dove, representing the Holy Spirit. Thus all three Persons of the Trinity are involved in this act of redemption. What then are we to make of the large lion? And what about the two knights fighting (Fig. 47)? Theirs is a very dramatic action—one has a sword raised high, while the other knight plunges a spear in his opponent's leg. A local theory maintains that the knights are Ralph de Baskerville, lord of the manor of Eardisley in the early 12th century, and his father-in-law Lord Drogo. Ralph challenged his father-in-law to mortal combat to settle a dispute over land, and the latter died of his wounds. After this tragedy, Ralph sought pardon from the Pope, and later became a monk at Gloucester. Was the font commissioned by Ralph to commemorate these events? And does the lion represent evil, from which Ralph is being saved?[27] It is a persuasive suggestion, impossible to prove. But if the theory is true, what are we to make of the Monmouth slab (see below), which also shows two knights fighting?

The font at St. Michael, Castle Frome: Fig. 48 (left) shows the Baptism of Christ;
Fig. 49 (right) The Man (or angel) of St. Matthew holding his Gospel

Fig. 50 (top) St. Andrew, Bridge Sollers: a feline head
and dragons on the west impost of the south doorway

Fig. 51 (lower) St. Mary the Virgin, Bishop's Frome:
sculpture with a grotesque head and ?foliage

The superb font at Castle Frome is possibly the latest work of the School in the county. The font stands on three crouching figures, of which only one retains its head; these are thought to show Italian influence, and may symbolise demons crushed by the power of the Church. Around the rim of the bowl there is plaiting, and on the stem interlacing. In between are carved the Baptism of Christ (Fig. 48), together with the symbols of the four evangelists. The small figure of Christ is represented in the Jordan, with fish swimming on each side; on Jesus' right is a large figure of John the Baptist and above is the Hand of God the Father, with the dove representing the Holy Spirit. Moving round the font there is the Man (or Angel) of St. Matthew holding his gospel (Fig. 49), the Eagle of St. John, the Lion of St. Mark and the Bull of St. Luke. Two doves fill the remaining space, perhaps symbolising purity after baptism.[28]

Two other churches in Herefordshire have carvings which are probably related to the Herefordshire School. At Bridge Sollers, the imposts on the doorway show, on the left,

Fig. 52 Corbels at Peytoe Hall

the head of a cat with two dragons' heads issuing from its mouth (Fig. 50), and on the right a single dragon. And at Bishop's Frome, in the south wall of the chancel externally, on each side of the priest's door, are two slabs of carving terminating the string courses; on the left a grotesque head with a foliage pattern (Fig. 51), and on the right a winged creature with a twisted body. These slabs had not been noted by the Royal Commission on Historical Monuments, nor by Pevsner; but it is interesting to record that they had been noticed by Sir Stephen Glynne, who visited the church on 26th April, 1873. He wrote, 'On the south (of the chancel) are three Norman windows and part of an original horizontal band with grotesque animal figures'. A fragment from the Norman font from Edvin Loach, now stored at the English Heritage stone store at Atcham near Shrewsbury, has recently been described.[29] It shows a series of rather worn medallions, two of which are inhabited with birds. Finally, at Peytoe Hall (a quarter of a mile from Wigmore Abbey) I was shown two mutilated carvings which had been stored in the loft (Fig. 52). I sent photographs of these, and of the Bishop's Frome sculptures, to Professor Thurlby, who agrees that they could possibly be attributed to the Herefordshire School.[30]

Works attributed to the Herefordshire School outside the county
The team responsible for the work at Shobdon and Kilpeck was in demand over a wide area of the West Midlands and Welsh Marches—so much so that in a recent review, Zamecki suggested that it would be more appropriate to name it the School of the Welsh Marches.[31] The works generally attributed to the School are as follows:

1. Chaddesley Corbett (Worcestershire) font, a fine work portraying four dragons apparently swallowing serpents.
2. Stottesdon (Shropshire) font, also excellent, with medallions containing the Agnus Dei, beasts and a human figure.
3. Ruardean (Gloucestershire) tympanum, with St. George slaying the dragon, very similar to, but less accomplished than, the work at Brinsop.
4. Llanbadarn Fawr (Radnorshire) tympanum, showing a rather primitive Tree of Life and various animals etc.
5. Ribbesford (Worcestershire) tympanum, depicting an archer, birds and an animal.
6. Pedmore (Worcestershire) tympanum, with a fine representation of Christ in Majesty, as at Shobdon, Rowlestone and St. Giles Hospital, Hereford.
7. Romsley (Worcestershire) tympanum, a poorer rendering of the same subject.
8. Billesley (Warwickshire) slab, discovered in 1980 behind a skirting board in the church, probably part of a tympanum,[32] showing a dove and a trousered figure typical of the School.
9. Monmouth slab , found in the wall of a shop in the town, and now in the Monmouth Museum. Two knights are fighting, as on the font at Eardisley. Its provenance is unknown.

10. Rock (Worcestershire). The chancel arch has carvings with a variety of motifs, including human figures and a lion.
11. Alveley (Shropshire). Some carvings at the former Bell Inn, next to the church, show unmistakable links with the Herefordshire School.[33]
12. Aston Eyre (Shropshire) tympanum has long been attributed to the School. It is a magnificent portrayal of the Entry into Jerusalem, a reflective, almost devotional, piece, very different from the beasts and dragons of other works of the school; recently its relationship to the School has been doubted.

Towers and Spires

The church towers of Herefordshire are, in general, not lofty structures dominating the landscape, as in, say, Somerset or East Anglia: instead they are mainly fairly short, not to say humble. In a border county with turbulent invaders on its doorstep, one might expect to see towers built for defence and as a refuge—as for example in Northumberland or near the coast in East Anglia. But in truth few give much indication of this. The tower at Garway (Fig. 60) seems to be so designed, the walls at Ewyas Harold are seven feet thick, while those at Kington and Bosbury are nearly six feet thick. At Monnington-on-Wye, Pevsner drew attention to the arrow-slits in the battlements, but when one realises that this is a Perpendicular, not a Norman tower—14th century at the earliest—one wonders whether these slits are decorative rather than functional. However, there is a remarkable group of seven towers detached from the church (out of about 40 in the whole country)—originally there were 11, for the towers at Eardisley, Ewyas Harold, Kington and Weobley used to be detached. These probably owe their origins in part to providing a place of safety for local inhabitants. Otherwise, motte-and-bailey castles abound, and perhaps these were sufficient to shelter the populace in time of need.

It therefore seems that the principal function of the great majority of the towers is what it was in the rest of the country—to mark out the church as a place of worship, to house the bells, and later, in many cases, to embody the pride of the parishioners in their parish church. But, apart from the detached towers already mentioned, there is one other point of note—there are a number of towers whose upper stages are half-timbered, giving a very striking appearance in this county of black-and-white villages.

Of medieval church towers (126 in total) 102 (81%) are built at the west end of the church; nine (7%) are to the north (Bredwardine, Eardisley, Hampton Bishop, Hereford All Saints, Kinnersley, Marden, Norton Canon, Walford-on-Wye and Weobley) and of these all are north-western except Hampton Bishop and Walford; five (4%) are to the south (Canon Pyon, Colwall and Leintwardine south-western, Hereford St. Peter south-eastern, and Kington southern); and only three (2%) are central (Bromyard, Fownhope and Much Marcle; Mordiford had a central tower until c.1811). The remaining 7 towers are detached.

Difficulties abound in the dating of towers; though no-one would mistake a typical squat Norman tower with a stately battlemented Perpendicular one, in practice it may not be so easy. Often parts of the tower were built at widely differing periods, thus the lower stages might be Norman or Early English, and the belfry Perpendicular. And windows can be a trap—they were often inserted later into an earlier struc-ture, so that a Decorated or Perpendicular window may adorn a Norman or Early English tower. After excluding all doubtful examples (towers which were transitional between two successive medieval styles, and towers which clearly belonged to more than one style), I estimate that out of 69 towers in Herefordshire, only 9 (13%) are Norman; 29 (42%) are Early English; 16 (23%) Decorated; and 15 (22%)

Fig. 53 (left) St. Margaret, Wellington: Norman tower

Fig. 54 (above) St. Mary Magdalene, Little Hereford: Early English Tower

Fig. 55 (right) St. Michael, Kingsland: Decorated tower

Fig. 56 (left) St. Clydog, Clodock: Perpendicular tower

Fig. 57 (centre) St. James, Kinnersley: Tower with saddleback roof

Fig. 58 (right) St. Mary, Pembridge: The detached bell-tower

Perpendicular. This confirms the general impression that the heyday for church building in Herefordshire was the 13th century.

Norman towers tend to be squat, plain, solidly-built, with thick walls, e.g. Stanford Bishop (Fig. 211, p.107) and Wellington (Fig. 53). At belfry level, there are often two round-headed windows divided by a shaft, with a larger round-headed arch surmounting both, as at Fownhope. The roof may be flat and plain, but can be pyramidal. Wellington's tower is most unusual—round-headed windows pierce the flat buttresses, and on either side of the buttress are shafts with capitals. Kington (Fig. 216, p.112 is unique in Herefordshire in having a double pyramid roof, with a broach spire above; double pyramid roofs of this sort may be seen over towers in Shropshire (Clun, Hopesay, More) and in mid-Wales (Knighton, Kerry). Buttresses in the 12th century usually clasp the angles of the tower.

Early English towers as at Clehonger and Little Hereford (Fig. 54) have pointed lancet windows (though these were often inserted into pre-existing Norman towers), and the belfry windows tend to become more prominent. Buttresses in the 13th century were usually placed at each corner, at right-angles to each other. The projection of the buttresses diminishes towards the top of the tower, and was reduced stepwise with a sloping set-off to shed rainwater.

Decorated towers as at Kingsland (Fig. 55) and Aymestrey tend to be grander affairs—often of four storeys in other counties. Belfry windows may exhibit tracery typical of the Decorated style, and buttresses are often diagonal, placed at the four corners as at Aymestrey and Eastnor.

In the Perpendicular period (Much Marcle—Fig. 2, p.xi, St. Weonard's, and Clodock—Fig. 56), towers are usually topped by a battlemented parapet, below which may be a decorative frieze. Parapets were developed when lead roofing was introduced and lowered the pitch of the roof. Previously, the roof was supported at the eaves by a corbel-table (see Kingsland), overlapping it so that rainwater was thrown clear of the walls. When the roof became flatter, it ended in a gutter behind the parapet, and the water then escaped through spouts (gargoyles) often fantastically carved into grotesque shapes which project from the wall just below the parapet.

Kinnersley (Fig. 57) is now unique in the county in having a gabled roof known as a saddleback. Although the tower is plain, and looks early, it dates from the 14th century. The old church at Yazor, now in ruins, previously had a saddleback roof, described by Glynne in 1846.

The seven detached towers of Herefordshire offer interesting contrasts. The noblest and best-known is undoubtedly Pembridge (Fig. 58)—a sturdily-built structure composed of stone below, surmounted by a tall pyramidal section, followed by a weather-boarded belfry, then a second truncated pyramid, a second weather-boarded stage, and finally a short spire. Internally there is a massive timber structure which has been recently dated by dendrochronology to 1207-1223, with secondary timbers dating to 1668, and which rises to the higher of the two pyramidal roofs. Rather similar, but less complex, is the tower at Yarpole (Fig. 59)—this again has a stone base, with a truncated pyramid above, and a weather-boarded belfry with short spire. Inside stand four massive timber posts supporting the bell-stage. Sir Stephen Glynne described Yarpole's belfry as rude but picturesque, 'something savouring of the pigeon house'!

Fig. 59 St. Leonard, Yarpole:
Another detached bell-tower

Fig. 60 (left) St. Michael, Garway: 13th-century detached tower
Fig. 61 (centre) St. Bartholmew, Richard's Castle: 13th-century detached tower
Fig. 62 (right) St. Bartholomew, Holmer: Detached tower with half-timbered upper storey

Fig. 63 (left) St. Michael and All Angels, Ledbury: Detached tower with recessed spire
Fig. 64 (centre) St. Mary, Orcop: Tower with weather-boarded upper storey,
then a truncated pyramid, a belfry and spire
Fig. 65 (right) St. Michael, Brampton Abbotts: Timbered bell-turret with pyramid spire

Fig. 66 (left) St. Michael, Brimfield: Tower with half-timbered upper storey
Fig. 66 (centre) St. Mary Magdalene, Stretton Sugwas: Victorian tower with timbered upper storey
Fig. 67 (right) St. Giles, Goodrich: Broach spire

The detached towers at Garway (Fig. 60) and Bosbury are plain, unbuttressed Early English structures of the 13th century, with lancet windows. Richard's Castle (Fig. 61) is later 13th-century, the windows showing Y-tracery. Both Garway and Richard's Castle have a pyramid roof. Also of the 13th century are the lower parts of the towers at Holmer (Fig. 62, see below), and Ledbury (Fig. 63).

Timbered structures supporting the bell-stages as at the detached towers of Pembridge and Yarpole can be seen inside several churches in Herefordshire. At Orcop (Fig. 64), the lower part of the west tower is of stone; above is a weather-boarded stage, then a truncated pyramid roof, then the bell-stage and finally a spire; internally a complex timber structure rises from the base of the tower. At Brampton Abbotts, the simpler timbered bell-turret (Fig. 65) is again supported internally by tall posts at the west end of the nave. A similar arrangement exists at Vowchurch.

Towers with a half-timbered upper storey make a picturesque scene in the countryside; they occur at Brimfield (Fig. 66), Burrington, Hampton Bishop, Holmer (Fig. 62), Letton, Stretton Sugwas (Fig 67) and Winforton. Timber-framed buildings are notoriously hard to date, but the timber-framed storeys at Holmer and Winforton have been assigned to the 16th century, and at Brimfield to the 17th century. The splendid tower at Stretton Sugwas is Victorian, and was consciously modelled on the structure at Holmer.

Spires were usually developed in the Decorated or Perpendicular eras—i.e. from the late 13th century onwards—and in general are of two anatomical types: either broach spires, in which semi-pyramidal pieces of masonry effect a smooth transition to the usually octagonal spire; or recessed spires, in which the spire is set within a parapet. Excellent examples of each kind occur in Herefordshire.

The finest stone broach spires are at Goodrich and Sellack. At the former (Fig. 68), there is a Decorated west tower, with a tall broach spire; lucarnes (small windows) at the base of the spire exhibit Decorated

Fig. 69 St. James, Kimbolton: Shingled broach spire

Fig. 70 St. Peter and St. Paul, Weobley: Recessed spire with flying buttresses

tracery. The tower at Sellack is also Decorated, the broaches being very small. Shingled broach spires are seen at Fownhope, Kimbolton (Fig. 69), Kington (Fig. 216, p.112) and Orleton (Fig. 194, p.95).

The finest recessed spires are at Weobley, Ross-on-Wye, Stretton Grandison and Withington. Weobley has the most elegant spire in the county (Fig. 70)—Decorated, adorning a 14th-century tower, and the only spire in Herefordshire graced with flying buttresses which connect crocketed pinnacles with the spire. At Ross, there is an early 14th-century west tower, diagonally buttressed and a tall spire which is a well-known local landmark (Fig. 266, p.172). Pevsner commented adversely on the corner pinnacles, which he considered oversized and an unhappy restoration.[1] The elegant spire at Stretton Grandison gives distinction to an otherwise unremarkable church, and is well seen across the valley of the Frome. Similarly at both Withington and Llangarron a rather more austere spire rests on a late 13th-century or early 14th-century tower with diagonal buttresses. The two medieval churches in Hereford (All Saints and St. Peter's) have recessed spires, and so does the church at Stoke Edith. At Linton-by-Ross, the tower is Perpendicular, and bears a tall spire. At Ledbury (Fig. 63), the detached tower bears a spire—also a well-known landmark—which was constructed in the early 18th century, replacing a shingled spire. Finally, at Bodenham (Fig. 197, p.94), is a spire that was never finished, and looks rather comical: the late 13th-century tower has an incomplete Decorated spire at the top of which is a tiny pyramidal roof.

Porches

In the Middle Ages, many ceremonies took place at the church door. Here was performed the early part of the baptism and marriage services; penance, the churching of women and pronouncements of outlawry were made there.[1] In general it was not until the 14th century that porches were erected to give shelter, usually, but not always, over the south door.

Herefordshire has a splendid array of timbered porches, too numerous to be listed here. The porches at Humber, Kinnersley (Fig. 71) and Sarnesfield are probably all 14th-century, and each has traceried bargeboards over the entrance, concealing the horizontal timbers within. Inside the porch at Sarnesfield are cusped wind-braces at each side, and tie-beams. The fine porch at Eye is very similar. Less elaborate is the porch at Orleton. The porch at Aconbury (Fig. 72) is one of the best. Here is an impressive structure from the late 14th or early 15th century, consisting of two bays. Inside, tie-beams are present, supported by angels. Along the open side-walls are a series of wooden columns with ogee-headed lights.

Fig. 71 (left) St. James, Kinnersley:
14th-century porch

Fig. 72 (above) St. John the Baptist, Aconbury:
Two-bay porch

Fig. 73 (above left) St. Mary, Dilwyn: Stone porch with Decorated windows

Fig. 74 (lower left) St. Peter, Peterchurch: porch with ball-flower decoration

Fig. 75 (above right) St. Dubricius, Ballingham: A plain Perpendicular porch

The porch at Vowchurch is early 17th-century, with balusters on each side. The Victorian porch at Wigmore is built in the style of the fourteenth century: the lower part is of stone; the wooden superstructure has cusped and ogee-headed bargeboards, and quatrefoils in the spandrels of the arch.

Stone porches are not so frequent, but some good examples exist. The greater town churches—Ledbury, Leominster, Ross-on-Wye—all have stone porches of the 14th century. The Decorated porch at Pembridge is vaulted inside and has flowing tracery in the windows. But some village churches also have stone porches. Dilwyn (Fig. 73) is notable, with fine Decorated windows on each side. Peterchurch (Fig. 74) has a display of ball-flower around the entrance door. At Wellington, the Decorated south porch has a fine roof of cusped tie-beams, struts and wind-braces. The porch at Kingsland is remarkable for the chapel which leads off it (Fig. 199, p.96). Plainer is the south porch at Ballingham (Fig. 75); there is a Perpendicular straight-headed arch over the doorway, and in the spandrels are shields; the interior is vaulted, with diagonal and ridge-ribs. The side-walls each have a window of two trefoiled lights in a square head.

Roofs and Vaults

In medieval churches, the timber framework of the roof supports the actual waterproofing material. In the earliest days, this would have consisted of primitive thatching with turf or heather (or occasionally reed), but by the end of the 12th century in eastern England clay roofing-tiles had been introduced. Alternatively, long pointed tiles made of split wood (shingles) were used and pegged to boarding beneath. In the early Middle Ages, the pitches of roofs in northern countries were steep to prevent lodging of vast amounts of snow in winter. Following the widespread introduction of lead as a roofing material later in the Middle Ages, it became necessary to lower the pitch to prevent the sheets of lead 'creeping' down the roof.

Church roofs may be divided into two basic types:either single-framed roofs, in which there are no principal rafters, all rafters being the same size, each pair being pegged together at the apex, and stabilised by a linking collar-beam and bracing; or double-framed roofs which are divided into bays by the principal rafters. Simple single-framed roofs are usually, but not always, held to originate relatively early in the Middle Ages—each pair of rafters, trussed or not, is an independent unit of the roof. Scissor-bracing may help to support such a roof; scissor-beams are timbers which support the common rafters above the level of the collar-beams. (Figs. 77 and 78 illustrate the complex array of timbers found in roofs.)

Fig. 76 St. Lawrence, Weston-under-Penyard:
A trussed-rafter roof with tie-beams

There are a good number of single-framed trussed-rafter roofs in Herefordshire; one 14th-century example occurs at Ballingham. At Hentland and in the nave at Holmer scissor-bracing is also seen. At Weston-under-Penyard (Fig. 76), the roof is a single-frame trussed-rafter with scissor-bracing, but there are also three tie-beams. Other trussed-rafter roofs occur at Bosbury, Bridge Sollers (Fig. 220, p.119) and Hampton Bishop.

Tie-beam roofs are frequent. Tie-beams were inserted to tie the wall-plates together to prevent them slipping off the tops of the

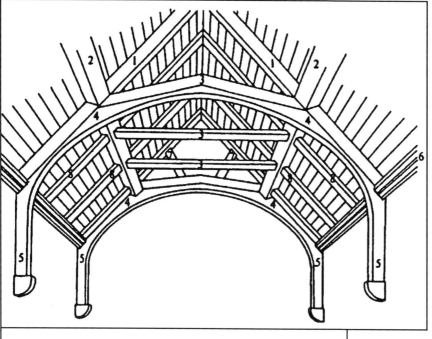

Figs. 77 & 78 The Timbers of a Roof. On the left are examples of (above) an Arch-Braced Roof and (below) a King-Post Roof construction. Various timbers are identified thus:

1. Principal (sometimes Principal Rafter)
2. Purlin
3. Collar-beam
4. Arch-brace
5. Wall-post
6. Wall-plate
7. Longitudinal Strut
8. Common Rafter
9. Tie-beam
10. King-post
11. Transverse Strut (queen-posts if there is no king-post)
12. Ridge-piece or -board

Fig. 79 St. Lawrence, Bishopstone: A complex roof with tie-beams, king-posts amd struts; beyond is a wagon-roof

side-walls. In the chancel at Bishopstone (Fig. 79), a series of tie-beams stretch from wall to wall; from the centre of each, a king-post rises vertically to support the ridge-piece. The principal rafters rise from the ends of the tie-beams to the ridge-piece (the common rafters between them are hidden by the ceiling). There are two purlins on each side parallel to the ridge-piece. Other struts and timbers are added to form a decorative pattern. Beyond, in the nave is a wagon-roof (see below). At Sarnesfield (Fig. 80), two

queen-posts arise from each tie-beam, projecting upwards and sideways to support the purlins and principal rafters. Between the tie-beams, collar-beams are supported by arched braces. There is one tier of foiled wind-braces laterally. The roof at Leysters (Fig. 81) is simpler—a single tie-beam, arched braces supporting collar-beams, and tiers of cusped quatrefoiled wind-braces. At Colwall (Fig. 83) there is a single tie-beam; there are two collar-beams in each unit, one above the other, the lower collar being supported by an arched brace arising from the wall-plate. On each side are two tiers of wind-braces, the inferior surface of the lower tier being carved into a foiled pattern. At Wigmore, tie-beams are placed in alternate units, and above each tie-beam is a collar supported by an arched brace. A single tier of wind-braces is present on each side. The wall-plate is supported by a series of corbels projecting from the walls (a corbel-table). The roof at Mathon (Fig. 84) is similar—three tie-beams, collar-beams

Fig. 80 (top) St. Mary, Sarnesfield: Two queen-posts arise from each tie-beam; above are collar-beams supported by arched braces

Fig. 81 (centre) St. Andrew, Leysters: Collar-beams supported by arched braces; a single tie-beam is seen

Fig. 82 (left) St. Bartholomew, Vowchurch: Tie-beams resting on posts inside the walls, with queen-posts supporting the collar-beams above

Fig. 83 (left) St. James, Colwall: Two collar-beams in each unit, the lower supported by an arched brace. Two tiers of wind-braces laterally

Fig. 84 (right) St. John the Baptist, Mathon: Tie-beams, collar-beams on arched braces and wind-braces laterally

Fig. 85 (lower left) St. Mary Magdalene, Leintwardine: A low-pitched panelled and boarded roof, with bosses at the intersections

Fig. 86 (below) St. Barnabas, Brampton Bryan: A double hammer-beam roof, resting on wall-posts

supported by arched braces, and a single tier of foiled wind-braces on each side. At Vowchurch (Fig. 82), the tie-beams rest on timber posts set inside the walls and are supported by arched braces. From the tie-beams, queen-posts ascend to support the collar-beams above. This roof was probably constructed *c*.1613. At King's Pyon (Fig. 235, p.134), there are tie-beams, collar-beams with arched braces, two tiers of wind-braces on each side, and in addition, two longitudinal beams just above the tie-beams.

When the pitch of the roof had become flatter, the roof was often panelled and boarded, and decorative bosses were often used at the intersections. Such roofs were seen especially in association with Perpendicular architecture, and so are not as common in Herefordshire as in other counties, such as Cheshire. Leintwardine (Fig. 85) is, however, an example—the tie-beams are supported on each side by vertical wall-posts, and are cambered upwards to support the ridge-piece and purlins directly. Sometimes in roofs of low pitch, a wagon-roof was formed by using soft-wood boards to cover the undersides of the rafters, collars and bases. Such roofs are characteristic of the West Country, but are infrequent in Herefordshire. At Turnastone (Fig. 87), the wall-plates can be seen on each side, and a single

Fig. 87 St. Mary Magdalene, Turnastone: A photograph of the interior in 1903, showing a tie-beam spanning the nave, with wall-plates on each side, a wagon-roof above

Fig. 88 St. Michael, Michaelchurch Escley: A wagon-roof with tie-beams below; the painting of Christ of the Trades may be seen on the left

tie-beam spans the nave between them. Above is a wagon-roof; the ridge-piece, purlins and principal rafters can be seen, the rest being hidden by the ceiling. There is a notable wagon-roof at Michaelchurch Escley (Fig. 88), with tie-beams below. Wagon-roofs also occur at Orcop, St. Weonard's (Fig. 159, p.68) and Welsh Newton (Fig. 158, p.68), and in the nave at Bishopstone and the chancel at Hereford All Saints (Fig. 232, p.131).

Fig. 89 (left) St. John the Baptist, King's Caple: Rib-vaulting over the Perpendicular chapel

Fig. 90 (right) Holy Trinity, Bosbury: Fan-vaulting in the Morton chapel

Hammer-beam roofs are particularly associated with East Anglia, where they are often extravagantly decorated with angels and other carving; they are seldom seen in Herefordshire but plain examples occur in the north aisle of All Saints, Hereford, the chancel at Holmer and also at Brampton Bryan (Fig. 86).

The provision of a stone vault was beyond the means of the great majority of parish churches in the Middle Ages, and there is no church in Herefordshire with a vaulted nave. There are, however, a few vaulted chapels. At King's Caple (Fig. 89), the Perpendicular north chapel has a rib-vault, with a boss over the intersection of the diagonal and ridge-ribs. Also Perpendicular is the north chapel at Sellack and the fan-vaulting in the Morton chapel at Bosbury (Fig. 90). The Decorated porch at Pembridge is vaulted and so is the Norman apse at Kilpeck.

Fonts

Baptism is the rite of admission to the Church, and in medieval times the first part of the service was conducted in the porch, or at the entry into the church. The traditional site for the font was centrally at the western end of the nave. The earliest fonts were probably constructed of wood, but none of these survive.

The styles of medieval fonts mirror the characteristics of the parish churches, and they may be approximately dated using similar criteria to those used in dating architectural features (see p.75). Thus Norman fonts, if adorned at all, may be enriched with a variety of geometrical patterns—zigzag, plain and cable mouldings, saltire crosses, scallops and other recognised Norman motifs. If arcades are present, they are round-headed. Human figures are not frequent, but when present may be rude and sometimes bizarre. In the 13th century (the Early English era), arcades become pointed, following the general adoption of the Gothic arch; sculpture became more realistic, and may include foliage (e.g. Knill) and human figures (e.g. Hope-under-Dinmore). In the 14th century (the Decorated era), arcades may exhibit ogee patterns and cusping, while Perpendicular fonts frequently display quatrefoil panels, rosettes, fleurons etc.

In 1949-51, Marshall anaylsed 201 fonts in Herefordshire, and dated them as follows:

Norman	87
13th century	20
14th century	23
15th century to Reformation	24
1550 - 1660	8
1660 - 1830	24
After 1830	15

Thus 43% of the total were of Norman origin. This contrasts markedly with an analysis of Suffolk fonts by Cautley;[1] he found that of 505 fonts, only 18 (3.5%) were Norman, and 'the majority' were Perpendicular (say, from 1350 to the Reformation). Even more pointed contrasts can be made between the west and east of England: in Herefordshire, the finest fonts are all Norman, including two which rank as the finest in the country; in contrast Perpendicular fonts are relatively modest structures. In Suffolk, the Norman fonts are plain and undistinguished, whereas some of the Perpendicular fonts are tremendously impressive, especially the 14 so-called Seven Sacraments fonts which are outstanding examples of Perpendicular workmanship.

*Fig. 91 (above) A plain Norman font with fine
Jacobean cover at St. Andrew, Evesbatch*

*Fig. 92 (above right) A huge Norman font supported
on five legs at St. Andrew, Bredwardine*

*Fig. 93 (below right) A Norman font with interlace
around the bowl, arcades around the stem, a chain
and saltire crosses below at St. Peter, Birley*

Norman fonts

Of the 87 Norman fonts in Herefordshire, half (44) are
plain and unadorned tubs typified by Evesbatch (Fig.
91). Here is a plain upright bowl resting on a stem of the
same circumference, hewn from brown sandstone. The
font at Kingstone is of this type—it was thought by
Marshall to be possibly Saxon rather than Norman
because, uniquely among this group, the thickness of
the rim is only one and a quarter inches;[2] in all the
others, the rim is between three and five inches thick. It
would be tedious to enumerate the plain Norman fonts:
all of them were originally tub- or bucket-shaped,
though a few (Sellack, Bridge Sollers, Ballingham)
have been pared into octagonal or hexagonal form.

A group of five fonts (Dormington, Monkland,
Much Marcle, Welsh Newton and Little Hereford) have
one or more plain mouldings around the circumference
of the bowl, either at the rim, the middle or lower,
thought to resemble hoops of willow which would have

previously been used to bind the waist of wooden fonts. Another group of five (Humber, Peterchurch, Little Birch, Kington, and Blakemere) have a band of cable moulding running round the waist of the bowl; Peterchurch (Fig. 248, p.151) and Kington also have chevron patterning running round the top of the rim.

Four fonts (Bosbury, Bredwardine, Kilpeck and Madley) were originally supported on five legs; Madley lost its legs when damage was sustained during the Civil War. The bowls of Bredwardine (Fig. 92), Kilpeck and Madley are very similar; all are huge, and hewn from the same limestone (breccia) found in the Golden Valley. The bowl of Bosbury is different, being of square outline above and circular below.

Twenty Norman fonts are enriched with varying degrees of geometrical patterns—Norman motifs such as chevron, saltire crosses, lozenges, arcades, scallops, either alone or in various combinations. Thus Whitchurch has arcades around the bowl; Thornbury a zone of lozenge pattern; Middleton-on-the-Hill triangles with a 'flame' inside each. More complex are Cusop with saltire crosses around the rim and lozenges around the whole of the bowl; Birley (Fig. 93) with an interlacing pattern around the upper bowl, arcades on the stem and saltire crosses around the base; and Michaelchurch (Fig. 94) with intersecting arcades around the rim, then two bands of saltire crosses and below interlacing chevron and diamond patterns. Bromyard (Fig. 95) has a running tendril-like motif around two thirds of the bowl, but the rest is decorated with a simplified form of the Tree of Life;[3] below is a rather flat zigzag pattern.

A group of five fonts have sculptured figures, with or without geometrical carving. Whitbourne (Fig. 96) has a band of interlocking stars, with a single mutilated carving of the Agnus Dei. How Caple has an octagonal bowl, carved with what Pevsner describes as haphazard vegetable and geometrical motifs, and also a damaged Agnus Dei. The bowl of Sutton St. Michael is plain, but around the base are sculpted four lions. In Hereford Cathedral, the font has the same lions around the base, but the bowl is intricately carved with an arcade of 12 arches, between which are the mutilated figures of the apostles. Around the rim is a key pattern, possibly a reference to St. Peter. The apostles figure also in the splendid font at Burghill (Fig.

Fig. 94 (left) A Norman font with intersecting arcades around the rim, then two bands of saltire crosses and a diamond pattern below at St. Michael, Michaelchurch

Fig. 95 (centre) A Norman font with a tendril-like motif, and below a zigzag pattern at St. Peter, Bromyard

Fig. 96 (right) A Norman font with a band of stars at St. John the Baptist, Whitbourne

Fig. 97 (left) A Norman font with a lead bowl on a stone stem carved with the figures of Christ and the apostles at St. Mary, Burghill

Fig. 98 (centre) Pointed arcades on a 13th-century font at St. Mary, Collington

Fig. 99 (right) A 13th-century font carved with panels of various designs at St. Michael, Knill

97): this is a lead bowl (see below), standing on a stone stem, carved with the 12 apostles and also the figure of Christ. Again the figures are much defaced.

The remaining four Norman fonts are the work of the Herefordshire School of Carvers, and have already been described—Castle Frome (Figs. 48, 49, p.20) and Eardisley (Figs. 46, 47, p.19) exhibit sculpture of the highest quality, and can claim to be the finest Norman fonts in the country, while Shobdon (Fig. 44, p.18) and Orleton (Fig. 45, p.18) are a little less distinguished.

The 13th Century (Early English)

The change from semicircular arches to pointed ones was reflected also in the decoration of fonts; and as the century proceeded, fewer bowls were rounded and a great variety of shapes evolved. Of 20 Early English fonts, 12 have octagonal bowls and only four are now circular; possibly a few of the octagonal bowls were originally circular and were later converted

Fig. 100 Figures of apostles on the 13th-century font at St. Mary-the-Virgin, Hope-under-Dinmore

40

into an octagonal form. The remaining 13th-century fonts are Marden (12-sided); Pembridge and Brimfield (4-lobed); and Lyonshall (8-lobed).

Collington (Fig. 98) could pass as a Norman font, but for the pointed arcades. Yarpole, another early 13th-century font, has been restored—only the central portion of the bowl appears to be medieval, and the arcades are thought originally to have been pointed.[4] The panels of the font at Knill (Fig. 99) are carved with a variety of crosses, quatrefoils, palm-leaves—quite different from Norman sculpture. The 12-sided font at Marden is carved with blank trefoiled arches—Marshall speculates that these may originally have carried paintings of the 12 apostles.[5] The font at Hope-under-Dinmore (Fig. 100) is the finest of the 13th-century fonts: on its eight sides are carved figures of Christ, with St. Peter, St. Paul and St. John the Baptist, and the four evangelists.[6] The figures are under cinquefoiled arches—this is accomplished sculpture of a high order.

Of the multi-lobed fonts, Pembridge and Brimfield are similar; both are plain, and have four lobes, and may well be the work of the same man. Lyonshall is more complex—the eight marble columns of the stem are Victorian, but above are capitals with upright stiff-leaf foliage of the 13th century leading to the plain bowl.

The 14th and 15th Centuries (Decorated and early Perpendicular)

During the Decorated era, the majority of the fonts are plain octagonal bowls. A few have simple arcading: Bodenham (Fig. 101) has an elementary ogee arcade with cusping, Foy and Weobley more complex patterns. Perpendicular fonts are similar, but a number exhibit carving, usually with a liberal display of quatrefoils. Stretton Grandison is the only hexagonal font in the county, and on each face of the bowl is a simple quatrefoil. Canon Pyon's font is composed of four blocks of stone: the upper has a frieze of small quatrefoils; the second and fourth are plain, but the third has more carving. At Brampton Abbotts (Fig. 102), the bowl has a quatrefoil on each face, with central enrichment, and on the trumpet-shaped stem, panelled and traceried faces. Above is an excellent modern font-cover. The bowl at Hentland (Fig. 103) is carved with two heads and roses, and the underside of the bowl and the stem are also carved. The finest Perpendicular fonts in Herefordshire are at Llangarron (Fig. 104) and Walford-on-Wye (Fig. 105): both have a combination of quatrefoil panels on the bowl,

Fig. 101 A 14th-century font with ogee arcades at St. Michael, Bodenham

Fig. 102 A Perpendicular font with quatrefoils on each face at St. Michael, Brampton Abbotts

Fig. 103 (left) A Perpendicular font with roses and heads at St. Dubricius, Hentland

Fig. 104 (centre) A Perpendicular font with quatrefoil panels on the bowl and rosettes and fleurons on the stem at St. Deinst, Llangarron

Fig. 105 (right) Octagonal Perpendicular font with quatrefoil panels on the bowl and leaf patterns around the foot of the stem at St. Michael, Walford-on-Wye

Fig. 106 A plain narrow font —?Roman, at St. Michael, Kenchester

carving on the underside of the bowl, and traceried panels on the stem. Llangarron also has rosettes and fleurons on the stem, while Walford has additional leaf patterns around the foot of the stem.

There remain two ancient fonts in Herefordshire which cannot be fitted into any classification, because they apparently are of Roman origin, though differing by a thousand years in the degree of antiquity. At Kenchester, near the Roman town of *Magnis*, is a plain narrow circular font (Fig. 106) which the Royal Commission on Historical Monuments believed may be a re-used Roman object. More bizarre is the font at Lea, near Ross. This Italian object (Fig. 107) was given to the church in 1907 in memory of Sarah Decima Bradney. Apparently it was bought from a dealer and its provenance is unknown. It is quite unlike anything ever produced in England. The bowl has a lovely frieze of foliage inhabited by human and animal figures, mermaids and a two-tailed merman. The bowl is supported by a slender shaft, which has rams on its capital and a knot around its middle. The shaft stands on an elephant whose saddle is enriched by figures of saints and bordered with mosaic executed in an Italian technique known as Cosmati work; a similar mosaic is around the rim of the bowl. Cosmati work flourished in Rome in the 12th and 13th centuries, which is therefore likely to be the date for the production of this 'font'. The font at Lea is therefore a quite unexpected exotic to find in an English parish church: it is worth seeing.

Fig. 107 (left) An exotic Italian font from the 12th or 13th centuries at St. John the Baptist, Lea
Fig. 108 (centre) A lead font dated 1689 at St. John the Baptist, Aston Ingham
Fig. 109 (right) An early Georgian font at St. James, Cradley

Post-Reformation fonts

At Sutton St. Michael, in addition to the Norman font, there is on a window-sill a small urn supported by the figure of an angel clasping a book. This most unusual object is thought to date from the mid-17th century. At Aston Ingham is a lead font (Fig. 108) decorated with foliage, the initials WM and the year 1689, indicating its origins in the reign of William and Mary. Lead fonts are rare—that at Burghill was noted above, and all told there are about 30 in the country. Most of them date from the 12th or 13th century, so Aston Ingham's is unusually late.[7] From the 1720s comes the handsome font at Tyberton, a graceful bowl carved with heads and standing on a fluted stem. Contemporary with this is the font at Cradley where the bowl stands on a decorated curvaceous stem (Fig. 109). Further fonts of the 17th and 18th centuries may be seen at Fownhope, Holme Lacy, How Caple, Llanwarne, Ross-on-Wye, Stoke Edith, Woolhope and elsewhere.

Fig. 110 (right) A richly decorated Victorian font at St. Margaret, Welsh Bicknor

There are about a dozen Victorian or later fonts in Herefordshire, and three deserve special mention. That at Welsh Bicknor (Fig. 110) stands on a group of columns with richly carved capitals, and around the rim is a series of heads and rosettes. The font at Adforton (Fig. 111) was designed by the architect J.P. Seddon (who also designed Hoarwithy); the bowl stands on four columns and around the sides are fishes swimming. The font at Brockhampton-by-Ross was also designed by the architect, in this instance W.R. Lethaby; it shows interwoven friezes of vines.

Fig. 111 (right) Fish swim round the bowl of this Victorian font at St. Andrew, Adforton

Memorials and Monuments, 1250-1850

There are a large number and range of memorials and monuments in the county's churches and it is not possible here to refer to more than a small proportion of them. Some ancient churches have an impressive array of coffin-lids, effigies, slabs, tomb-chests, statues, and tablets, ranging from the 13th to the 20th centuries. Herefordshire was rarely in the vanguard of progress, so as a general rule memorials tend to be conservative, often retaining features at a time when they have become largely archaic in the rest of the country. Although the majority, especially of the 18th and 19th centuries, are mediocre, there are some from every century which are excellent. In particular, the churches at Ledbury, Much Marcle and Ross-on-Wye have assemblies which can compare with any parish church in the country; other churches with several good monuments include Holme Lacy, Kinnersley and Much Dewchurch. For convenience, I have gathered in this section the best that the county can offer, so that the reader may appreciate the gradual evolution of style over a period of 600 years; in nearly every case, further information about each subject is in the entry for the church concerned.

The Middle Ages (1250-1550)
The earliest of all memorials to the dead is the Roman tombstone now built into the outer south wall of the chancel at Upton Bishop. It shows the upper part of a human figure with the right hand raised. Next is the funerary slab at Clodock, thought to belong to the 9th century, which has an indistinct Latin inscription. Apart from these oddities, the earliest memorials are coffin-lids. These were the carved lids of stone coffins which were allowed to remain exposed on the floor of the church to provide a permanent memorial to those buried beneath.[1] This practice apparently began in the early 12th century and persisted for about 200 years. Examples in Herefordshire from the 13th and early 14th centuries may be seen at Aconbury, Bosbury, Brinsop, Clehonger, Dilwyn, Linton-by-Ross, Llanwarne, Mansell Gamage, Mordiford, Much Dewchurch, Richard's Castle, Tarrington, Weobley, and Woolhope; the best are at Richard's Castle and Weobley. Most of these coffin-lids are incised with a foliated cross, of varying complexity, and they commemorate unknown persons, with the exception of that at Weobley (Fig. 112) which is to Hugo Bissop of Norton Canon. The lid at Richard's Castle shows in relatively high relief a cross, with leaves sprouting from the stem and the limbs of the cross.

In some of the early coffin-lids elsewhere in England, an effigy of the deceased was carved in low relief on the lid, one of the earliest examples being at Westminster Abbey (Abbot Crispin, c.1118). The earliest effigies in the 12th century were of ecclesiastics, but later, effigies of knights, civilians and ladies became increasingly frequent. Gradually during the 12th, 13th and early 14th centuries, some effigies instead of being carved out of the slab were fashioned in raised low relief by cutting back the surrounding

Fig. 112 (left) 13th-century coffin-lid with foliated cross
in St. Peter and St. Paul, Weobley

Fig. 113 (above) Effigies of the two wives of a knight
at St. Michael and All Angels, Edwyn Ralph

Fig. 114 (lower left) Late 13th-century effigy of a priest,
St. Michael, Ledbury

slab. Later, there was progressive undercutting of the sides of the effigy until finally the effigy was freed from the underlying slab.

This process can be seen in a group of effigies spanning the years from about 1250-1325. Probably the earliest is the lady at Wolferlow. She lies rigidly, with garments clinging closely to her in stylised folds. Rather similar is the lady at Welsh Bicknor. At Bishop's Frome is the effigy of a knight drawing his sword, with legs crossed, and wearing a mail coif. The earlier of the two knights at Edwyn Ralph also has a mail coif; this has become heavier by the time of the second effigy in this church. Next to him are very fine effigies of his two wives (Fig. 113). Of the same period (c.1300) is the knight at Dilwyn; he is holding the hilt of his sword with his right hand. Somewhat later is the knight and his lady at Stretford. The finest monument of the late 13th century is undoubtedly the figure of a priest at Ledbury (Fig. 114); he is portrayed with great sensitivity. Finally in this group are two ladies for comparison with the lady at Wolferlow. The lady at Brampton Bryan (Fig. 115) is holding her heart in her hands, (and so is one at Ewyas Harold), while the lady at Bodenham is infinitely more relaxed than her predecessors at Wolferlow and Welsh Bicknor; her left hand is posed gracefully on her chest, while her right hand tenderly caresses the baby at her side. Did she, I wonder, die in childbirth? Other effigies of this period may be seen at Abbey Dore, Little Hereford, Llangarron, Upton Bishop and Westhide.

All these effigies are of stone, but other materials were sometimes used. Wooden effigies are nowhere frequent; in all there are fewer than 100 in the country, but there are two in Herefordshire (and it is known that previously there was a third at Abbey Dore, probably of a bishop).[2] Of the surviving effigies, the earlier one, at Clifford, dates from c.1300 and is of a priest; the stylised vestments remind one of the drapery of the ladies at

Fig. 115 Early 14th-century effigy of a lady holding her heart in her hands at St. Barnabas, Brampton Bryan

Wolferlow and Welsh Bicknor. More realistic is the later (c.1360-70) oaken effigy at Much Marcle (Fig. 116): carved from a single block of oak, six feet four inches long, this unknown gentleman with staring eyes and bearded face makes an impressive appearance. In the larger churches, abbeys and cathedrals, some effigies were made of imported Tournai marble, or of Purbeck marble (e.g. at Temple church, London). For the rich, gilt bronze was occasionally used, but there are no examples of the use of these materials in Herefordshire parish churches.

The dating of effigies is often difficult; even when the date of death is known, this gives no more than an approximate estimate, for in the Middle Ages the memorial was sometimes constructed before death, or sometimes not for several decades afterwards. Details of style and costume are of great use in dating. The earliest 12th-century effigies of knights have the legs uncrossed, but from around 1250, for about a century, the legs are usually crossed; this was long thought to indicate a crusader, but this is not now generally believed. During this century (1250-1350) knights are often depicted actively drawing or sheathing their swords. The head often rests on a helmet, and at the feet may occasionally be a lion. In the later Middle Ages, from c.1350, it became more usual for the hands, even of knights, to be clasped in prayer, in an attitude of repose. Effigies of ladies followed a similar trend: the earlier ones are stiff and stylised, later they become more relaxed, and representations of costume become more realistic. The head usually rests on a pillow, sometimes flanked by representations of angels, and there is often a dog at the feet. Effigies of bishops are rarely found in parish churches, but in cathedrals they are often depicted in the act of blessing.

As the effigy became gradually freed from the slab beneath, so from the early 13th century onward it became common for the effigy to be placed on a tomb-chest, the coffin usually lying in a vault beneath. This immediately gave great scope for medieval craftsmen to exhibit their skills in adorning the sides of the chest. At first, this took the form of simple arcading—'Early English' arcades in the 13th century, later becoming cusped, and, in the Decorated period, ogeed. The arcades were in the beginning blind, but later were furnished with shields, angels or human figures (known as weepers, representing family members, especially the children of the deceased), and occasionally religious scenes were portrayed. Other forms of decoration were common: quatrefoils and circles, with or without flowers and foliage, were often employed. Tomb-chests were either free-standing, or set in recesses in the wall. In the latter case, there was usually a canopy over the effigy, and in the Decorated period this was often cusped and ogeed, and adorned with ball-flower. Occasionally the effigy remains to this day in its tomb-recess,

Fig. 116 Wooden effigy of a gentleman c.1360-70 at St. Bartholomew, Much Marcle

Fig. 117 (above) Effigy of a knight on a tomb-chest c.1330 at St. Michael, Moccas

Fig. 118 (right) Tomb-chest and effigy of Blanche Mortimer, Lady Grandison at Much Marcle—the finest memorial in any Herefordshire church

but the majority of recesses are now empty, or worse, furnished with modern church paraphernalia. Canopies over free-standing tomb-chests are often seen in cathedrals, but are unusual in parish churches.

The next group of illustrations from Herefordshire churches shows effigies in the latter half of the Middle Ages—1330-1550. At Moccas (*c.*1330) is the tomb of a knight, still bearing his shield, but the hands quietly folded in prayer (Fig. 117). Around the sides of the tomb-chest is a tier of large quatrefoils containing shields, and below a row of fleurons. The tomb-chest and effigy of Lady Grandison (d.1347) at Much Marcle are superb—this is the finest memorial in any Herefordshire church (Figs. 8, p.*xiv*, and 118). The tomb-chest is in a recess, with a gorgeous canopy of cusped arches with an array of shields above. On the sides of the chest is arcading furnished with more shields. The effigy is exquisite: the face beautiful, the hands delicate, the drapery natural, and flowing over the sides of the tomb-chest in an endearing manner. Such an arrangement of drapery may also be seen at the contemporary memorial at Ledbury (Fig. 119); here the effigy lies on a fine Decorated tomb-chest also enriched with heraldic shields. At Clehonger are two memorials to Sir Richard and Lady Pembrugge. Sir Richard's effigy (Fig. 120) with uncrossed legs lies on a plain tomb-chest. His left hand is on his shield, and he is portrayed turning slightly to the left. His wife's monument is less ambitious and more formal. At King's Pyon there is an elegant early 14th-century Decorated tomb-recess, and within it lie *late* 14th-century effigies, the stone effigy of a lady and an alabaster one of a knight; and at Pembridge are two pairs of 14th-century effigies on a stone tomb-chest. In addition to the Grandison memorial, there is at Much Marcle a memorial with two stone effigies on an elaborate tomb-chest, dating from *c.*1400. The armoured knight again has uncrossed legs, his head resting on his helmet, a lion at his feet. His elegant lady wears a long gown with hanging sleeves, angels at her head, puppies playing at her feet. The side of the chest is divided into panels displaying shields.

Fig. 119 The Pauncefoot memorial c.1360 at Ledbury

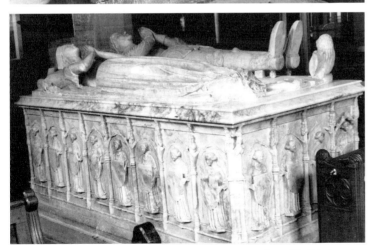

From the 15th century, similar effigies are commonly made of alabaster. Alabaster is a compact marble-like form of gypsum (calcium sulphate), and was quarried at Chellaston near Derby and at Tutbury, Staffordshire. The earliest use of alabaster is in the west doorway of the Priory Church of St. Mary, Tutbury, *c*.1160-70, but it was not until the early 14th century that alabaster was first used in effigies (at Hanbury, Staffordshire). Gardner pointed out that alabaster is soft, easy to work and well-suited for taking colour and gilding.[3] (Effigies were brightly coloured in the Middle Ages, and even now traces of the original colour can occasionally be found.) Because of these properties, it became the favoured material for memorial effigies for over 300 years. The industry was first centred on Nottingham, whence alabaster was sent all over the country and also to the continent in the late 14th and 15th centuries. In the later 15th century, however, Nottingham's supremacy was increasingly challenged by workers at Burton upon Trent. From then onward, Nottingham concentrated on religious statuary, and Burton became the dominant centre for monumental effigies and slabs. The Burton workshop continued to predominate until the middle of the 17th century when the centre of production moved to London.

The earliest alabaster effigy in Herefordshire is the knight at King's Pyon, dating from the second half of the 14th century, so Herefordshire was not exactly in the van in the use of this material. But from about 1430, for 200 years, the majority of effigies were of alabaster. In the 15th century, these included effigies at Weobley, Burghill, Bredwardine, Kington and Stoke Edith. At Weobley, are the effigies of Sir William Devereux, *c*.1430 (Fig. 121), Dame Alice Crutwell and Sir John Marbury, d.1437. At

Fig. 120 (top) Mid-14th-century memorial to Sir Richard Pembrugge at All Saints, Clehonger

Fig. 121 (centre) Alabaster effigy of Sir William Devereux c.1450 at St. Peter and St. Paul, Weobley

Fig. 122 (lower) Tomb-chest and alabaster effigies of Thomas Vaughan and his wife (d.1469) at St. Mary, Kington

Burghill, there are Sir John and Lady Milbourne, *c.*1440; at Bredwardine, an unknown knight, *c.*1450; at Kington (Fig. 122), the fine tomb-chest and effigies of Thomas Vaughan and his wife (d.1469), with angels holding shields around two sides of the chest; and at Stoke Edith an unknown lady wearing a butterfly head-dress, now enclosed behind wrought-iron railings.

From the early 16th century, similar effigies are at Croft, Ross-on-Wye, Eye, and from the 1570s at Much Dewchurch, Holme Lacy and Madley. At Croft church (Fig. 123), adjacent to the castle, is the splendid tomb-chest of Sir Richard and Lady Croft (d.1509), with effigies and angels. Above is a Perpendicular canopy and at the west end of the chest is a wall with four saints. At Ross-on-Wye (Fig. 124) is the tomb-chest and alabaster effigies of William Rudhall and his wife (d.1530); there are saints along the sides of the chest, and figures kneeling before a representation of the Annunciation. At Eye are two memorials: the first is to Sir Rowland Cornewall (d.1520), the alabaster effigy of a knight with his gauntlets by his side (Fig 125). He lies on a modern tomb-chest, and is wearing the SS collar. The second, a generation later, is a splendid memorial to Sir Richard Cornewall (d.1540) and his wife; around the chest are kneeling angels and shields, mourners and an Annunciation (Fig. 126). The beginnings of Renaissance influence may be seen in a pilaster at the north end.

The three memorials from the 1570s are the last from the sequence of the Middle Ages; in spirit they look back to the medieval past rather than forward to the (Protestant) future. At Much Dewchurch are two effigies of John and Walter Pye (*c.*1570)—two men lying in repose. Much more sophisticated is the memorial at Holme Lacy to John

Fig. 123 (top) Monument to Sir Richard and Lady Croft (d.1509) at St. Michael, Croft

Fig. 124 (centre) Tomb-chest and alabaster effigies of William Rudhall and his wife (d.1530) at St. Mary, Ross

Fig. 125 (lower) Alabaster effigy of Sir Rowland Cornewall (d.1520) with gauntlets by his side at St. Peter and St. Paul, Eye

Fig. 126 *The Annunciation on the end of Sir Richard Cornewall's tomb-chest, Eye*

Scudamore (d.1571) and his wife: fine alabaster effigies on a tomb-chest, with angels and shields around the sides. The edges of the chest are chamfered and furnished with an inscription. Finally, at Madley, is the memorial to Richard Willison and his wife (d.1575): mutilated effigies in stone, the chest displaying blank arches, shields and figures. It is the work of John Guldo of Hereford (see below).

Less costly than memorial effigies were incised slabs, of stone or alabaster; these range in date from the 13th to the 16th centuries. Two of the best are illustrated: from Stretton Sugwas (Fig. 127) to Richard Grevelhey and his wife (d.1473); and from Turnastone (Fig. 128) to Thomas ap Harry and his wife (d.1522). Further slabs are at Aymestrey, Eardisland, Edwyn Ralph, Hope-under-Dinmore, Ledbury, Sollers Hope and Westhide.

Monumental brasses became exceedingly popular during the second half of the Middle Ages, especially in the eastern parts of England. In Herefordshire, they survive at Brampton Abbotts, Burghill, Clehonger (perhaps the finest), Colwall, Ledbury and Llandinabo. At Allensmore, Canon Pyon and Dilwyn and also at Hereford Cathedral are monumental slabs from the late 14th or early 15th century in which there are inlays not of brass but of a cement composition;[4] such slabs are extremely rare before the 17th century. The Allensmore slab is inlaid with the figure of a knight in armour and his lady in a long

Fig. 127 *(far left) Incised slab to Richard Grevelhey (d.1473) and his wife at St. Mary Magdalene, Stretton Sugwas*

Fig. 128 *(left) Incised slab to Thomas ap Harry and his wife (d.1522) at St. Mary Magdalene, Turnastone*

Fig. 129 Monument to John Harford at Holy Trinity, Bosbury

gown; above each is a cinque-foiled canopy.

To conclude this section on medieval memorials there are two late 13th-century shrines, at Bridstow and Goodrich. Each has cusped arcading around the sides, and the one at Bridstow has also a shield and cross under a gabled canopy.

Post-Reformation Monuments

For some years after the Reformation, memorial effigies continued to be displayed recumbent, the hands clasped in prayer. Gradually, however, a new spirit became apparent. The hands were often depicted lying relaxed at the side, and in late Elizabethan and Jacobean monuments there was an increasing tendency for the deceased to be portrayed kneeling in prayer, most often the husband and wife kneeling at a prayer-desk, and sometimes accompanied by children and occasionally other members of the family. In the 17th century, some figures were shown reclining, usually uncomfortably on one elbow; a few were shown seated or even standing.

Two churches in Herefordshire have Elizabethan monuments, which, though not outstanding, are unusual and interesting. At Bosbury, on either side of the sanctuary, are the huge memorials to John Harford (d.1573) and Richard Harford (d.1578). The former monument (Fig. 129), at least, is by John Guldo of Hereford, who was also responsible for the Willison tomb at Madley referred to above and the memorial to Judge Evans at Abergavenny. It is perhaps remarkable that the same sculptor could produce two such memorials, the Madley one medieval, the Bosbury Renaissance, during the same decade. At Bacton (Fig. 130) is the unique memorial to Blanche Parry (d.1590), maid of honour to Elizabeth I, where Blanche is depicted kneeling before the seated queen—something which would have been unthinkable 50 years earlier.

In the 17th century, some memorials still consisted of effigies lying on a tomb-chest (though they were passing out of fashion), and at Bishopstone and Much Cowarne one could be forgiven for feeling that little had happened to change medieval ways. Stone effigies still lie on tomb-chests, hands clasped in prayer; at

Fig. 130 Blanche Parry (d.1590) kneeling before the Queen at St Faith, Bacton

Bishopstone to John Berinton and his
wife (d.1614), and at Much Cowarne to
Edmund Fox and his wife (d.1617) and
to Sybil Reed (d.1624)—these are rustic
works, of very conservative style.
Around the Fox monument are ten
kneeling figures and three babies in a
cradle. Behind Sybil Reed are four
kneeling figures and a rounded gable.
Their late date is revealed by the
costumes, for at both these churches the
effigies are depicted wearing the ruff
which was so popular at that time.

Kneeling figures at prayer are present at
Mathon, Bacton and Much Dewchurch. At Mathon
there is the monument to Jane Walweyn (d.1617):
above the plain tomb-chest is a panel carved with
two figures kneeling at a prayer-desk. Rather
similar is the monument at Bacton to Alexander
Stanton (d.1620) and his wife. Much more elaborate
is the wall-monument at Much Dewchurch to
Walter Pye (d.1625) and his wife (Fig. 258, p.163),
again depicted at prayer, with 13 kneeling children
below. The major effigies are flanked by classical
columns, and above are an arch and superstructure
with obelisks and shields—denoting the growing
enthusiasm for 'architectural' surrounds for
funerary monuments. Even more striking is the
memorial to Francis Smalman and his wife (d.1635) at
Kinnersley (Fig. 131). The kneeling figures face each other

below a canopy held aloft by cherubs blowing trumpets;
the children kneel below, in various directions. Beneath are
corbels of angels bearing shields in a purely medieval
manner.[5] The contemporary memorial at Ledbury to
Edward Skynner (d.1631) and his wife (Fig. 132) is
another grand affair, with the kneeling couple facing each
other and between them, on the floor, an effigy of a little
girl; their ten surviving children are portrayed below.

Infinitely more sophisticated, and breathing a totally
different spirit are the alabaster effigies at Castle Frome
from 1630-40 (Fig. 133). Here, the figures are portrayed

*Fig. 131 (top) Detail on the Smalman monument
at St. James, Kinnersley*

*Fig. 132 (centre) Large wall-monument to
Edward Skynner (d.1635) and his wife at Ledbury*

*Fig. 133 Alabaster effigies of the Unett family c.1630-40
at St. Michael, Castle Frome*

with the arms relaxed, the right at the side
holding a book, the left placed across the
chest. Even more polished is the memorial at
Much Marcle to Sir John Kyrle and his wife
(*c*.1650), who lie on an expensive tomb-
chest of black and white marble (Fig. 134).
Their hands are indeed clasped in prayer, but
the figures breathe an air of satisfied
opulence. Around the chest are cartouches
with wreathes. The memorial at Ross-on-
Wye (Fig. 135) to John Rudhall (d.1636) has
been identified as the work of the same
sculptor who was responsible for the
Smalman monument at Kinnersley and the
Kyrle monument at Much Marcle; here
again are alabaster effigies on a black
marble top, with the children around the
sides of the tomb-chest. Esdaile has identified further monuments by the same hand in
a group of churches, including Elmley
Castle, Wickhamford, Inkberrow
(Worcestershire), Ditchley, Wroxton

(Oxfordshire) and
Lydiard Tregoze
(Wiltshire).[6] She
claimed that these
are the finest
group of monu-

*Fig. 134 (upper) Effigies of Sir John Kyrle and his wife
(d.1650) at Much Marcle*

*Fig. 135 (lower) Memorial to John Rudhall (d.1636)
and his wife at Ross*

ments by one hand in the country, and pointed out that all are costume pieces
of a high order, and betray the work of an artist trained in heraldry, and also
in the Gothic tradition (just when it was becoming unfashionable!). Other
memorials of this period in Herefordshire are at Kentchurch, Lugwardine and
Abbey Dore.

The Civil War is recalled in the free-standing memorial at Ross-on-Wye
(Fig. 136) to Colonel William Rudhall (d.1651) who is shown armed, clad in
Roman dress and rather arrogant. Another colonel, John Birch (d.1691), is
shown standing at Weobley in a niche flanked by Corinthian columns, with an
open pediment above (Fig. 137). He commanded the Parliamentary forces
besieging Goodrich and Ludlow castles in 1646 and was later MP for
Leominster and Weobley. His long and colourful career is described in West
and West.[7]

In the second half of the 17th century, the English Baroque evolved, to be
followed in the next century by rococo (both rather restrained in England
compared with the extravagancies seen on the continent). There was a vogue for
standing wall-monuments with urns, obelisks and sarcophagus, without effigy

Fig. 136 Standing memorial to Col. William Rudhall (d.1651) at Ross

Fig. 137 (left) Monument to Col. John Birch (d.1691) at Weobley

Fig. 138 (centre) Marble wall-monument to Paul Foley (d.1699) at St Mary, Stoke Edith

Fig. 139 (right) Memorial to James Scudamore ((d.1668) but the memorial is much later) at St. Cuthbert, Holme Lacy

but often with scrolls, cherubs, and displays of flowers and foliage. Good examples of these wall-monuments may be seen at a number of Herefordshire churches; at Brinsop is the memorial to William Dansey (d.1708); other memorials may be seen at less well-known churches such as Dormington, Evesbatch, Foy, Hatfield, Humber, Llangarron, Mansell Lacy, Mordiford, and Walford-on-Wye. Effigies became much less frequent, but where they persist (as at the memorial to James Scudamore at Holme Lacy (Fig. 139)) they tended to become more flamboyant with a wide range of posture and gesture. Ostentation rather than piety was the order of the day.

At Stoke Edith is the fine marble monument to Paul Foley (d.1699); there is no effigy, but a sarcophagus and urn, and above a pediment (Fig. 138). The finest display of late Stuart memorials is at Holme Lacy (see p.160): here are the memorials to Jane Scudamore (d.1699), her husband James (d.1668), and to John Scudamore, Viscount Sligo (d.1716) (Fig. 140).

But Herefordshire is a county of contrasts: from these sophisticated memorials one can turn to the remote church of St. Devereux (Fig. 141), where a naive rustic monument to Ann Goode (d.1668) shows the subject at prayer (a late date

Fig. 140 Memorial to John Scudamore, Viscount Sligo (d.1716) at Holme Lacy

Fig. 141 (left) Rustic monument to Ann Goode (d.1668) at St. Dubricius, St. Devereux

Fig. 142 (centre) Memorial to Lady Morgan (d.1764) at Kinnersley

Fig. 143 (right) Detail of Earl Conyngsby at St. Mary-the-Virgin, Hope-under-Dinmore

Fig. 144 (left) Detail of the Countess Conyngsby with her infant son, Hope-under-Dinmore

Fig. 145 (centre) Memorial to Capt. Samuel Skynner (d.1725) by Thomas White at Ledbury

Fig. 146 (right) Memorial to Viscount Bateman (d.1804) by Joseph Nollekens
at St. John the Evangelist, Shobdon

for this typical Elizabethan or Jacobean posture), a world away from the wealth and the worldliness of Stoke Edith and Holme Lacy.

In the 18th century, tomb-chests and kneeling figures at prayer-desks are no longer seen; effigies (of which there are relatively few in Herefordshire) may be depicted seated, standing, or reclining; and the enthusiasm for urns, cherubs and sarcophagi was supplemented as the century proceeded by the frequent depiction of pyramids or obelisks as a background instead of architectural surrounds with columns and pediments. As an alternative to effigies, busts in medallions or later on pedestals were often employed.

At Ledbury, the effigies of Anthony Biddulph (d.1718) and his wife (d.1706) are reclining in front of a tall back-plate. The fine memorial at Kinnersley to Lady Morgan (d.1764) depicts an angel with a medallion bust of the deceased, and a funerary urn (Fig. 142). This is by Nicholas Read who worked from c.1749 till his death in 1787 and who had been apprenticed to Roubiliac, and took over his studio in 1762 after Roubiliac's death. His work at Kinnersley is more satisfying than some of his more grandiose memorials elsewhere.[8] At Hope-under-Dinmore is another fine monument to the Earl and Countess Conyngsby; Pevsner dates this monument by an unknown sculptor to c.1760. The effigies (Figs. 143, 144) are shown seated, flanked by Corinthian pilasters, and an open segmental pediment above. Towards the end of the century are three memorials at Eastnor designed by James Stuart (a leading figure in the Greek revival) and carved by Thomas Scheemakers (1740-1808).

Much more numerous than effigies or standing monuments are the hanging wall-tablets, which by the 18th century had replaced memorial brasses and incised slabs. The tablets can vary from the simplest form to memorials of distinction; it is neither possible nor desirable to refer to them all here—few parish churches are without any memorial tablet—but some of the best are as follows.

At Brampton Bryan are the monuments to the second Earl of Oxford (d.1724) and Mrs. Sarah Harley (d.1721). The former is an impressive memorial, with an architectural frame with garlands, and above an urn. Mrs. Harley's monument is smaller, but again with an architectural surround. At Ledbury is the memorial to Capt. Samuel Skynner (d.1725) by Thomas White, consisting of a bust in front of naval trophies (Fig. 145). Perhaps the finest of all is the monument at Canon Pyon to George Sawyer (d.1753). This is a very chaste composition in white marble, featuring a draped urn. The sculptor was Louis Francois Roubiliac (1702/5-62), 'probably the most accomplished sculptor ever to work in England'.[9] At Much Dewchurch is the monument to John Symons (d.1763) in white and pink marble, and with three cherubs' heads at the foot. At Ross-on-Wye, the monument to John Kyrle was erected in 1776, though he had died in 1724. He was a great local philanthropist, known as the Man of Ross. The monument is by a local sculptor named Marsh; above the inscription are two medallions, one with a likeness of the deceased and the other portraying two Virtues. At Stretton Grandison is the unusual memorial to William Jauncey (d.1794) by Thomas King of Bath (1741-1804); it shows a column broken in two. Other works by the same sculptor are at Tyberton. A late monument in the rococo style is the memorial at Shobdon to Viscount Bateman (d.1804); above the inscription is a portrait medallion with a cherub in front of an obelisk (Fig. 146); the sculptor is Joseph Nollekens (1737-1823), and in the quick movement of the cherub the work is certainly rococo in inspiration rather than Greek, which was then coming into fashion. Nollekens had used the motif of the child and a portrait medallion previously, at Bruera and at Cartmel.[10] Even later in this style, still with an urn before an obelisk is the memorial at Much Dewchurch to Thomas Symons (d.1818).

The end of the 18th and the first half of the 19th centuries witnessed the Greek revival, which replaced the earlier penchant for things Roman (in the Baroque and rococo eras). Interest in Greek antiquities was fostered by two young architects, James Stuart and Nicholas Revett; and popular attention increased when Lord Elgin, British Ambassador at Constantinople from 1799-1803, studied the ruins of the Parthenon in Athens, and brought the Elgin marbles back to England because they were in great

danger of neglect and destruction. Later, in the 1820s, the Greek struggle for independence caught the public imagination, especially when Lord Byron became involved (he died during the Greek war of independence in 1824). From about 1810 to 1830, Greek churches were built up and down the land, and church monuments took on a decidedly Greek style. Colour was eschewed, and the use of white marble was almost universal. Figures were often carved in relief, and the depiction of angels ministering at the point of death was a frequent theme. Women mourning over the deceased were also commonly depicted.

This theme was introduced by an unknown artist in a small roundel below the monument to John Parkinson (d.1804) at Kinnersley (Fig. 147); and a few years later at Brockhampton-by-Bromyard (Fig. 148) in the monument to Lydia Bulkeley by John Bacon the Younger (1777-1859), said by Whinney to have little originality.[11]

The work of two of the leading sculptors of this time, John Flaxman (1755-1826) and Sir Richard Westmacott (1775-1856) may be seen at King's Caple and Ledbury. Flaxman's great gift was in linear design: smoothly rounded limbs, delicate clean contours—'His sentiment is that of his age, drenched with nostalgia for the past ... but ... applied to the present with a freshness, a lack of self-consciousness that gives him a special place among neo-classical artists, for few have his innate sincerity and charm'.[12] These properties may be discerned at Ledbury, where the monument to William Miles (d.1803) shows a woman reading in front of an obelisk (Fig.

Fig. 147 (top) Roundel from the monument to John Parkinson (1804) at Kinnersley

Fig. 148 (centre) Memorial to Lydia Bulkeley (d.1812) by John Bacon junior in the new chapel, Brockhampton-by-Bromyard

Fig. 149 (left) Memorial to William Miles (d.1803) by Flaxman at Ledbury

149); and at King's Caple, where the monument to Mrs. Holcombe Ferguson (d.1814) shows a young woman seated by an urn, with her son on her knee.

Sir Richard Westmacott was a sculptor more difficult to assess. "His best work borders on greatness ... (but) most of his very considerable work is far more commonplace'.[13] He had a greater feeling of form than Flaxman, but not the latter's gift of linear design. There are two of Westmacott's works at Ledbury: the monuments to Robert Myddleton Biddulph (d.1814) and to Daniel Ellis Saunders (d.1825); the former shows a woman mourning by an urn, with reliefs of three children (Fig. 150), and the latter shows a family group—both are excellent.

Fig. 150 Memorial to Robert Biddulph (d.1814) by Sir Richard Westmacott at Ledbury

The monument to Eliza Woodhouse (d.1833) at King's Caple, erected by her grand-daughter 'in gratitude for her parental care' is also full of feeling,, and is reckoned one of the sculptor's better works.

Another fine monument in the Greek style is that to Thomas Westfaling (d. 1817) at Ross-on-Wye, by William Theed senior; a bust of Westfaling rests on a plinth, and on one side of the plinth is a relief of Charity teaching children (Fig. 151).

Fig. 151 (left) The Westfaling monument at Ross: charity teaching children
Fig. 152 (right) Monument to Richard Harcourt Symons (d.1850) at St. David, Much Dewchurch

On a less exalted plane may be mentioned the monument at Wigmore to Edward Davies (d.1814) by Thomas Denman; Denman was Flaxman's brother-in-law, and the memorial features weeping willows, with an urn above. The same tree (obviously a symbol of mourning) is shown even more prominently in the memorial to Richard Harcourt Symons (d.1850) at Much Dewchurch, by an unknown sculptor (Fig. 152). Finally, at Ledbury is the marble memorial to a child, John Hamilton (d.1851) by Mary and Thomas Thornycroft; John is portrayed asleep, and behind are two angels (Fig.153).

Halfway through the 19th century, monuments and memorials virtually cease in Herefordshire. The Greek revival has expired; elsewhere, the Gothic revival is in full swing, but of this there is very little evidence in the county's monuments—certainly none of the first rank. The best of the later monuments are those at Eastnor to the first Earl Somers (d.1855) by Sir George Gilbert Scott, and to the third Earl Somers (d.1883) by Sir J.E. Boehm.

Fig. 153 Memorial to a child, John Hamilton (d.1851) by Thomas Thorneycroft and his wife at Ledbury

Stained Glass

Eight or nine Herefordshire churches have significant displays of medieval stained glass, and many more have fragments of slighter importance. The finest glass and the most extensive array is at Eaton Bishop, but Credenhill, Dilwyn, Madley, Moccas and Ross-on-Wye all have some excellent work.

Oddly enough, the earliest recorded glass in the county no longer exists: this was the grisaille window in the presbytery at Abbey Dore, which showed a 'fish-scale' pattern. The glass was discovered during excavations at the beginning of the 20th century, but was lost during repairs to the window in 1973.[1] It was thought to be contemporary with the building of the abbey, between 1180 and 1250. The only other mid-13th-century glass in a Herefordshire parish church is at Madley, where in the upper part of the central east window are roundels, some of which depict the life of St. John the Evangelist.

The 14th century witnessed the golden age of medieval English stained glass, and glass in the Decorated style may be seen at Thruxton, Dilwyn, Kingsland, Moccas, Madley, and above all at Credenhill and Eaton Bishop. The tiny church at Thruxton (Fig. 154) possesses just one treasure—a small representation of the Crucifixion in a window in the south wall of the chancel. It is a sombre piece—Christ is shown wearing a brown loin-cloth, with yellow foliage on each side; the cross itself is dark green, and there is a red border. At Dilwyn, there is a lovely quatrefoil panel of a pair of angels swinging censers. At Moccas, there are a series of canopies, similar to those at Eaton Bishop, each containing two small figures; the glass was installed by the de Fresnes family. The 14th-century glass at Madley is part of a Tree of Jesse, similar to the Trees at Tewkesbury, Bristol and Ludlow. At Brinsop, St. George, the patron saint of the church, is shown in the east window with the saint depicted wearing armour, his red cross on the shield, with a ground of lattice-work as at Eaton Bishop. Above St. George is the Virgin Mary with the infant Jesus, and below St. John the Evangelist.

Credenhill's greatest treasure is the glass in the south chancel window. This portrays side by side St. Thomas à Becket of Canterbury and St. Thomas Cantilupe, bishop of Hereford from 1272–82 (see back cover). The vest-

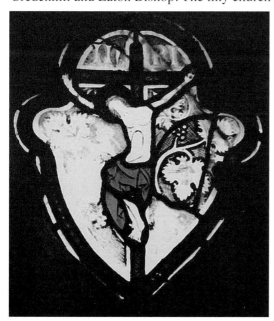

*Fig. 154 The Crucifixion
at St. Bartholomew, Thruxton*

ments are coloured in a gorgeous array of blue, green, red and yellow; on either side is a border of castles and fleurs-de-lis. Above are the names Cantuar and Cantulopo, doubtless chosen to strengthen the links between the two bishops by a play on words.[2] Indeed, it has been persuasively argued that this panel was part of the campaign to promote canonisation of Cantilupe by his successor at Hereford, Richard Swinfield (bishop from 1283-1316). The date of the panel is thought to be very early in the 14th century: canonisation was accomplished by 1320.

The glass at Eaton Bishop has been said to stand at the peak of English glass-painting at its most glorious period,[3] and has been dated to **c**.1330 (Figs. 155, 156 and back cover). The glass came from the same workshop that produced the glass at nearby Madley and Moccas, and further afield at Tewkesbury, Ludlow and Bristol.[4] As at Brinsop, the figures stand against a ground of rich lattice-work. The finest glass is in the east window. The lowest row of panels are the donor panels, kneeling figures with some words below. Above, from north to south, is the finest panel, the Virgin and Child, next St. Michael weighing souls in his balance, then a bishop holding a book, the Archangel Gabriel raising his right hand in benediction, and the head of Christ. In the south window of the chancel, figures include an angel, a Crucifixion, and Christ in Majesty at the top; in the north window, there is a small Crucifixion at the top. Pevsner draws attention to the typical Decorated colour scheme of brown, green and yellow, with little red and less blue, and notes that the tall canopies are typical of Decorated glass.[5]

Three churches have good glass from the 15th century. In the east window of the chancel at Ross-on-Wye are four figures which came from the bishop's chapel at Stretton Sugwas. There has been a lot of debate about the identity of the figures, especially in the central panels. Reading from left to right, the panels are now thought to show St. Ethelbert; the Virgin and Child holding an open book with a bishop kneeling (possibly the donor Thomas Spofford, bishop of Hereford from 1422–1448); St. Joachim (father of the Virgin); and St. Thomas Cantilupe with crozier in his left hand, the right raised in blessing. In the east window of the north aisle at Goodrich are white and yellow figures of angels with shields. And at St. Weonard's, the figure of St. Catherine in the east window of the north aisle is original glass of the 15th century; the rest of this window is Victorian. Nearby is a panel of Flemish glass from the late

Glass at St. Michael, Eaton Bishop:
Fig. 155 (top) The Virgin and Child
Fig. 156 (lower) The Archangel Gabriel

15th century, depicting the call of St. Peter; this glass was bought in Hereford market and given to the church in 1952 (see back cover).[6] Glass from the 15th century may also be seen at Weobley.

Glazing came to an abrupt halt at the Reformation, but was revived in Herefordshire 80 years later at Abbey Dore and Sellack, and in 1675 also at Foy. The occasion for this unexpected recrudescence was provided by Lord Scudamore's rescue of Abbey Dore, and the influence behind it was the High-Church theology of William Laud, Bishop of London from 1628 and Archbishop of Canterbury from 1633. The east window at Abbey Dore comprises three lancets: in the outer windows are two bands of figures—the upper band depicts the four Evangelists, each identified by his symbol, Matthew and Mark in the north window, and Luke and John in the south; in the lower band are the first four disciples, Peter and Andrew in the north, and James and John in the south. The taller central window has a jumble of fragments in its upper part; below this are the figures of Moses and John the Baptist; and in the lowest part a dramatic portrayal of the Ascension. It has been pointed out that the outer windows and the upper figures in the central window look back in style to the Gothic past, but the portrayal of the Ascension 'belongs firmly to the first half of the seventeenth century'.[7] 'No stained glass of this type had been produced for some three hundred years'—a clear case not of Gothic survival but of Gothic revival. Nevertheless, one cannot but feel that this glass looks back to the past rather than forward to the future.

The same must be said of the glass at Sellack and Foy. At Sellack, also funded by Lord Scudamore, the east window was reglazed in 1630, re-using some fragments of glass of the previous two centuries but with the addition of some contemporary glass; the scenes depicted include the Nativity and Crucifixion,

Fig. 157 Victorian stained glass at St. Peter, Pudleston

and portrayal of several saints. In 1675, the glass at Sellack was copied at Foy, under the will of John Abrahall. Netherlandish glass from the 17th century is present at Llanwarne.

Victorian stained glass is, of course, to be found in almost every church in the county—much of it uninspired and sentimental. But good glass of the 19th century has long been undervalued, and it is now clear that the best Victorian glass can withstand comparison with that of any age. With such an abundance of material, it is impossible here to do more than indicate some churches where excellent glass is found. Many of the well-known Victorian artists are represented in the county, but there is not much by the pre-Raphaelites—though two windows at Ledbury were made in the William Morris workshop to the design of Sir Edward Burne-Jones, and one window at Hoarwithy is believed to be by him. At St. Paul's, Tupsley, Hereford, are four windows by Henry Dearle who had close links with Burne-Jones and William Morris (p.193). There is said to be glass by Pugin at Clehonger, Kilpeck and Pudleston; by Charles Eamer Kempe at Bridstow, Colwall, Eastnor, Evesbatch, Ledbury, Leominster, Llandinabo and Much Marcle; by Hardman at Goodrich, Monkland, Pudleston (see back cover), Tedstone Delamere and Upton Bishop; by Clayton and Bell at Canon Frome, Ullingswick and Upton Bishop; and by Burlison and Grylls at Eardisland. Other churches with good Victorian glass include Almeley, Bridge Sollers,

Hoarwithy, Welsh Bicknor and Yazor. The anonymous glass at Hoarwithy is particularly impressive (see back cover).

From the 20th century, there is work by Sir Ninian Comper at Brinsop, by Martin Travers at Leominster and by A.J. Davies at St. Margaret's (a representation of St. Margaret as a sheperdess, carrying a replica of the church); see also the representation of the parable of the sower at Hereford, St. James. There is also glass of this time at All Saints, and St. Francis of Assisi, Hereford and at How Caple. But perhaps the best is at Lethaby's church at Brockhampton-by-Ross. Here in the east window are depicted seven saints and two angels, the work of Christopher Whall (whose work may also be seen at Ledbury).

Wall-paintings

In the Middle Ages, wall-paintings were frequent in parish churches. In an illiterate age, they were used by the Church to reinforce its teaching, to encourage reverence, and to rebuke and warn of sin and the Last Judgment. Doubtless the general artistic standard was low, and the colouring to our eyes garish. The painting was done in distemper (colour with water as a medium, and bound with white of egg or size—a gluey material) on dry and finished plaster-work (in contrast to frescoes, in which painting was done on wet plaster and permanently incorporated with it). Sometimes painting was repeated: 13th-century painting could be executed on fresh plaster applied over the paintings of the previous century or so. Because distemper was fugitive and easily damaged, very few good examples remain. Their number was further depleted when at the Reformation many paintings were destroyed, or more fortunately covered over—sometimes to remain hidden for hundreds of years. A recent discovery of 11th-century wall-paintings hidden by plaster in the ruined church of St. Mary the Virgin, Houghton-on-the-Hill, Norfolk strongly suggests that yet more exciting discoveries await to be made—perhaps in Herefordshire.[1]

At present, however, Herefordshire is not a good county for wall-paintings: only a handful of churches exhibit work from the medieval period, notably Byford, Madley and Michaelchurch Escley, and none is of a particularly high standard. There is certainly nothing which can compare with the marvellous paintings in the old church at Kempley, just over the border in Gloucestershire (which were re-discovered in 1871).

The commonest subject for medieval wall-painting was the figure of St. Christopher, patron saint of travellers; his figure was usually found on the wall opposite the entrance to the church, providing assurance to visitors that no harm would come to them that day, but there is no good example of this in Herefordshire. At Byford are 14th-century paintings of St. Margaret and an unidentified lady in the south transept. This saint is often depicted holding a long cross, thrusting this into the mouth of a dragon,[2] but whether she is doing this at Byford it is hard to say. At Brinsop are much defaced paintings of the Annunciation, Visitation and Crucifixion. Further medieval painting may be seen at Madley and Clodock, where a medieval painting of the Virgin (from an Annunciation scene) in the splay of a south window has recently been restored. Purely decorative wall-painting may be seen at Aston and at Michaelchurch.

The wall-painting at Michaelchurch Escley is the most interesting in the county. Here on the north wall is portrayed *Christ of the Trades*: a large figure of Christ surrounded by implements of many kinds—scissors, shears, axes, etc. (Fig. 88, p.35). This is a well-recognised but infrequent theme in medieval art—at Hessett, Suffolk, there is even a playing card, the six of diamonds, among the tools. Other churches which have this theme are Ampney St. Mary, Gloucestershire, West Chiltington, Sussex and four in Cornwall (Breage, Lanivet, Poundstock and St. Just-in-Penwith).[3]

More frequent in Herefordshire than medieval wall-paintings are post-Reformation paintings of biblical texts. At Abbey Dore are a series of 17th-century paintings in the crossing, including a skeleton leaning on a spade (the Remembrance of Death), and a figure of Time with his scythe and hour-glass. Below this are the Royal Arms of Queen Anne. A series of biblical texts around the crossing and the transepts dates from the 1630s (when the abbey was re-opened) and the reign of Queen Anne (1702-14). Even more striking are the texts which embellish the church at St. Margaret's. These have recently been beautifully restored, and now complement the rood-loft in that church (Fig. 163, p.69). A Royal Arms, Ten Commandments and Lord's Prayer are painted on the walls at Clodock.

Victorian decorative wall-painting can be seen at various churches; among the best are the designs by Bodley at Kingsland (Fig. 200, p.97) and Kinnersley (Fig. 217, p.113).

Rood-screens and lofts

In the later Middle Ages, screens had two functions—firstly, to act as a partition between the nave and chancel, and secondly to support the great rood—the image of Christ crucified, flanked by the figures of the Virgin Mary and of St. John the Evangelist. The rood-loft was a gallery above the screen, to which access was frequently provided by means of a stone stair-case; these stair-cases sometimes survive, and may now be the sole evidence of the previous existence of a loft. Sometimes the rood-loft would also house an altar, in which case a piscina high up on the south wall may remain to indicate its past location (as at Burghill and Little Hereford). Normally the rood-screen and rood-loft were part of the same fabric, but this was not universally the case, and in some churches they were independent structures. At the Reformation, the great rood and the rood-lofts were almost universally destroyed; many screens (or partitions as they were then termed, the word 'screen' appears to have come into general use only at the end of the 16th century) were also destroyed, but a fair number were spared. Where they were destroyed in the 16th century, they were often replaced in the High-Church revival from the 1840s onwards: so Victorian screens greatly outnumber medieval survivals. Above the great rood, extra decoration was sometimes applied to the roof, to act as a canopy of honour, or ceilure; these are not frequent, the best in Herefordshire being at Almeley.

Good medieval screens may occasionally be found almost anywhere in England, but those in Devon and East Anglia are recognised as of outstanding quality. In Herefordshire, many are rude and rustic in workmanship, but nonetheless attractive and appropriate for remote churches; a few are of superior quality. There are three rood-screens and lofts which are outstanding: the 14th-century stone screen at Welsh Newton, the Perpendicular screen at Aymestrey, and above all the superb rood-loft at St. Margaret's, one of the greatest treasures in the county. Rood-lofts are rare: only about a dozen remain in England, but there are more in Wales, some exhibiting exquisite wood-carving. The loft at St. Margaret's is clearly Welsh in character, and the church is very close to the Welsh border.

Medieval stone screens are rare, and that at Welsh Newton is the sole example in Herefordshire. It is an elegant structure (Fig. 158) dating from the early 14th century and consists of three arches, the central arch having a more acute angle than the lateral ones. It is supported by two octagonal piers with moulded capitals. The moulded arches are decorated with ball-flower, and there is also ball-flower on the cornice above. A dormer window on the south side gives light to the rood-screen.

There are about 14 medieval wooden screens in Herefordshire, and nearly all date from the first half of the 16th century—though some, especially the rudest, are extremely difficult to date. Simplest of all, and devoid of diagnostic tracery, is the screen at Pixley—genuine rustic carpentry, fashioned entirely with the use of pegs and no nails, and contributing greatly to the atmosphere of this humble little church. At nearby Aylton, the 15th-century screen has traceried spandrels, the central bay with cusping. A curious feature is the sequence of five traceried panels above the bressummer (the transverse beam)—surely this is not their original position? But as at Pixley, the screen at Aylton is entirely appropriate for its surroundings. At Stretford (Fig. 204, p.101), there are twin naves, and the screen extends across the entire church. Again the tracery has large forms, and the dado (the lower part of the screen) and the bressummer above are plain. Plain also is the screen at Michaelchurch—a compound of old and later woodwork.

Somewhat more complex is the screen at Sutton St. Nicholas: here the tracery is still of large form and relatively simple, but linenfold panelling in the dado proclaims its origin in the early 16th-century. Above the tracery, the cornice is moulded but plain. Rather more intricate are the screens at St. Weonard's: here a screen separates the chancel and nave, and two parclose screens enclose the chapel at the east end of the north aisle (Fig. 159). The tracery is again pure and of fairly large form but more complex, and again there is linenfold panelling in the dado. Above is a simple leaf frieze. In the Victorian church at Stoke Lacy is another sixteenth-century screen with a leaf-frieze in the cornice and below open panels with cusped ogee heads, crockets and tracery above. The dado is plain. At Withington the dado is of stone; the tracery of the screen is still of large form but is remarkable for the leaves on the cusps and small rosettes at junctions. The cornice is moulded but plain, and above is a continuous cresting. At Moreton-on-Lugg an excellent Perpendicular screen has been re-positioned at the west end and now encloses the organ. At Pipe and Lyde, the screen has gone, but the beam survives, beautifully carved with two friezes of foliage.

Fig. 158 (top) 14th-century rood-screen in stone at St. Mary, Welsh Newton

Fig. 159 (centre) Parclose screen with linenfold panelling in the dado at St. Weonard, St. Weonards

Fig. 160 (lower) A fine screen with upward coving, ribs and bosses at All Saints, Eyton

Fig. 161 (top) Another fine screen at St. Dinabo,
Llandinabo

Fig. 162 (centre) Exquisite vaulting over the screen, the
finest in Herefordshire, at St. John the Baptist and
St. Alkmund, Aymestrey

Fig. 163 (lower) Transverse cornice at the base of the
soffit carved with foliage; below a painted text from the
18th century at St. Margaret, St. Margarets

Further medieval or part-medieval screens may be seen at Eardisland and Kenderchurch; the screen at the latter church is mostly Victorian, but the cross-beam above the coving is carved with running vine-ornament.

The finest screens are the final group of four, all dating from the 15th or early 16th century: Burghill, Eyton, Llandinabo and Aymestrey. The screen at Burghill is tall and elegant, with deep coving above, enriched with ribs and bosses and supported by four posts. There are two bands of foliage in the cornice, and above is cresting running from side to side. The tracery is delicate, the dado plain. The obscure, humble church at Eyton is a surprising place to find a treasure; yet here is an original late-medieval screen (Fig. 160) with a central doorway and five single-light divisions on each side; there is tracery with ogee arches and quatrefoils, upward coving with ribs and bosses and a cornice with two trails of foliage. Llandinabo is another little-known church with a fine screen (Fig. 161): here the vertical mullions dividing the screen into three bays on each side are themselves decorated with geometric patterns, the exuberant tracery is very pretty, and the cornice carved with angels, dolphins, a mermaid etc. The dado is plain, but the upper part is pierced with a series of trefoil-headed elevation squints, four on the north and five on the south.[1] And so to Aymestrey: a much more substantial parish church, like Burghill, and with a screen unrivalled in delicacy in the county (Fig. 162). It dates from the early 16th century, and is especially notable for the exquisite vaulting, with ribs in the coving producing stellate effects. An uncommon aspect is the series of pendant arches under the cornice, which has three friezes of foliage. Above the cornice is cresting. The screen has one-light divisions, with linenfold panelling in the dado. The adjacent parclose screens are plainer, but also have linenfold panelling.

Finally, the rood-loft at St. Margaret's, a miracle of wood-carving (Fig. 7, p.*xiii*). It has often been pointed out that this loft is Welsh in character: a similar structure survives at Patrishow in Breconshire, which is less than ten miles away. Other celebrated rood-lofts in the area include those at Llanfilo (Breconshire), Llananno (Radnorshire), and Llanwnnog (Montgomeryshire). The loft at St. Margaret's stretches right across the church, the front of the loft being divided into 20 plain panels. Above and below the panels are friezes of running vine-foliage and at the top there is a delicate cresting. The loft is supported by two elaborately carved posts, and in each there is an empty niche: these would previously have held small statues. The soffit, or underside, of the loft is slightly coved (Fig. 163); it is divided into panels by moulded ribs, with carved bosses at the intersections representing human faces, foliage etc. (Fig. 164). A further transverse cornice at the base of the soffit is also carved with foliage.

Post-Reformation screens do not display the same delicacy of carving: the main screen at Dilwyn is tall with fan-vaulting above which may not be original; the tracery is more complex, and as expected the parclose screens are less elaborate. The screen is believed to date from *c*.1600. The screens at Foy and

Fig. 164 (top) Bosses at the intersections of the ribs on the underside of the rood-loft, St. Margarets

Fig. 165 (lower) The screen by John Abel dated 1634 at St. Mary, Abbey Dore

Michaelchurch Escley are also only partly original (17th-century), the rest being Victorian reconstruction. Wholly original, and a good example of rustic craftsmanship of its date (1613) is the screen at Vowchurch. Above the central arch are two dragons, and on either side two human figures known locally as Adam and Eve. But the contrast between this crude woodwork and the exquisite carving at St. Margaret's is painful. Quite the best 17th-century screen in Herefordshire is that at Abbey Dore, dated *c*.1634. This rather ponderous screen (Fig. 165) divides the chancel from the crossing and transepts, and the carving betrays a mixture of Gothic and classical detail; it is believed to be the work of John Abel (1577-1674). The screen is divided into five bays by Ionic columns which support an entablature with shaped consoles above each column.[2] The elegant screen at Monnington-on-Wye has a wide central opening with four bays on each side, the open upper panels being separated by twisted posts. An unusual screen from the last decade of the 17th century is at How Caple.

Notable Royal Coats of Arms in the county include Elton (Elizabeth I), Abbey Dore (Charles I), Monnington-on-Wye (Charles II), How Caple (William III) and Tyberton (George I). The Elton Arms is carved of wood with the initials ER and the inscription 'God save the Queene'.

Pulpits, Pews and Chancel Furnishings

Pulpits surviving from the Middle Ages are not common in England, and in Herefordshire there is only one, perhaps two. That at Stretton Grandison is hexagonal, the panels delicately carved with blind tracery showing ogee curves with cusping. The cornice has a frieze of running foliage. The pulpit at Wigmore is probably a little later—16th-century certainly, but whether before or after the Reformation it is difficult to say. It is notable for the vertical linenfold panelling. The pulpit at Kinnersley (Fig. 166) contains Flemish allegorical figures, dating from around 1530, but the pulpit itself is later.

After the Reformation, much greater emphasis was placed on the preaching of the Word, and pulpits suddenly become plentiful: Pevsner counted 36 Jacobean pulpits in the county, though some are probably later than the reign of James I (1603-25).[1] Many of them are decorated with the characteristic short blank arches (e.g. Colwall), but in addition there are often arabesques (Wormsley, Fig. 167), balusters (Mathon) or even dragons

Fig. 166 Pulpit with Flemish allegorical figures c.1530 at St. James, Kinnersley

Fig. 167 Jacobean pulpit with arches and arabesques, St. Mary, Wormsley

Fig. 168 Jacobean pulpit adorned with dragons at St. Mary, Pembridge

(Pembridge, Fig. 168). Several retain their testers or sounding-boards hanging above, as at Hereford All Saints; here are blank arches below, and within and above the arches further enrichment with various motifs. The pulpit at Moreton Jeffries (Fig. 169) is very elaborate for such an obscure church. The pulpit at King's Caple is unusually tall and stately, that at Bishopstone plain but elegant.

Fig. 169 An elaborate pulpit in the rustic church of Moreton Jeffries

In the succeeding century pulpits tend to be plainer, as, for example, at Clodock. An exception is the early 18th-century octagonal pulpit at Letton, which is very ornate—a minor baroque masterpiece. Each face is carved with a panel festooned with foliage, fruit and flowers, and above is the sounding-board replete with a panelled soffit.

Victorian pulpits are too numerous to list; but one at Stoke Lacy is carved in stone, and the pulpit at Welsh Bicknor is a real eye-catcher—carved with heads and adorned with marbles (Fig. 170).

For a county so abundantly wooded as Herefordshire, and with such widespread use of timber in the construction of houses, there is relatively little good woodwork in parish churches, except for the screens previously noted. By far the best set of choir-stalls is at Hereford All Saints, dating from the 14th century. The backs are carved with two tiers of ogee arches with cusping, and above runs a delicately carved cresting. Under the seats are a delightful set of misericords; though said to be cruder in execution than those in Hereford Cathedral,[2] there are lively representations of mermaids, beasts, grotesque human figures etc. (Fig. 171). Other stalls and misericords in the county are at Hereford St. Peter, Holme Lacy, Canon Pyon (Fig. 172) and Leintwardine; at the last may be seen an Annunciation and a Resurrection, and at Canon Pyon, St. Catherine's wheel. Carved stalls or pews can be seen at Almeley and Wigmore. Behind the stalls at Kimbolton is linen-fold panelling from the early 16th century.

On a much lower level of workmanship, ancient rustic pews survive in a number of village churches, those at Huntington near

Fig. 170 Exotic stone pulpit adorned with marble at St. Margaret, Welsh Bicknor

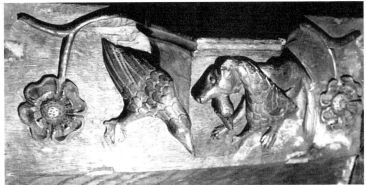

Kington being a good example; it is not possible on stylistic grounds to date them, but they are probably from the 17th century. Richard's Castle has a set of carved pews (Fig. 173), and also a family pew. A more sophisticated family pew may be seen at Madley. Clodock has a great variety of woodwork from the 17th and 18th centuries; in addition to the pulpit already mentioned, there is an excellent set of communion rails around three sides of the altar (Fig. 174), and many box-pews (Fig. 246, p.148). At Dulas there is again much woodwork from the 17th century—pulpit, lectern, desk etc.

A number of churches have reredoses of distinction. Those at Hampton Bishop and Leintwardine are of stone, much mutilated, and date from the late medieval period. A typical 17th-century reredos is seen at Brampton Bryan. At Tyberton and in the south chapel at Hereford All Saints are structures from the early 18th century. That at Hereford is a plainer version of those seen at Wren churches in London; at Tyberton, however, the oak panelling behind the altar is carved with emblems of the passion and other religious motifs (Fig. 269, p.180). At Kinnersley, there is a reredos composed of Jacobean panels (Fig. 175). The church at Putley has an elaborate reredos of alabaster and

Fig. 171 (top) Misericord at All Saints, Hereford

Fig. 172 (2nd from top) Misericord at St. Lawrence, Canon Pyon

Fig. 173 (2nd from bottom) Carved pews at St. Bartholomew, Richard's Castle

Fig. 174 (bottom) Communion rails at St. Clydog, Clodock

Fig. 175 (top left) Reredos with Jacobean panels at St. James, Kinnersley

Fig. 176 (lower left) An elaborate Victorian reredos of alabaster and mosaic at St. John the Baptist, Putley

Fig. 177 (top right) An ornate Victorian reredos at St. Mary, Yazor

mosaic (Fig. 176)—a Victorian extravaganza. Another excellent Victorian reredos is at Yazor (Fig. 177). At Monkland is a distinguished 20th-century reredos designed by Goodhart-Rendel (Fig. 278, p.188). This has a background of Salviati's mosaic, which is also in evidence at Moreton-on-Lugg. Finally, at Rowlstone is a unique pair of candle-brackets (Fig. 249, p.152).

Medieval Styles

Over 200 churches were built in Herefordshire during the Middle Ages; for the sake of readers who may be unfamiliar with medieval churches, a brief description of the styles used may be helpful.

There are no churches in the county dating from the Anglo-Saxon period, so the description begins with the arrival of the Normans in 1066. I have retained the traditional names for the medieval styles introduced in Thomas Rickman's classification, published in his *Attempt to discriminate the Styles of English Architecture* in 1817, terms which have been accepted ever since. He divided medieval styles into four groups: Romanesque or Norman (1066-1200), and three Gothic styles, Early English (1200-1300), Decorated (1300-1350) and Perpendicular (1350-1550). These dates are approximate, and must be treated with considerable caution. In Herefordshire, most medieval churches date from the 12th or 13th centuries—the Norman and Early English periods; the amount of building declined early in the 14th century, though there are some notable Decorated churches in the county. Perpendicular is seen least of all.

Fig. 178 Herringbone masonry at St. James the Apostle, Wigmore

Early Norman architecture (1066 until *c*.1100) is sometimes characterised by herringbone masonry, which was a style of building continued from Saxon times. Rows of stones were laid diagonally, each row leaning alternately to the right and left (Fig. 178), and it occurs at Bredwardine, Edvin Loach, Hatfield, Letton, Mathon, Munsley and Wigmore.

Another sign of early Norman building is the extensive use of tufa—a type of limestone in which new rocks have been formed by spring-water laden with calcium carbonate bubbling through sphagnum moss. The calcium carbonate was deposited in the form of a precipitate and gradually hardened. When the rock dries out, it develops a characteristic pitted appearance, like a petrified sponge.[1] The church at Moccas is largely built of tufa, and the material is also present at Blakemere, Bredwardine, Edvin Loach, Hatfield, Letton, Little Hereford, Monkland, Tedstone Delamere, Tedstone Wafer and Wigmore; it will be noted that there is a correlation between the use of herring-bone masonry and tufa .[2] The use of tufa declined during the second quarter of the 12th century.

The 12th century witnessed a tremendous programme of church building throughout the entire country: cathedrals, monastic houses and parish churches were built in abundance. Norman churches are characterised by solidly built arcades and towers: the arches are rounded, the cylindrical columns supporting the arcades massive (Fig. 179). The columns or piers are surmounted by square-edged capitals, as at Bridge Sollers (Fig. 220, p.119), which effect the transition from the round column to the square abacus above which supports the arch. The lower surface of the capital is often carved into a cushion (a rounding-off of the lower angles into the cylindrical shaft below), scallop— (Fig. 179), a further modification in which the surface is elaborated into a series of truncated cones)—or volute (spiral scrolls). In Herefordshire, a variant of the scalloped capital is frequently seen in which each scallop assumes a concave or trumpet shape (Fig. 180).[3] Towards the end of the 12th century, a few capitals are

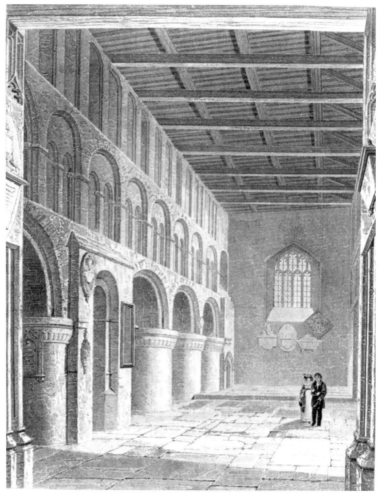

Fig. 179 The North Nave of Leominster Priory, looking east

enriched with decoration known as water-leaf—a broad leaf turning up towards the angle of the abacus (Fig. 181), as, for example, at Bishop's Frome, Clehonger, Garway and King's Pyon.

Semicircular arches are the hallmark of Norman or Romanesque building, and in addition to the nave arcades are found above doors and windows. They were often decorated by geometric designs, especially the ubiquitous chevron or zigzag (Fig. 22, p.9), which was introduced very early in the 12th century. Other Norman ornamental motifs are beakhead (the repeated use of stylised heads of birds or mammals with long beaks), billet (short raised rectangles repeated at regular intervals) and nailhead (small pyramids similarly repeated). Very early in the Norman period (1070-1100) a sunken-star pattern may be seen, together with rosettes and other motifs. Norman windows are usually small and round-headed, and deeply splayed internally to maximise the provision of light, glass being expensive.

The smallest Norman churches began as just a nave and chancel—this is to be seen in its purest form at Heath chapel in Shropshire—a building perfectly preserved and virtually unaltered for over 800 years. In Herefordshire, Kilpeck and Moccas are similar, but at the eastern end of the chancel is an apse, a semi-circular projection very common on the continent but unusual in England. There is an apse also in the quite exceptional four-cell church at Peterchurch. Other small two-cell churches in the county include Aston, Munsley and Yatton.

The population steadily grew throughout the 12th and 13th centuries, and it was often necessary to enlarge the small two-cell churches. This was frequently done by lateral enlargement of the nave in the form of aisles, separated from the nave by arcades of semicircular arches supported by massive piers or columns. Norman arcades are not very frequent in Herefordshire— many have been replaced in later centuries—but occur in, for example, Bridge Sollers (Fig. 220, p.119) and Linton-by-Ross (Fig. 264, p.170). For Norman building on a grand scale, there is nothing to compare with the 12th-century nave at Leominster (Fig. 179) (except, of course, the cathedral).

The introduction of the pointed arch, which ushered in Gothic architecture, and which was to revolutionise church building, was primarily for structural reasons, such an arch being able to transmit a larger proportion of the thrust directly to the ground.[4] It appears to have been first used at Autun Cathedral in France, around 1120-1130. In England, it is present from about 1160-1200 side by side with semicircular arches and massive Norman columns (the Transitional period) (Fig. 180); other examples of Transitional arcades occur at Sarnesfield (Fig. 218, p.115), Kingstone, and Bosbury. After about 1200 semicircular arches are seen no more, the columns become less substantial, and the Early English style has begun. This lasted throughout the whole of the 13th century. Arches are acutely pointed; the less massive piers at first remained mostly cylindrical (Fig. 182), but later became octagonal or multi-shafted. Capitals became usually rounded rather than square, and were sometimes decorated with 'stiff-leaf' foliage (Fig. 183)—more exuberant than

Fig. 180 (top) Transitional arcade with trumpet-scallop capitals in St. John the Baptist, Byford

Fig. 181 (centre) Water-leaf capitals at St. Mary the Virgin, King's Pyon

Fig. 182 (lower) Early English columns and arcades in St. Mary the Virgin, Dilwyn

water-leaf, the leaves often being multilob-ular. A frequent ornamental motif in the 13th century is dogtooth—a series of four-cornered stars placed diagonally and raised pyrami-dally. The other major characteristic of the Early English style is the lancet window—until the Victorians imitated it, a sure indica-tion of the 13th century. The lancet is a tall narrow window with an acutely pointed upper end (Fig. 243, p.145). Often they are paired, or grouped in a series of three or more, some-times provided with a common hood-mould to throw rain-water clear of the window. Later in the century, the area enclosed by a common hood-mould was often pierced, resulting in plate or Y-tracery (Fig. 218, p.115); from this germ, the development of complex tracery in the next century evolved. A very frequent pattern in Herefordshire is a group of three stepped windows often under a common arch,

Fig. 183 Stiff-leaf capital in St. Lawrence, Canon Pyon

with the mullions flanking the middle light running up to the arch above (Fig. 184); this usually indicates a date around 1300. This type of window is often referred to later in this book as the 'Herefordshire Window'.

The Decorated style was introduced around 1300, and lasted for about 50 years. Decorated arches are not so acutely pointed, and the piers are often octagonal or multi-shafted in cross-section (Fig. 185). Carvings on the moulded capitals are freer and more elaborate, and when foliage is seen it is more realistic than the stiff-leaf carving of the previous century. Y-tracery developed into intersecting tracery (Fig. 263, p.169), in which each vertical mullion branches into two carved bars. The most characteristic Decorated feature, introduced very early in the 14th century, is the ogee arch—two shallow S-shaped curves meeting upwards in a sharp point (Fig. 186), often embellished with crockets and other ornamental features. There was nothing functional about the ogee arch—it was an exuberant artistic fancy. In windows it led to complicated patterns of flowing tracery (Fig. 187)—geometrical, curvilinear or reticulated. Leaf patterns—trefoil, quatrefoil, cinquefoil, even sexfoil—are frequent in Decorated adornments, the leaves often separated by cusping. Another characteristic motif of the Decorated age was ball-flower ornamentation—a small ball enclosed by three petals forming a glob-ular flower; this was often set in rows on mouldings on windows, above tomb-recesses and elsewhere. The masons of Herefordshire had a particular fondness for ball-flower—at Ledbury and Leominster (Fig. 187), for instance, carrying it to extreme lengths,

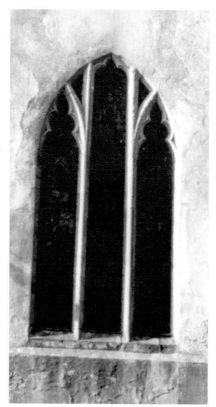

Fig. 184 A typical Herefordshire window at St. Bartholomew, Ashperton

with entire windows encrusted with it. There are some distinguished Decorated churches in Herefordshire, notably in a small area characterised by the black-and-white villages—Pembridge, Weobley, Dilwyn, Lyonshall and Kington. After a detailed study of the mouldings employed, Morris postulated the existence of a local workshop.[5]

Around 1350, the Black Death engulfed the country, and a quarter, perhaps a third, of the entire population died. At about this time, coincidentally or not, there was a reaction against all things Decorated, and a sterner, plainer style emerged—Perpendicular. This was in contrast to France, where Decorated became ever more extreme, producing the Flamboyant style. But Perpendicular remained exclusively British, the only medieval style to have evolved in, and been confined to, this island. In Perpendicular building, the emphasis

Fig. 185 (top) Decorated arcades and columns, the latter polygonal in cross-section with hollows in the diagonals in St. Michael, Kingsland

Fig. 186 (centre) Tomb-recesses with ogee arching above and cusping at St. Mary Magdalene, Little Hereford

Fig. 188 (lower) The chancel with a Perpendicular east window in St. Peter and St. Paul, Weobley

Fig. 187 A complex Decorated window, heavily adorned with ball-flower at Leominster Priory

throughout is on verticality; straight lines replace the sinuous tracery of the Decorated style; the pointed arches become flatter. This 'alters the proportions of the arcade: a large part of its height is now taken up by the piers. The piers being both taller and thinner make the arcade appear loftier and produce the impression of height and lightness of structure that is so characteristic of the Perpendicular style ... the preference for straight lines shows particularly clearly in window tracery. There the vertical mullions that divide a window into its lights rise almost without interruption to the head of the window, ruling its tracery into tiers of vertical compartments' (Fig. 188).[6] The steeply sloping roofs of earlier centuries were now often replaced by low-pitched roofs (Fig. 85, p.34), thus enabling the side walls of the nave to be heightened and allowing for the insertion of a clerestory. Although the Perpendicular style is thought to have originated in Gloucester *c*.1350, in neighbouring Herefordshire there is relatively little Perpendicular building. This is in marked contrast to Cheshire, and to areas of the country enriched by the trade in wool, where glorious Perpendicular churches may be found, as in the Cotswolds and East Anglia. The inference must be that Herefordshire in the 15th century remained relatively poor, with a static population, and that church extensions were unnecessary. The main examples of the Perpendicular style in the county are the church at St. Weonard's, the towers at Little Dewchurch, Bridstow, Hentland, Holme Lacy, Lugwardine and Much Marcle (Fig. 2. p.*xi*), and subsidiary chapels in Birley (Fig. 196, p.93), Bosbury (Fig. 90, p.36), King's Caple (Fig. 89, p.36) and Sellack.

Monastic Foundations

Although this book is primarily concerned with parish churches, a number of churches had close links with monastic foundations. It seems artificial to ignore these and a brief account is given here of Herefordshire's religious houses.

The battle of Hastings in 1066 swept away Anglo-Saxon England for ever, and William the Conqueror lost no time in imposing Norman rule on his new subjects. The new regime embarked on ambitious building programmes—castles for defence against the Scots and Welsh and to maintain the subjugation of the English, and cathedrals, parish churches and monastic foundations for the Church. Cathedrals are outside the scope of this work, and the Norman contribution to the building of parish churches is referred to earlier (pp.75-77)

Monastic foundations were not, of course, so numerous as parish churches. Nevertheless Herefordshire eventually possessed more than 20, and of these, 16 date from the Norman period (1066 - c.1200, see Table I). The major foundations in Herefordshire were Dore and Wigmore abbeys, and Leominster Priory. Priories tended to be smaller than abbeys, and many of the priory cells were very small, often housing only two or three monks sent from the owning house to exploit a distant estate. The alien priories were so called because they were founded by French religious houses; later in the Middle Ages, at the time of the wars with France, they became very vulnerable, and most of them were suppressed in the 15th century, although some escaped by purchasing naturalisation.

At the time of the Conquest, monastic life in Herefordshire was at a low ebb: there had been two Anglo-Saxon foundations—Leominster Priory, and the Priory of St. Guthlac in Hereford. Leominster was probably founded as a nunnery in the 9th century, and came to an end in 1046 when Swein (son of Earl Godwin) dragged out the abbess by force and seduced her;[1] it was not to be re-founded until 1123, when Henry I established it as a cell of Reading Abbey (p.97). The date of the foundation of St. Guthlac's is uncertain; it may have been as early as the 8th century,[2] and at the time of the Conquest the church stood on Castle Green. The Domesday survey (1086) records that St. Guthlac's had extensive properties, including the manors of Almeley, Brampton Abbotts, Dormington, Hope-under-Dinmore, Moccas and Whitney. St. Peter's, Hereford was granted by Hugh de Lacy in 1101 to the abbey of Gloucester, intending it to become a dependent priory. St. Guthlac's was united with this priory in 1143, when it was moved from Castle Green to Bye Street, the new establishment being the Priory of St. Peter, St. Paul and St. Guthlac.

Most of the orders of religious houses were represented in the county, the Benedictine foundations being most numerous (Table I). These houses followed the Rule laid down by St. Benedict in the 6th century. For five hundred years they were the dominant influence in monasticism, and for much, and especially the early part, of this period, they were the major repositories of learning and literature throughout western Europe. The Benedictines did not, however, constitute a single religious order, for each

Foundation	Order and status	Founded	Dissolved	Subject to
Hereford St. Guthlac	Benedictine Priory	?8th century	1538	Gloucester
Leominster	Benedictine Priory	?9th century	1046	
Monkland	Benedictine alien cell	c.1100	1414	Conches
Liver's Ocle	Benedictine alien cell	1100	1414	Lyre
Ewyas Harold	Benedictine priory cell	after 1100	1359	Gloucester
Titley	Tironian alien cell	1120 - 21	1391	Tiron
Leominster	Benedictine priory	1123	1539	Reading
Clifford	Cluniac priory	1129 - 30	1536	Lewes
Wigmore	Augustinian/Victorine abbey	1131 - 35	1538	
Kilpeck	Benedictine priory	1134	1428	Gloucester
Dore	Cistercian abbey	1147	1536	Morimond
Hereford St. Giles	Knights Hospitallers	1158	-	Dinmore
Garway	Knights Templars	1180	merged 1410	
Dinmore	Knights Hospitallers	1189	leased 1535	
Limebrook	Augustinian canonesses priory	1189	1539	
Colwall	Benedictine priory cell	1199		Great Malvern
Wormsley	Victorine priory	1200	1539	
Aconbury	Augustinian canonesses priory	1216	1539	
Bosbury	Knights Templars	1217 - 19	merged 1410	
Craswall	Grandmontine alien priory	1220 - 25	1462	Grandmont
Hereford Greyfriars	Franciscan	before 1228	1538	Bristol
Hereford Blackfriars	Dominican	1242	1538	Oxford
Flanesford	Augustinian priory	1346	1536	

Table I: The Monastic Foundations of Herefordshire
(Most of the data in this Table is from Knowles, D. and Hadcock, R.N. (1971))

monastery was autonomous. In Herefordshire, the major Benedictine establishments were the old Anglo-Saxon foundations of Leominster and St. Guthlac's. Kilpeck Priory was also Benedictine; it was founded in 1134, and given by Hugh lord of Kilpeck to the Abbey of St. Peter at Gloucester (the famous church being an endowment of the priory).[3] The priory was united with Gloucester in 1428.[4] In addition, there were small Benedictine cells at Colwall (Brockbury), Liver's Ocle, Monkland, and Ewyas Harold. Liver's Ocle and Monkland were alien cells, subject to French abbeys, and these were suppressed in 1414.

The loose Benedictine monopoly was not challenged until 910, when a Benedictine abbey was established at Cluny, and here was instituted a stricter observance of St. Benedict's Rule. Furthermore, the abbey sponsored an extensive series of subsidiary houses, known generally as priories. These were often favoured by the aristocracy, and many Cluniac foundations became wealthy. In England, the leading Cluniac priory was at Lewes in Sussex, and the small priory at Clifford in the Wye valley, founded in 1129-30 by Simon fitzRichard, was subject to Lewes. Being ultimately subservient to Cluny, it ranked as an alien priory; in common with most other Cluniac foundations, Clifford purchased naturalisation (thus it became 'denizen') in the mid-14th century.

By about 1100, there was a general desire for reform of monasticism: the Benedictines were seen as too lax, the Cluniacs as too wealthy. To meet these perceptions, three orders were founded at about the same time: the orders of Tiron, Grandmont and Cîteaux. The first two remained relatively small, with only a handful of dependencies in England. Each, however, had one in Herefordshire—Titley, of the order of Tiron, was founded in 1120 - 21, Craswall, of the order of Grandmont, not until 1217 - 22. As alien establishments, they were suppressed early—Titley in 1391, and Craswall in 1462. The Cistercians, from Cîteaux, became large and extremely influential, transforming the face of monasticism in the 12th century; and they had a major foundation in Herefordshire at Dore Abbey. Their great expansion was largely the

Fig. 189 Flanesford Priory in a 1798 engraving

work of Bernard of Clairvaux (1090 - 1153); Cistercian monasteries were characterised by extreme asceticism, combined with hard physical labour on their estates. Their architecture, at least at first, was plain and elegant, eschewing decorative sculpture. Dore Abbey was founded in 1147 at the height of Cistercian prestige; by the end of the 12th century, the movement had lost some of its impetus; discipline had tended to decline, and some of the abbeys departed from their original convictions by accumulating wealth.

The remaining major movement of reform in the 12th century was that instituted by followers of St. Augustine's Rule. St. Augustine of Hippo (392 - 430) had never laid down a strict Rule like St. Benedict; and his precepts could therefore be widely interpreted. The Augustinian canons (sometimes known as Austin canons) lived together under a moderate rule: asceticism was discouraged, and they were much given to good works—'They ran hospitals and retreats for the aged and for lepers; they were school-teachers, chaplains ... above all, they assumed the responsibility for the parish churches'.[5] The major Augustinian house in Herefordshire was Wigmore Abbey. This was founded in 1131 by Oliver de Merlimond, steward of Hugh Mortimer, following his stay at the Abbey of St. Victor outside Paris during his pilgrimage to Santiago di Compostela (p.11). The Abbey of St. Victor was then at the height of its intellectual eminence,[6] and Wigmore became a Victorine abbey (the Victorines were a branch of the Augustinians). The abbey had a chequered career in its infancy; it began at Shobdon, then moved to Eye, then to Wigmore village (where they found the speech of their neighbours 'very vulgar and coarse'), then to Byton, back to Shobdon, and finally settled on their permanent site one mile north of Wigmore in 1172.

Smaller Augustinian houses were Wormsley Priory (founded c.1200 by Gilbert Talbot for Victorine canons) and Flanesford Priory (founded in 1346 by Richard Talbot, lord of Goodrich). In addition, two houses for nuns at Aconbury and Limebrook were established—Limebrook Priory was founded by Robert de Lingen (or possibly by one of the Mortimers) in 1189. Aconbury Priory was founded by Margery de Lacy in 1216 as a hospital for the sisters of St. John of Jerusalem attached to the preceptory of Dinmore;[7] in 1237 the foundation was changed to the Augustinian canonesses and it appears then to have become an educational establishment (p.155).

By 1200, the great majority of religious houses in Herefordshire had been established, and in the following century some of the impetus for expansion was lost. Instead, the early 13th century was characterised by the arrival in England of two orders of mendicant friars—the Dominicans and the Franciscans. The friars relied mostly on charity for subsistence and on wealthy donors for the cost of their buildings. They preached a more personal faith, bringing men and women directly to God rather than relying on the intercessory roles of the monks. Such an approach suddenly became more in tune with the times (more 'relevant' in today's parlance), and the friars soon established themselves in almost every cathedral city and county town in England. The Franciscans (the grey friars) came first to Hereford (before 1228), their establishment being in the west of the city, outside Friars' Gate and followed the teachings of St. Francis of Assisi (c.1182 - 1226). He founded the order based on poverty, chastity, and obedience, renouncing all idea of property and it spread very rapidly during the last years of his life. The Dominicans (the black friars) arrived in Hereford in 1242, following the teachings of St. Dominic (c.1170 - 1221); they imitated the Franciscans in eschewing property, and living a life of rigid poverty. The

Dominicans first established themselves in the Eign Gate suburb of Hereford, and in 1322 acquired a site in the Widemarsh suburb. The orders of mendicant friars expanded rapidly throughout the 13th century, and by 1300 their establishment was virtually complete.

The remaining religious houses in Herefordshire were those of the Knights Hospitallers and the Knights Templars. The Knights Hospitallers (the knights of the Order of St. John of Jerusalem) were founded in the 11th century to care for pilgrims in Jerusalem, and after the capture of that city by the crusaders in 1099 they guarded Christian possessions in the Middle East. In the mid-12th century, they were given land in the county, at Dinmore, where in 1189 they built a manor-house and chapel. The estates of Dinmore were extensive, spreading into Shropshire and Wales. Their other establishment was St. Giles' Hospital in St. Owen Street in Hereford, founded in 1158; here (as at Garway) they built a church with a round nave. The Knights Templars were founded in the early 12th century to protect pilgrims on their way to the Holy Land and in 1180 they were given land in Garway by Henry II. The order also founded a small house in Bosbury in 1217 - 19. In 1312, the Templars were overthrown by King Philip IV of France, and their properties in Herefordshire passed to the Knights Hospitallers. Other hospitals in Herefordshire in the Middle Ages included St Katharine's Hospital, Ledbury, founded by Hugh Foliot, bishop of Hereford, before 1230; the hospitals of St. Mary and of SS Clement and Katharine in Leominster; the hospital of SS John the Baptist and Mary Magdalene in Richard's Castle; and the hospital of St. John in Widemarsh Street in Hereford, which was later given to the Knights Hospitallers.

From the 14th century onwards, the story of monastic establishments in England was one of decline in vigour and influence, an increasing laxity of spiritual observance, loss of reputation, and reduced numbers of monks and nuns. During the wars with France, most of the alien priories were either suppressed or else escaped by purchasing naturalisation. By the time of the Reformation, most of the remaining religious houses were weak and demoralised, and Henry VIII brought this chapter of religious history to a close by the Dissolution of the Monasteries in 1536 - 40.

After the Dissolution, the religious houses passed into private hands and over the centuries nearly all the monastic foundations in Herefordshire have crumbled into ruin. Substantial remains are seen at Abbey Dore, Aconbury, Dinmore, Garway and Leominster (q.v.), where in each instance part or all of the church survives.

The remnants at other foundations are as follows:[8]

Clifford Priory: a 13th-century doorway reset in the basement of Priory Farm.

Craswall Priory: the ruins lie one mile north-west of the present church. They comprise the south wall of the nave and chancel, and part of the walls of the apse, together with the doorway from the apse south into the sacristy. There is also evidence of the shafted entrance to the chapter house and remains of the windows and the two circular piers within.

Flanesford: a 14th-century range containing the refectory on the upper floor (Fig. 189).

Garway: excavation of the round nave (p.157), and the medieval dovecot south of the church with an inscription dated 1326.

Hereford Blackfriars: ruins of the range west of the cloisters, and the preaching cross. Excavations have revealed the north wall of the church and the south walk of the cloister.

Hereford St. Giles' Hospital: the reset 12th century tympanum from the former chapel (Fig. 39, p.17).

Limebrook Priory: ruins of one 13th-century building.

Wigmore Abbey: The abbey church was the burial place of the Mortimers. The surviving fragments comprise part of the south and west walls of the south transept dating from the late 12th century. The 14th-century abbot's lodging also survives, with a two-storey building adjoining to the west and a further separate 14th-century building.

There are no surviving remnants of the monastic foundations at Bosbury, Hereford Greyfriars, Hereford St. Guthlac, Kilpeck, Titley and Wormsley.

Medieval Churches
in the Regions of the County

Mortimer Country

St. Giles, Aston**

Aston, or more properly Pipe Aston, is a small settlement in Mortimer Forest, on the minor road between Ludlow and Wigmore. There are two tumps or mounds, one only 120 yards north-east from the church, indicating old defensive works. St. Giles' church consists simply of a nave, chancel, south porch and western bell-turret but possesses one outstanding treasure in the Norman tympanum set above the north doorway (Fig. 35, p.15).

There are Norman windows in the north wall of the nave and chancel. The windows in the south wall of the nave are taller, and include chevron and nailhead decoration in the arch. It appears that the chancel was rebuilt in the 13th century: the east window has three stepped lancets under a common arch, and on the south a pair of trefoil-headed lights. Inside there is a good roof with tie-beams, collar-beams and wind-braces. There is some medieval wall-painting on the walls of the nave. The 12th-century holy water stoup,[1] carved with a lion and winged dragon, referred to on p.15 now serves upside down as the font.

St. John the Baptist and St. Alkmund, Aymestrey**

St. Alkmund was the younger son of Alhred, king of Northumbria in Anglo-Saxon times, and other churches dedicated to him are at Whitchurch, Shropshire; Derby (now demolished); and Blyborough, Lincolnshire. The reason for the dedication at Aymestrey is not known. Aymestrey was a large parish in the Middle Ages, with four townships. The name means Aethelmund's tree,[2] the second element being derived from OE *treow* (tree, post or beam). It has been thought that in small parishes *treow* may indicate a boundary tree, but in large parishes such as Aymestrey, Oswestry (Oswald's tree) or Coventry (Cofa's tree) Gelling speculates that the word may signify internal boundary marks between the divisions of a large estate.

However that may be, Aymestrey is now a delightful village either side of the A4110 and on the river Lugg, with an interesting church with one outstanding treasure—the screen. The church is of Norman origin, and there are Norman windows with tufa surrounds in the chancel; above on the outside is some herringbone masonry. The arcades separating the nave from the aisles are also 12th-century, though Marshall suggested that they have either been re-set or imported (perhaps from Wigmore Abbey).[3] The tower is later, probably around 1300.

The screen (Fig. 162, p.69) dates from the early 16th century, and is of high quality—the finest in Herefordshire (see p.69). Vallance compared it with the screens at Denbigh and

Fig. 190 The south parclose screen with linenfold panelling in the dado at Aymestrey

Gresford (Denbighshire), Mobberley (Cheshire) and Hughley (Shropshire)—all works of the finest stamp.[4] The parclose screens are also fine, and have linenfold panelling in the dado (Fig. 190). In the north wall of the chancel is an incised alabaster slab to Sir John Lingen and his wife (1506).

A notable curate of Aymestrey was the Reverend T.T. Lewis, a founder-member of the Woolhope Club; he spent years painstakingly researching the geology of the local limestone, and as a result of his work (which received belated recognition) Aymestrey limestone is known to geologists throughout the world.

St. Michael, Croft*

Standing next to the castle (which is in the care of the National Trust), St. Michael's church (Fig. 191) makes a pretty sight with its pink stone bell-turret, surmounted by a balustrade and a lead ogee-shaped cap. The church is older than the castle, which now dates mainly from the 15th and 16th centuries; and the manor has been in the hands of the Croft family since just after the Norman conquest (with a break from 1746 to 1923). The church consists simply of nave and chancel, built around 1300; two of the windows in the north wall of the nave show Y-tracery of this period. On the south side are straight-headed windows, with pairs or triplets of trefoil-headed lancets.

Fig. 191 Croft church

The interior is attractive, with its set of box-pews and an 18th-century west gallery. But the great feature of the church is the tomb-chest (Fig. 123, p.50) to Sir Richard Croft and his wife (d.1509). This was formerly sited in a chapel on the north side of the chancel, which was demolished c.1800.[5] On the chest are the alabaster effigies, (Sir Richard wearing the armour in which he fought at the battle of Tewkesbury in 1471) and above their heads an intricately carved canopy, replete with crockets and finials. Behind the heads of the effigies, in the west wall of the monument, are four figures of saints—St. Anthony, St. Roche, St. Margaret and St. Sitha. Further figures are present in a series of recesses along the south side of the tomb-chest, each with an ogeed and crocketed head. The workmanship of the whole monument is excellent. Note also the painted 17th-century ceiling, with carved angels' heads, and on the floor some medieval tiles. There is public access to the church during service times on Sundays; at other times it is likely to be locked.

St. Mary the Virgin, Elton

This little church makes a very pretty picture next door to the Georgian hall; it is of medieval origin, though much altered in Victorian times. The south doorways survive from the 12th century, and there is one Norman window in the chancel. There is a Jacobean pulpit, and a good screen which is at least partly original. Perhaps the best artefact in Elton is the Royal Coat of Arms of Elizabeth I carved in wood.

St. Peter and St. Paul, Eye**

Fig. 192 The 17th-century pulpit and the arcade into the north chapel at Eye

Eye, to the north of Leominster, means 'island' (from OE *eg*), and is so called because it lies between two streams. The church is attractively situated next to the fine 17th-century manor-house, and dates mainly from the 13th century. The tower is a Victorian rebuilding, with few older features. The church is entered via a fine 14th-century wooden porch showing ornate tracery. Both north and south doorways are Early English, the north being flanked by columns with capitals bearing leaf foliage. The arcades are also Early English, the south with scalloped capitals being a little earlier than the north, where the capitals are round and moulded. In the roof over the nave is a carved tie-beam. High on the south wall of the chancel is the figure of an angel with a shield, of uncertain origin.

The chancel opens via a two-bay arcade into a north chapel (Fig. 192) which houses some excellent monuments. This arcade was built later in the 13th century—the capital of the pier showing stiff-leaf foliage. The 17th-century pulpit has two tiers of arabesque panels, and in between enriched arches; it is dated 1681, but is probably earlier.[6] In the chapel are two 15th-century tombs attributed to the Cornewall family (Figs. 125, 126, see pp.50, 51). The Cornewalls were the original owners of the Berrington estates, which later passed into the hands of Thomas Harley from Brampton Bryan. He built Berrington Hall (*c*.1780) and his memorial is in the chapel. Note also the hatchment of John Blount (d.1629) and Elizabeth his wife; and Sir Reginald Blomfield's moving memorial to the three sons of Lord Cawley, the later owner of Berrington, all killed in the First World War.

All Saints, Kinsham

This little church is in the grounds of Upper Kinsham in the Lugg valley. It dates from around 1300, though the windows have been renewed. In the south wall of the chancel is a fine piscina, with a trefoiled arch above, dating from *c*.1310; there is a further piscina in the south wall of the nave. Some fragments of medieval glass are in the east window. There is a memorial to Thomas Harley, d.1738.

St. Mary Magdalene, Leintwardine**

Leintwardine, in the far north of the county, has an ancient history, being known in Roman times as *Bravonium*, when it was a strategic settlement on the road north from Kenchester to Wroxeter. The first element in the name is probably a river-name *Lent* (the village is at the confluence of the Teme and the Clun rivers—which one was the Lent?), the second element is from OE worbign meaning 'an enclosed settlement'. Leintwardine was a place of considerable importance in Saxon times, being the centre of a hundred extending into Shropshire and Radnorshire, as well as Herefordshire, and the manors were held by the king, Edward the Confessor, in the 11th century. At the time of the Domesday survey (1086), the manor was owned by Ralph de Mortimer, based on nearby Wigmore Castle. A hundred years later, Hugh de Mortimer gave the church to Wigmore Abbey.

Sir Stephen Glynne visited Leintwardine on 20 April, 1846, and was not impressed: 'The nave is unhappily fitted up in a conventicle fashion with large gallery, crooked pews and a huge pulpit in the centre of the nave near the chancel arch which it completely masks. The chancel in its neglected and decaying state presents a still more melancholy sight ... There is an arcade of three bays between the chancel and its north chapel which is walled up and the chapel appropriated to various unworthy purposes ... school, vestry, and coalhole!' Fortunately, radical changes in 1865 brought great improvement—perhaps we tend today to look too much askance at Victorian restorations.

The church stands on elevated ground above the river Teme, commanding an extensive view up the valley; it consists of a nave with north and south aisles, a chancel with a north chapel and a south-west tower opening into the south aisle. The chancel is said to be built over the east bank of the Roman station. This is the reason why the floor of the chancel and north chapel is so much higher than that of the nave.[7] Although there is a late Norman west doorway with a round arch and leaf capitals on the shafts, the building is essentially of the 13th and 14th centuries. Entrance to the church is through the porch under the south-west tower; the latter was built in the early 14th century, with Decorated windows of two lights in the belfry. The south doorway is earlier, 13th century, with a pointed arch and deep mouldings. The nave (Fig. 85, p.34) is spacious, and divided from the aisles by two different arcades: the south is Early English, with round piers and capitals, the north Decorated with octagonal piers and capitals. The chancel arch and most of the chancel were rebuilt in 1865; thus the east window with intersecting tracery is Victorian. To the north of the chancel is an arcade of three bays and two octagonal piers leading to the north chapel; both the arcade and chapel are Decorated (early 14th century), and the north windows of the chapel have reticulated tracery. Over the nave is a Perpendicular clerestory and, unusual in Herefordshire, a low-pitched roof, panelled and embossed (Fig. 85, p.34).

In the chancel, on either side of the altar are the remains of a stone reredos—tall carved panels probably dating from the 15th century. Below the dado-rail is a range of cinquefoil-headed panels and above, four tiers of similar panels. It appears that this reredos formerly extended between the two surviving sections, the central portion being cut away in 1865 to make room for the window.[8] There are also some stalls, which are thought to have come from Wigmore Abbey. These contain misericords with the usual mixture of the sacred and profane—scenes of Annunciation and Resurrection, and under other seats wrestlers and mermaids. In the north aisle is the mechanism of an ancient clock. The north chapel contains a memorial by Peter Rouw to General Sir Banestre Tarleton (d.1833) a colourful character who served with distinction in the War of American Independence. Later he became a close friend of the Prince of Wales (afterwards George IV) before retiring to enjoy the country life at Leintwardine House.

St. Andrew, Leinthall Earls

This is a small Norman church, restored in 1823, with undivided nave and chancel, a timbered bellcote, a tie-beam roof with queen-posts, and a Jacobean pulpit.

Fig. 193 Orleton church

St. Mary Magdalene, Leinthall Starkes

This is basically a Norman church, with small round-headed windows remaining in both chancel and nave. There was originally a Norman west doorway, of which traces remain; the doorway is now blocked up by a buttress.

St. George, Orleton**

Orleton, north of Leominster, means 'settlement among the alders'. It is an attractive village and is the presumed birth-place of Adam de Orleton who rose to be bishop of Hereford (1316-27). Coming from the land of the Mortimers, perhaps it is not surprising that he supported Queen Isabella and her lover Roger Mortimer, and forced Edward II to abdicate,[9] perhaps conniving at his subsequent murder in Berkeley Castle. When Edward III struck back at Mortimer and executed him, it is perhaps unexpected that Adam prospered, becoming successively bishop of Worcester and Winchester. He is buried in Hereford Cathedral.

Fig. 194 The nave and chancel at Wigmore

There are Norman vestiges in Orleton church (Fig. 193), notably a window in the west of the nave now blocked by the tower, and two round-headed doorways, one in the chancel now leading into the vestry and a west doorway in the tower. Otherwise the church is of the 13th and 14th centuries, with lancet windows in the chancel and Decorated windows in the nave. There is an excellent tie-beam roof with king-posts and queen-posts. Some fragments of medieval stained glass are present in the windows of the nave. Note also the fine Jacobean pulpit which has four panelled sides with tiers of arabesques and arched panels. Over the tower is an attractive broach spire. The wooden porch was built in 1686; the gable shows moulded barge-boards, and at the sides the open panels are separated by turned balusters. The excellent font (Fig. 45), the work of the Herefordshire School, is described in detail on p.19.

St. Bartholomew, Richard's Castle**

Richard's Castle takes its name from Richard le Scrob, who was a Norman living in England at the time of Edward the Confessor; around 1050, he built a castle here which antedated the Norman Conquest, and is therefore one of the earliest Norman castles in England. By the time of the Domesday survey (1086), Richard's Castle was already a borough; it was held by Richard's son, but later it fell into the hands of the Mortimers. Its subsequent history was one of decline, a borough that never realised its potential. Perhaps it was overshadowed by the growing importance of Wigmore to the south and Ludlow to the north.

Next to the castle, on the hillside to the west of the village, is the ancient parish church, well known for its detached tower which may have had a defensive function. Church and castle stand on a hillside to the west of the present village, which straddles the Herefordshire/Shropshire border; a new church was built in 1892 at Batchcott in Shropshire, and the old church is no longer used for regular services. Yet it is well worth visiting—the site breathes the air of history, and inside the church are some notable furnishings.

Fig. 195 The nave with box-pews, and chancel, Richard's Castle

The tower stands to the east of the church (Fig. 61, p.26)—a squat building, dating from around 1300. There is Y-tracery in the windows of the belfry. The church itself is partly older, for the nave is Norman, with two round-headed windows in the north wall. In the 14th century were added the chancel, north transept and south aisle—all showing features of the Decorated style (Fig. 195). The elaborate curvilinear tracery of the east window of the chancel, with a 'leaf-stem' motif in the centre, has been compared by Morris to contemporary windows in the north transept at Ludlow, three miles distant, and in the porch at Pembridge.[10] He tentatively assigns a date as late as the 1340s or 1350s for this work. The presence of a battlemented capital on the arcade to the north chapel would imply a later date. The arcade consists of clustered piers, each with four octagonal shafts. There is much ball-flower on the capitals of the arcade and on one of the windows of the south aisle. The west window of the nave is Perpendicular (15th century). The north transept was built as a chantry chapel for the Knights Hopsitaller of St. John, whose local base was at Dinmore. In the north wall of the transept is an unusual window with a six-pointed star. Under part of the nave and chancel is a crypt, which was probably built as an integral part of the original church. After the Reformation, it was walled up, filled with earth and used for burials. In the 19th century, the floor of the chancel was relaid with tiles, destroying all traces of the roof of the crypt. The crypt was excavated in 1988.[11]

There are some excellent wooden furnishings (Fig. 173, p.73). In the north transept is a 17th-century canopied pew of the Salwey family, who have held the manor for nearly 400 years. At the west end of the nave a further pew rises, and there is a good set of box-pews. By the font is a 13th-century coffin-lid enriched with a foliated cross.

St. James, Wigmore**

In the 11th and 12th centuries, the Normans built castle, church and abbey—probably in that order—and Wigmore was famous for centuries as the stronghold of the Mortimers. It was then a borough of some note—now castle and abbey are in ruins, the borough is no more, but the church stands proudly on its eminence overlooking what is now a village.

The church was probably built towards the end of the 11th century, judging by the very extensive herringbone work in the north wall of the nave (Fig. 178, p.75). There is one blocked Norman window on the south side of the nave now looking into the south aisle. This spacious aisle was added around 1300, the arcade dividing it from the nave consisting of octagonal piers with plain capitals. The chancel arch and chancel are Decorated (Fig. 194). High up on the wall separating the chancel and nave is a piscina which was originally used in conjunction with an altar on the rood-loft (as in Little Hereford).[12] A north aisle was added in the 15th century, but the eastern half of this was subsequently demolished. There are good roofs—that over the south aisle dates from the 14th century, with tie-beams, arched braces and foiled wind-braces laterally. The pulpit is late Perpendicular with vertical linenfold panels. There are some late-medieval stalls with traceried fronts. The very attractive porch is Victorian. The monument to Edward Davies (d.1814) with weeping willows is by Thomas Denman.

Around Leominster

St. Peter, Birley*

This little-known church, situated just to the east of the old Roman road (now the A4110) to the north of Canon Pyon, looks particularly fine from the south, where the most striking features are the Norman tower and the half-timbered gable of the Perpendicular chapel. There are typical Norman windows in the lower stages of the tower; above the belfry is a pyramid roof.

Internally, the tower arch to the nave is late Norman, with crocketed capitals. The chancel is Early English, with lancet windows. The chancel arch is handsome: this is Decorated, with much ball-flower embellishment; the capitals and shafts have human and animal heads. On the south is a Perpendicular chapel, with straight-headed windows (Fig. 196). The excellent Norman font (Fig. 93, p.38) has an interlaced pattern below the rim, and on the stem semicircular arches; below a chain, and then a band of saltire crosses.

Fig. 196 Perpendicular chapel with a straight-headed window, Birley

St. Michael and All Angels, Bodenham*

Bodenham, which lies to the east of the A49 at the side of Dinmore Hill, is a Saxon name meaning 'Boda's land in a river-bend',[1] and this is certainly apt here, for the river Lugg makes a great detour around Dinmore Hill, and the village is on the north bank of the river. It is a rather self-consciously pretty village, and has a fine church (Fig. 197) made memorable by its truncated, unfinished spire.

Unusually for Herefordshire, the church is mostly Decorated. It is a spacious building, consisting of a west tower, nave with north and south aisles, gabled transepts which do not project beyond the aisles, a north porch, and chancel. The tower is large and has three stages, and above is a moulded parapet with square-based pinnacles at the corners; within is the lowest part of a recessed

Fig. 197 Bodenham church in 1850

octagonal spire. There is ball-flower decoration over the doorways. The tower arch to the nave is lofty, and so are the arcades dividing the nave and the aisles—these were apparently heightened in the 16th century. The east window of the chancel is Decorated; the transepts have tall Perpendicular windows. There is a lovely 14th-century effigy of a lady with her coif and wimple; her right hand rests on the shoulder of her child—a moving portrayal of maternal protectiveness. The octagonal font has a wide and depressed ogee canopy (Fig. 101, p.41); it probably dates from the end of the 14th century.[2]

Fig. 198 Dinmore chapel

St. Michael, Brimfield

The most striking feature of St. Michael's is the tall 13th-century west tower, with its half-timbered upper storey (Fig. 66, p.27) dating from the 17th century. The font is Early English, and is plain, with four lobes. The rest of the church was drastically restored in the 19th century.

Dinmore Chapel* (St. John of Jerusalem)

Dinmore is Welsh *din mawr*—great hill, and the hill, rising to 500 feet above sea level is a landmark in central Herefordshire. Here, in the mid-12th century, the Knights Hospitaller of St. John of Jerusalem were given land, the founder of the establishment being Brother Thomas.[3] There they built their manor-house and chapel. The manor-house has long since gone, to be replaced by an attractive 17th-century dwelling, but the chapel remains. It stayed in the hands of the Knights until 1540 when the houses of the Order were dissolved.

The chapel (Fig. 198) is superbly situated next to the manor-house, and commands extensive views to the east as far as the Malvern Hills. The north buttresses and the door between date from the original building at the end of the 12th century, the buttresses being originally part of the walls of a range of dwellings extending towards the house.[4] Most of the rest of the church is 14th-century, including the tower and recessed spire, and the windows on the east and south walls with reticulated tracery. On the south wall are two medieval sundials. The interior is peaceful, and contains some fine modern woodwork.

Access: From Hereford, take the A49 north, and after about eight miles turn left into the drive leading to Dinmore Manor. Follow this for over a mile, right to the end, and park by the garden centre. Walk round the east side of the manor-house to the chapel.

All Saints, Eyton*
Visit this little-known church north-west of Leominster for one thing—the superb screen dating from c.1500 (Fig. 161, p.69). The church itself has one Norman window, and several ogee-headed lancets. The chancel roof has moulded tie-beams and collar-beams with arched braces.

St. Mary, Hope-under-Dinmore**
St. Mary's nestles under the northern slope of Dinmore Hill, an attractive situation marred only by the noise from the nearby A49. The church was largely rebuilt in 1879 and 1896 by the architect F.R. Kempson, who incorporated a small amount of older material. The building is unremarkable, but the church is worth visiting for the sake of three treasures within, though, unfortunately, the church is usually locked.

The 13th-century octagonal font is the finest of this century in the county, with figures of Christ and various saints (Fig. 100, p.40) under cinquefoiled arches. The font-cover dates from the late 17th century.

In the south wall of the north chapel is an incised slab to Humfry Conyngsby (d.1559) and his wife; he is depicted in plate armour, she with a French cap and costume of the period. This slab has been identified as the work of the Royley workshop at Burton upon Trent.[5]

Perhaps the best artefact is the huge memorial to the Earl and Countess Conyngsby (Figs. 143, 144, p.56): this shows seated effigies in front of a reredos of paired fluted pilasters with an open segmental pediment; the countess holds in her lap her infant son who choked to death on a cherry-stone in 1708. This fine work of the mid-18th century has in the past been attributed to Roubiliac, but this has not been confirmed.

St. Mary the Virgin, Humber
The oldest part of the church is the chancel, which is Early English work dating from around 1200. In the 13th century, the nave and west tower were added, the latter supporting a shingled broach spire. There is a fine timber porch of the 14th century, and the roof of the chancel is of the same period—it features tie-beams and king-posts. The plain Norman font has a prominent cable moulding.

St. James, Kimbolton*
Kimbolton lies on the A4112 north-east of Leominster, the church reached by a lane leading north from the village centre. Apart from two small Norman windows which survive in the chancel, this is essentially a church of the 13th century. The unbuttressed west tower is not tall, but is surmounted by a fine shingled broach spire (Fig. 69, p.28). The nave, chancel and south transept are all Early English, the south transept verging on the Decorated; in the south wall of this are two lancet windows, and above a two-light window

with trefoil above them under the containing arch, which has a hood moulding with head corbels.[6] Note the linenfold panelling of the 16th-century choir stalls.

St. Michael, Kingsland**

The villages of Kingsland, Monkland and Eardisland, all west of Leominster, share, as the second element in their names, the word *lene* now spelt 'land'. The same word is present in modified form in Leominster and Lyonshall. The *lene* appears to have been the land between the rivers Lugg and Arrow,[7] probably referring to their flowing waters. So the manors have been distinguished by their medieval proprietors, respectively king, monk and earl. After the Norman Conquest, William FitzOsbern became Earl of Hereford, but his son rebelled against the king in 1075, and forfeited his lands to the crown. In Domesday Book (1086), Lene was still described as 'King's land'. To the west of the church are a motte and bailey, the remains of a Norman castle.

Kingsland has been of some moment in English history; it was the probable site of the palace of King Merewalh of the Magonsaetan (p.3), and it was certainly the site of the battle of Mortimer's Cross, 1461. Here the young Edward, Earl of March defeated a Lancastrian army under Owain Tudor, avenging the fatal defeat six weeks previously of his father, Richard, Duke of York at the battle of Wakefield. Subsequently marching on London, he was crowned Edward IV, reigning until his death in 1483. The battle of Mortimer's Cross took place in the great west field of the manor of Kingsland.

In view of its history it is fitting that the parish church should be of greater than ordinary significance. It is quite a large church, and was thought to have been built around 1300,[8] a time when the Early English style was giving way to Decorated—though two very small lancet windows in the east transept may denote the presence of a wall earlier in the 13th century. Morris,[9] however, has presented evidence that the building is later, *c*.1320–40. The west tower is impressive (Fig. 55, p.24), with buttresses at the angles and windows consisting of paired lancets with Y-tracery on the ground floor and trefoil-headed tracery at belfry level; above this, the top of the tower is Perpendicular.

The most singular feature of St. Michael's is the little chantry chapel which arises to the east of the north porch (Fig. 199); this is known as the Volka chapel, and the origin of this name has been the subject of much speculation but little knowledge. Blount in 1675 wrote: 'On ye left dore into ye church is a little apartment, vulgarly sayd to be built by one Vaukel yt built ye church as a tomb for himself, and so goes by yt name, but more probably it was designed as a place for penitents, where they might look into the

church and hear prayers, but were not to be admitted into Communion till after they had shewed signs and proof of yr repentence and amendment'![10] R.H. George, writing in 1915, suggested that the chapel was the burial place of Walter de Mortimer, rector in 1315, the name Walter being later corrupted to Volka.[11] The chapel has a small east window with Y-tracery, and a straight-headed window in the north wall. On its south side, against the north aisle of the church, is a tomb-recess containing an open but empty stone coffin.

Fig. 199 The Volka chapel next to the north porch at Kingsland

Inside the church there are arcades of five bays (Fig. 185, p.79), the piers having four projections with hollows between. Above the spandrels of the arcades are sexfoiled clerestory windows. At the west end of the nave is a plain octagonal font, probably late 14th- or early 15th-century.[12] The nave roof has tie-beams and king-posts.

The chancel (Fig. 200) is the artistic treasure-house of St. Michael's. In the east window is some excellent 14th-century stained glass bearing the arms of Dame Matilda Mortimer, who presented the first known rector in 1285;[13] the main panels of the window represent four archangels (Michael, Raphael, Gabriel and Uriel), and above is the Coronation of the Virgin Mary and the figure of Christ holding a cross and seated on a rainbow. In the middle south window is the figure of an archbishop, with cross-staff and pallium; and there is further medieval glass in the north and south-east windows. The roof of the chancel was ceiled and painted during Bodley's restoration in 1866-68; Bodley also designed the pulpit, lectern and stalls. The encaustic tiles in the sanctuary are by Godwin, and the altar-piece in the Lady Chapel by Frank Brangwyn.[14]

Fig. 200 The chancel with ceiling decoration by G.F. Bodley at Kingsland

St. Andrew, Leysters*

The church, close to the A4112 north-east of Leominster, has a lovely situation, away from the village, and opposite a Norman motte. It comprises a low western tower with a pyramidal roof, nave and chancel. There is a Norman south doorway, with a plain lintel and tympanum, and a plain Norman font. The finest feature is the 14th-century roof (Fig. 81, p.33), with a tie-beam, collar-beams on arched braces and tiers of cusped quatrefoiled wind-braces.

The Priory of St. Peter and St. Paul, Leominster***

Leominster is thought to be the oldest Christian site in 'English' Herefordshire, the church there being founded by Merewalh *c*.660. So it is an ancient Christian site indeed; and during the Anglo-Saxon period developed as a minster church, serving a wide area of the surrounding countryside. By the time of the Domesday survey, it had been held by Queen Edith (wife of Edward the Confessor) and was a multiple estate of 16 members, including Aymestrey, Yarpole, Brimfield, Leinthall, and Edwyn Ralph. The prefix 'Leo' in the place-name derives from 'lene', (p.96) and this corresponds roughly to the area around the rivers Lugg and Arrow (which flow north and south of Leominster, and join two miles from the town).

The church at Leominster presents a very confusing picture, which can only be really understood by reference to its history. The Benedictine priory at Leominster seems to have been founded as a nunnery in the 9th century, and it was dissolved in 1046 and the nuns expelled. In 1121, following the tragic death of his son, Henry I founded Reading Abbey, where he was to be buried. Later in the same year, he was passing through Leominster *en route* to Wales, and there he refounded the monastery as a cell of Reading Abbey, and thus it remained until the Dissolution of the Monasteries.

Rebuilding of the church at Leominster quickly followed Henry I's refounding, and it was done on the grandest scale — second in size in Herefordshire only to the cathedral. The 12th-century monks' church consisted of the choir, transepts and crossing with a central tower above; to this was added the nave for parochial use by the townspeople (the rest of the church being monastic), completing a cruciform church. The eastern end of the church was semicircular or apsidal in shape, and from it radiated three chapels as at Reading. To the north was the cloister, with chapter-house, prior's house, refectory and dormitory surrounding it on three sides. Later in the Middle Ages, the church was extended: a second nave, parallel to the first was added in the 13th century, and a south aisle in the 14th century. Thus at the Reformation, there was the Norman nave, the 13th-century nave and the south aisle side by side (as today); but beyond the east end of the Norman nave was the crossing and transepts, and beyond the crossing the choir, with its radiating chapels. The monastery was dissolved in 1539 and after this the conventual buildings and the whole of the choir, crossing and transepts were demolished.

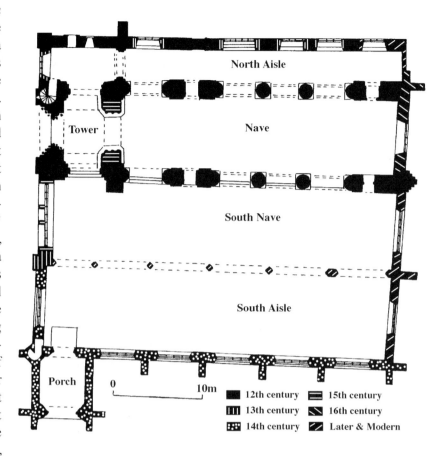

Fig. 201 *Plan of Leominster Priory*

The best way to understand the church is firstly to walk round the outside, beginning at the west end (Fig. 1, p.*xi*), and then proceed to the interior. At the west end, on the extreme left is a small circular Norman window above three lancet windows looking into the narrow Norman north aisle (the lancets must have been inserted later); then there is a noble Norman west doorway, which is discussed in detail on pp.12-13; this opens into the Norman nave and above it there is a large round-headed Norman window. Above this is the tower, which was added in the 15th century. To the right of the doorway is a very large west window of the 13th-century south nave; this window is Perpendicular, and was inserted in the thirteenth-century wall 200 years later. To the right of this is a Decorated window — the west window of the south aisle built in the 14th century, and festooned with the most lavish ball-flower decoration (Fig. 187, p.79), so typical of this period in Herefordshire.

Round the corner is the south porch; this is Early English, and must have been moved to its present site after the construction in the 14th century of the south aisle. Beyond the porch, there extends a very fine vista of the south aisle, a magnificent series of Decorated windows which can bear comparison with any in the country. Above is a panelled parapet.

The east end again has three components—the Decorated east windows of the south aisle and the south nave, and the round-headed window of the Norman north nave which was reconstructed in the 16th century after the Dissolution.

Now return to the south porch and enter the church. The south doorway is Early English, with columns and their stiff-leaf capitals on either side. Walk straight through the south aisle and south nave to the north, Norman nave—here there are two tremendous Norman arcades (Fig. 179, p.76), massive circular columns with scalloped capitals and semicircular arches—worthy of a cathedral. The arcades are irregular: it will be seen that, counting from the west end, the second and sixth bays are much narrower than the others, with sections of solid wall on either side. There has been some speculation about the reason for this—the Royal Commission on Historical Monuments thought that the fourth bay was also originally narrow, but was subsequently widened.[15] Above the arcades is a blocked triforium which originally opened into the Norman north and south aisles and which has remains of wall paintings on the south side towards the west end; and above this is a clerestory of round-headed windows, on the south side now looking into the south nave. The narrow north aisle has had windows inserted later—three stepped lancets at the west end, as seen from the exterior, and one of five stepped lancets in the north wall; other windows are much later, probably 18th-century.

The south nave was built in the 13th century, but one would never guess this now, for the west window is Perpendicular and the east Decorated—both inserted long after the nave was built; there must have been a pointed arcade separating the south nave from the south aisle, but this was dismantled in 1699 and replaced with incongruous Tuscan pillars; these in turn were replaced by Sir George Gilbert Scott in 1872-79 by the tall elegant arcade which one now sees.

The south aisle is a Decorated wonder—the windows are replete with ball-flower on the inside as well as the outside, and there is a Decorated sedilia with trefoiled heads and again much ball-flower.

Finally—the west doorway (Figs. 27-30) is the *pièce de résistance* of the whole church. It is described in detail on pp.12-13.

St. Mary Magdalene, Little Hereford*

Little Hereford, on the river Teme to the west of Tenbury Wells, appears to be so-named because the parish was a 'peculiar' to the canons of Hereford Cathedral, and thus outside the jurisdiction of the bishop.[16] The church has a pleasant situation beside the river Teme. It is surrounded by earthworks, of which the southern side runs along the bank of the river; a small mound south of the church may be the remains of a motte.[17] The church is mostly Early English, and the west tower (Fig. 54, p.24) is of this style; of an earlier building one Norman window remains in the north wall of the nave. Both the tower arch and the chancel arch are

Fig. 202 The nave, looking east at Little Hereford: above the chancel arch there is a central niche where an altar once stood on the rood-loft

impressive—the former is of three orders, the outer plain and the inner two moulded, the latter is duplex, with an east and a west arch and between the two the stairs rise to the former rood-loft. Above the chancel arch is a central niche with a projecting sill (Fig. 202), and at the south end of this is a piscina niche proving that there was once an altar on the rood-loft. The level of this altar is revealed by a slightly projecting ledge, and a little above this is another ledge which seems to have served for lights.

In the chancel are a set of sedilia with a piscina, and in the north wall two excellent Decorated tomb-recesses (Fig. 186, p.79), with ball-flower, ogee gables and crockets. In one of these is an incised slab with a very elongated effigy of a lady (c.1300) wearing a type of head-dress said to be unique in England.[18] Above the two recesses is the marble monument to Joseph Bailey (d.1850), showing a mourning lady under a cross. A further tomb-recess is in the nave. The font is plain.

St. Mary the Virgin, Middleton-on-the-Hill*
St. Mary's, north of Leominster and east of the A49, is an excellent Norman church, with round-headed doorways both north and south replete with chevron decoration; the blocked north doorway also has a band of the pellet motif. Set regularly along the north and south walls of the nave are flat buttresses almost like pilasters. Both the tower arch and the chancel arch are plain; above the latter is a Norman window which may once have opened into a chamber above the chancel. Further Norman windows may be seen in both nave and chancel. The tower is Early English, with lancet windows; it houses three medieval bells. The east window of the chancel, dating from c.1300, originally came from the church at Pudleston; it was inserted here in 1857.[19] The font is a Norman bowl, with a broad zigzag pattern.

St. Peter, Pudleston*
This church, which lies east of Leominster, to the north of the A44, was so extensively rebuilt in the 19th century that apart from the tower there is little that is really old; yet the restoration was so well done that appearances may well deceive the visitor. Sir Stephen Glynne was enthusiastic about the changes: he wrote, on 12 August, 1867, 'The interior richly arranged for high ritual ... The chancel is rather sumptuous in its fittings ... The reredos is of stone and has rich sculpture in medallions'.

The tower is old, and both the Royal Commission on Historical Monuments and Pevsner wondered whether the quoins and the rearrches of the windows could be Anglo-Saxon, but in the end both authorities concluded that the tower was Norman.[20] The west doorway certainly is, with its plain tympanum and arch with chevron decoration. Above the tower is a shingled spire. The chancel is Early English, with two lancet windows in the south wall. The east window of the chancel has complex Victorian tracery.

The nave and aisles belong to the 19th century (Fig. 203), the nave to 1813, the aisles and arcades to 1851. Some of the stained glass in one of the south aisle windows is possibly designed by Pugin. The stone pulpit, stone reredos and screen are Victorian. In the north wall of the chancel is a credence shelf, and on the south side a piscina.

Fig. 203 The east bay of the Victorian north arcade and the screen and chancel at Pudleston

St. Cosmas and St. Damian, Stretford**

One of the delights of church-crawling is to stumble upon a previously unknown church and to find a real treasure. Such an unexpected reward is provided by Stretford, a church without a village, nestling beside a farmhouse near the A4110 between Hereford and Leintwardine, just south of its junction with the A44. Part of this road follows the line of a Roman road (hence the name 'Stretford').

The church of St. Cosmas and St. Damian (previously known as St. Peter's)[21] is now in the care of the Churches Conservation Trust (previously the Redundant Churches Fund) having closed for regular worship in 1970. The exterior is plain and rather unprepossessing, and scarcely prepares one for the unexpected glories within. There is a timber bell-turret with a broach spire, and an excellent timber porch, said by the Royal Commission on Historical Monuments to be 16th-century, but looking older than that.

Internally, the church consists of twin naves and chancels separated by an arcade of three bays, the whole building spanned with an impressive timber roof. Churches with twin naves are rare (but there is one nearby at Leominster Priory). At Stretford, as at Leominster, the earlier nave is on the north, dating from the early-to-mid 12th century; and a Norman window and blocked Norman doorway remain in the north wall. The arcade and south nave followed a hundred years later in the Early English era, the arcade having pointed arches and the south wall lancet windows. In the 14th century (the Decorated era), both chancels were extended to the east, the windows in the east wall showing intersecting tracery with ogee arching.

Originally the twin naves were roofed separately with twin gables, but around 1540 the present roof was added together with the bell-turret which stands on a platform at the west end. One tie-beam spans the whole width of the church, with arched braces and collar-beams and laterally four series of wind-braces. The wall-posts are carved with coats of arms. Pevsner justly remarks that it is the roof that gives grandeur to the whole building.[22]

There is a plain Norman font, and two pairs of stone effigies in recesses in the north wall. These date from c.1340-50, the one in the chancel being a little earlier than that in the nave. It is thought that they commemorate Robert de la Bere (died after 1334) and his son John (died 1340-50) and their respective wives. The men are depicted in mail and plate armour, their wives with wimples and long gowns. Against the eastern respond of the arcade is a stone shrine, said to be that of St. Cosmas and St. Damian. Between the two chancels and naves are 16th-century screens of rude workmanship, stretching right across the church (Fig. 204). There is a Jacobean pulpit. The whole interior is a rustic delight.

Fig. 204 The rustic screen spans the twin naves and chancels at Stretford

St. Leonard, Yarpole*

Yarpole, north-west of Leominster, has a detached bell-tower, described and illustrated on p.25. The nave is Decorated, but in 1864 a north aisle was added and the chancel rebuilt by Sir George Gilbert Scott. The roof over the nave is single-framed, with tie-beams and king-posts. The octagonal font, probably late Norman, has arcading round the bowl.

Around Bromyard

St. Mary the Virgin, Bishop's Frome*

Standing sentinel over this attractive village in the Frome valley to the west of Frome's Hill and north of the main Hereford to Worcester road, in an area of hop-farms, is the church of St. Mary, an interesting amalgam of Norman and neo-Norman building. The neo-Norman style achieved a limited popularity in early Victorian times, and most churches built in that style date from the 1840s. Sure enough, the chancel at Bishop's Frome dates from 1847, the nave and north chapel following in 1861. The architect was F.R. Kempson of Hereford.

Fig. 205 Norman chancel arch and neo-Norman north arcade, Bishop's Frome

On each side of the priest's door in the external south wall of the chancel are slabs of sculpture (Fig. 51, p.20), probably a minor work of the Herefordshire School (see p.21). The west tower and the tower arch opening into the nave date from the 14th century. The south porch, nave and chancel are neo-Norman, but entering through the Victorian porch one encounters the fine, original 12th-century south doorway. There is a round arch of three moulded orders, the middle one with chevron decoration. The capitals show water-leaf carvings, dating the work to the latter part of the 12th century. Also original, but a little earlier, is the chancel arch (Fig. 205), with chevron decoration. The screen is partly late-medieval and partly Victorian. The north chapel and the arcade dividing it from the aisle is the work of Kempson.

In a recess in the south wall of the nave is a 13th-century stone effigy of a knight in armour; he is drawing his sword, bears a shield, and his crossed legs rest with his feet on a lion. The recess has ball-flower decoration. At the west end of the nave is a lead-lined Norman font. In the north Lady Chapel is the painted memorial to Margery de la Downes (1598) of Paunton Court in the parish; it shows two kneeling figures separated by a prayer-desk, a frequent motif in late-Elizabethan and Jacobean memorials.

St. Peter, Bromyard**

Bromyard, the market town for the north-east corner of Herefordshire, was an important Saxon minster (*monasterium*) in the 9th century. It became a collegiate church, the centre for an area which later developed many small parishes, but few churches of note. St. Peter's (Fig. 206) itself is fortunately an exception, and has many features of interest, though no trace of the Saxon minster survives. However, there are impressive Norman south and north doorways, with three orders of shafts and carved capitals. The arches above are decorated—the outer with embattled ornament, the middle with lozenges and the inner

Fig. 206 Bromyard church

with chevron at right-angles to the wall. Above the south doorway, part of the Norman tympanum, which is carved with a star and scale pattern, has been cut away, and over the arches is a figure of St. Peter, with his key (Fig. 14, p.7); this is thought to be 11th-century, either just before or after the Norman Conquest. Just to the east of this is a cross in relief, in a circle, similar to the Saxon cross at Stanton Lacy in Shropshire, which possibly strengthens the case for a Saxon origin of the adjacent figure of St. Peter. Taylor and Taylor accepted the St. Peter as Anglo-Saxon, but said that it was not *in situ*.[1] The tympanum over the north doorway is a 19th-century imitation of Norman carving.

Later than the doorways are the arcades of the nave; both the Royal Commission on Historical Monuments and Pevsner date the south arcade to *c*.1190, the north to *c*.1210: both arcades have circular piers, but the south capitals have trumpet-scallop carving while the north show stiff-leaf foliage.[2] The arcades were heightened at the restoration (better described as a 'mutilation') of 1805.[3] The church is cruciform, with a central 14th-century tower. There is a Norman tub-shaped font (Fig. 95, p.39), with zigzag decoration below and a scroll pattern above, with a 'tree of life'. The font has been thought to be older than the church, probably dating from the end of the 11th or beginning of the 12th century.[4] In the transepts and aisles are a number of fine 14th-century tomb-recesses. There is a piscina in both transepts, that in the north has dogtooth ornament.

St. Michael, Edwyn Ralph*

As often occurs in Herefordshire, there is an adjacent motte and bailey, in this case about 100 yards west of the church at Edwyn Ralph, itself just off the B4214 north of Bromyard. The present building is mainly 13th-century, but there is an earlier Norman window in the chancel, the arch externally having slight rope decoration, and a Norman south doorway, altered later. In the north wall of the chancel there are two ogee-headed 14th-century tomb-recesses, each surmounted by a carved head. These may have once housed the effigies now under the tower. The east window of the chancel has intersecting tracery.

Marshall states that the monuments were moved from the chancel to their present position in 1865.[5] In 1963, Sir Nikolaus Pevsner complained that the 'excellent' monuments in Edwyn Ralph were 'disgracefully placed under the tower'. Three decades later, the effigies are still there, still difficult to see; why are parochial authorities content to let their treasures remain so inaccessible and unappreciated? These fine effigies include a husband and wife c.1290, a husband and two wives (Fig. 113, p.46) of about a generation later; a small effigy of an early 14th-century lady, and an incised slab to Maud de Edefin, c.1325. The latter shows Maud, wife of Sir Thomas de Edefin, with a very high stiff wimple and sleeveless surcoat. The Latin inscription reads: 'Here lies the lady Maud; she was the wife of Sir Thomas de Edefin. To whomsoever shall say a Pater and an Ave for the soul of Maud de Edefin the lord Bishop of Worcester will allow thirty days of pardon, and the lord Bishop of Hereford sixty days of pardon'.[6]

St. Andrew, Evesbatch*

Evesbatch, south-east of Bromyard, means 'Esa's stream-valley'— the OE *baece* is used when a small stream flows in a fairly well-marked, but not dramatic, valley.[7] This is appropriate here, for Evesbatch stands at the head of the valley of the little river Leadon.

When Sir Stephen Glynne visited Evesbatch in 1873, he found the church 'small and mean ... the whole has a neglected look'. Fortunately, later Victorians put the matter right, for within four years the church was largely rebuilt, and the result is the very pretty church that the visitor sees today—it is certainly not neglected!

Small it remains, however—just nave and chancel of uncertain date, with a south porch and western timbered bell-turret. The interior (Fig. 207) is simple and appealing. The roof has trussed rafters and collar-beams, and is perhaps medieval. There are some ancient bench-ends and a 17th-century table and chest. The Norman font is a plain upright bowl (Fig. 91, p.38) but the Jacobean cover is quite exceptional; it is "of saucer form, cut from solid oak, with a central carved knot and radiating leaves'.[8] There are two wall-monuments, one of which shows Margaret Dobyns (d.1658) holding a baby, flanked by allegorical female figures.

Fig. 207 The interior looking west, Evesbatch

Fig. 208 The nave looking towards the west gallery, Hatfield

St. Leonard, Hatfield*

This small church, east of Leominster, is notable for its 11th-century origin—in the eastern part of the north wall there is herringbone masonry, both internally and externally. Tufa stone is employed in some of the external dressings and also in the chancel arch. The blocked north doorway has plain jambs with a heavy lintel comprising three stones joggled together (Fig. 15, p.7); above, a plain arch encloses a tympanum of square stones set diagonally.

The attractive interior (Fig. 208) has a western gallery and a plain Norman chancel arch. There are three uncommonly good 17th-century memorial tablets to members of the Colles family—the tablets have broken pediments above and are flanked by Ionic or twisted Corinthian columns.

Moreton Jeffries*

Methuen's 1930s *Little Guide* to Herefordshire pronounces, 'The little church is of no interest'.[9] But if you appreciate remoteness and seclusion and take pleasure in quaintness and antiqueness, then Moreton Jeffries is the church for you. For it is a real gem, the more exciting for being so utterly unexpected. The lane finishes about 150 yards from the church by dividing into two farm entrances, and so the visitor has to walk through a small field to reach a neglected, overgrown churchyard and then the church of no known dedication (Fig. 209).

Fig. 209 Moreton Jeffries church

From Bromyard, take the A465 south-west towards Hereford. One mile after Stoke Lacy, a lane on the right leads to Moreton Jeffries; where this lane divides into two, park the car and walk across the fields to the church. It is always open, but is no longer used for worship, being in the care of the Churches Conservation Trust since 1984. The manor is mentioned in the *Domesday Book* as belonging to the canons of Hereford, and the church dates from the 13th or early 14th century. It is small, without aisles, and there is no division between nave and chancel. At the west end is a timbered bell-turret. Its air of beneficent neglect contributes greatly to its atmosphere.

The great attraction is the 17th-century furnishings, especially the fine square Jacobean pulpit (Fig. 169, p.72), complete with sounding-board which has carved scroll-work and a cornice. Note also the clerk's desk, some of the pews and the panelling. The chancel roof, with tie-beams, dates from the same period. It is of two bays with three trusses—the tie-beams have curved braces. The roof of the nave is of trussed rafters and is probably medieval.[10]

St. Mary the Virgin, Much Cowarne**

Cowarne is a Saxon name meaning 'dairy-farming centre' which seems an apt description of the two villages of Much and Little Cowarne situated in the valley of the little river Lodon, east of Hereford, and south-west of Bromyard.[11] St. Mary's church (Fig. 210) stands on an eminence overlooking the valley, a short distance from the village. From the outside, the remains of the former north arcade are apparent in the north wall of the nave. The tower is massive and squat, and has lancet windows in the lower storey.

Apart from the tower, the church now consists of nave with south aisle and chancel. The former north arcade had round piers and capitals, and was built early in the 13th century. The south arcade comes from later in the 13th century—a graceful structure, with four clustered columns, and thin shafts between. Later still is the Decorated chancel, with a Perpendicular east window.

There are some good monuments: in the south aisle is a 13th-century stone effigy of a knight, much mutilated. Nearby lie the stone effigies of a Renaissance couple, Edmund Fox (d.1617) and his wife, with the figures of ten kneeling children round the tomb-chest. Both adult figures are clothed in contemporary costume, and at the end of the tomb are three babies asleep in a rocking-cradle. In the chancel is the effigy of Sybil Reed (d.1624) wearing a bonnet; on a panel above are her two daughters and two sons facing each other. These are rustic memorials, in a very conservative style for their date.

Fig. 210 (above) Much Cowarne: The remains of the former north arcade are seen on the north wall

Fig. 211 (right) Stanford Bishop

St. James, Stanford Bishop*

The site of this isolated church (Fig. 211) is evocative: on the highest point in the parish, commanding marvellous views of the countryside, the church is in a circular churchyard, generally held to denote a very ancient, possibly pre-Christian, site. Stanford means 'stone ford', presumably over the infant river Frome in the valley to the west. The manor was held by the bishop of Hereford. From Bromyard, take the A44 east towards Worcester, and after nearly two miles turn right into B4220 towards Ledbury. After two miles, turn right into a lane leading to Stanford Bishop; the church is on the left, up a short track.

When Sir Stephen Glynne visited on 26 April, 1873, he found that the church had 'rather a look of neglect and decay'. It is pleasing to record that this is not so now. St. Mary's is a late Norman and Early English church, with a squat tower, which opens into the church through a pointed (i.e. Transitional) late 12th-century arch. The south doorway is a little earlier, being round-arched, with trumpet-scallop capitals. The south porch also has a round-arched doorway, of uncertain age.

The interior is simple and peaceful, without arcades and with no division between nave and chancel. There is a plain Norman sandstone font at the west end. The pulpit is a restrained Jacobean structure. But the greatest treasure is 'St. Augustine's' chair, long believed to have been used by St. Augustine in the early 7th century when he met the British bishops of the Celtic church. But dendrochronology dates the chair to the medieval period. Even so, it is a rare example of a chair of that period, formed of posts and boards.

St. James, Tedstone Delamere

Access to the church is by a path across a field. Sir Stephen Glynne came here in 1860 and was full of praise for the church, which had been restored (and the chancel rebuilt) by Sir George Gilbert Scott in 1856-57. The church consists of a western timbered bell-cote, nave and chancel. Two Norman windows in the nave are surrounded by tufa, indicating a very early Norman date. There is a 15th- or 16th-century screen, an hour-glass stand (*c.*1700) in the porch, and Victorian stained glass by Hardman and Kempe.

St. Anna, Thornbury

While walking along the churchyard path, the visitor will probably be struck by the massive Early English west tower, and by the remains of a former south arcade clearly seen in the south wall of the nave. On the north wall is a rather fine blocked Norman doorway; there is volute on the east capital, saltire crosses on the west abacus, a band of cable moulding below the plain tympanum, and much chevron decoration in the arch. The Norman font has a complex frieze of lozenges.

St. Luke, Ullingswick*

Ullingswick (the dwelling-place or farm of Ulla)[12] is a parish six miles south-west of Bromyard. From Bromyard, take the A465 south-westwards; half-a-mile after Stoke Lacy, turn right, and after another half-a-mile, turn left. After one further mile, turn right, and right again down a 'no through road' to the church. The little church is a humble building—just a medieval nave and chancel, with a timbered bell-turret and porch added by the Victorians. The nave is Norman, with a small round-headed window in each of the north and south walls; in addition, there are two 12th-century lower jambs of two orders in the south doorway, though the rest of the doorway is later. There is a lancet window in the west wall of the nave, perhaps indicating that the nave was lengthened in the 13th century. The chancel was probably built very late in the 13th century, for the east wall has a typical 'Herefordshire' window (p.78) commonly built *c*.1300. The windows in the south wall of the chancel show Y-tracery. The south porch, originally of the 14th century, was restored and rebuilt in 1863.[13] The attractive bell-turret was probably added at the same time, the architect being F.R. Kempson, who also worked at Bishop's Frome nearby.

The finest artefact is the unusual memorial painting mounted on the south wall of the nave. This is to John Hill (d.1591) and shows an effigy of the deceased lying on a tomb-chest, flanked by kneeling members of his family, with shields-of-arms above. In the chancel is a 13th-century coffin-lid with foliated cross re-used in 1699. The stained glass in the east window is by Clayton and Bell.

St. Michael, Upper Sapey*

This village, on the Herefordshire/Worcestershire border some six miles north of Bromyard is much afflicted with modern executive housing; the visitor should ignore this and proceed directly to St. Michael's church, where there is much to admire. This is a 12th-century building with three spectacular Norman arches—the blocked north doorway, with capitals enriched with leaf and scroll-work; the similar south doorway; and best of all the tower arch. The last was originally built as the chancel arch, and was transferred to its present position in 1859-

Fig. 212 The tower arch, Upper Sapey

60. Each of the arches has two orders of shafts; the arches show zigzag, with (in the tower arch) unusual rows of pointed arches meeting along the edge of an arch order (Fig. 212), one row parallel with the wall, and the other at right-angles to it.[14] In the south wall of the nave is a plain tomb-recess, and in the south wall of the chancel a low-side window. The west tower is Victorian.

At the west end of the nave are some plain 16th-century benches, and there is good panelling also in the chancel, some of which looks Jacobean, and in the pulpit.

St. John the Baptist, Whitbourne

The church consists of west tower, nave and chancel, with a north aisle added in 1866 by A.E. Perkins. The south doorway is Norman, with chevron decoration and trumpet-scallop capitals. In the chancel are trefoil-headed lancet windows, but the east window is Perpendicular, as is the tower. The finest feature is the font (Fig. 96, p.39), which has a band of interlocking stars and a mutilated Agnus Dei.

St. Andrew, Wolferlow*

Wolferlow is about 5 miles north of Bromyard, to the west of the B4203. St. Andrew's was mostly rebuilt in Victorian times, but some good Norman work survives in the south and north doorways and the chancel arch. Outstanding is the late 13th-century stone effigy of an unknown lady; the drapery is displayed in parallel folds, and the lady's head is flanked by angels.

Black-and-White Villages

St. Mary the Virgin, Almeley*

St. Mary's is not the only religious building in Almeley which is worth visiting: there is also a half-timbered Friends' Meeting House which dates from 1672. The name of the village means 'elm wood', and it is now a peaceful backwater, away from main roads. It was not always so, for in earlier years it was on the main coach route from London to Wales, and later it had a railway station. In medieval times, it was even more important, boasting not one but two castles, the main motte being just south-west of the church.

Fig. 213 The ceilure over the former rood, Almeley

St. Mary's stands near the centre of the village to the south-east of Kington. The west tower is the oldest part of the church, being built around 1200. The whole of the rest of the church is Decorated; the arcades have octagonal piers, and both aisles have a gabled east end, with windows showing reticulated tracery; the east window of the chancel is also Decorated with geometrical tracery. The finest feature of the church is the painted boarded ceiling over the two easternmost bays of the nave (Fig. 213). This would have been above the former rood, and is known as a ceilure.

It is divided into panels, with a Tudor rose in the centre of each, dating it to the early 16th century. Ceilures are seen occasionally in parish churches, but are not at all frequent. Under the tower arch is a re-sited Jacobean screen.

St. Mary, Dilwyn**

The name means 'a secret or shady place', but now there is nothing secret or shady about Dilwyn.[1] On the contrary, the picturesque village is one of the stars of the 'black-and-white village trail', and lies just to the south of the A4112, about 6 miles west of Leominster.

Few churches can offer the amateur sleuth as great a challenge as St. Mary's, for on entering the church and looking left, the visitor will see that only the north half of the tower arch is preserved (Fig. 214), the south arcade running right against the apex of the arch. The reason is that the tower originally related to an earlier nave which has been demolished and replaced by the present nave. So the tower is the earliest part of the church, and does indeed show two Norman windows with double roll mouldings; also there are two curious small lancet windows with dogtooth decoration above—an Early English motif—presumably these windows were later insertions.

The arcades separating the nave from the aisles are Early English (Fig. 214): the piers are circular and solid, and some of the capitals have some geometric decoration; the easternmost pier of the south arcade has a bracket with dogtooth decoration. There is a great variety of windows in the aisles, but most date from around 1300, just as Early English was giving way to Decorated: thus there is plate tracery, with quatrefoils and cusping. The clerestory windows are most intriguing: above the spandrels of the arcades are the blocked-off windows of the 13th-century nave; these must have been sealed when the nave was heightened and the present roof added in the early 15th century.

The chancel is built on a substantial scale and is also Early English, the windows of the south wall being similar to those of the nave; but the impressive east window is early Decorated: three cusped lights, with above a large pointed trefoil. There is documentary evidence that the chancel was built around 1305 by Wormsley Priory, which would fit well with this window.[2] In the north wall of the chancel is a good Decorated tomb recess, with much ball-flower embellishment, crockets, and finials, indicating a date a little later in the 14th century. In the recess is a stone effigy of a knight wearing mail, with his hand on the hilt of his sword. This is said to represent Sir George Talbot, who died in 1387, but this seems a rather late date for this tomb recess.

To the Decorated period belong three other artefacts: firstly, the north window of the north transept, which shows reticulated tracery, though considerably restored. Secondly, in the angle between the chancel and the north transept is the staircase which formerly led to the rood-loft. The staircase opens above the screen, and the corbels which used to support the loft are still present. Thirdly, the impressive south porch (Fig. 73, p.30), which is not Perpendicular as usually stated, but Decorated—it was recognised as such

Fig. 214 The nave, looking west and showing the south Early English arcade impinging against the apex of the tower arch at Dilwyn

110

by Glynne, who described it as a very elegant Curvilinear porch. The windows have reticulated tracery on each side.

Finally, there are some excellent furnishings: the screen is very good, and the lower part at least is original 16th-century, with some fine carvings of human heads at floor level. Around the north-east chapel are ruder parclose screens, probably from the late 15th century. In the centre window of the south wall of the chancel is some beautiful medieval stained glass, with a pair of angels swinging censers. The glass in the other windows is good Victorian. At the west end of the south aisle is the plain 14th-century font, together with a number of medieval tiles and coffin-lids with foliated crosses.

St. Mary the Virgin, Eardisland

Many people regard Eardisland, on the river Arrow to the east of Leominster, as the prettiest of all the 'black-and-white' villages. St. Mary's church is not quite so outstanding, but there is, nevertheless, much to admire.

The church is mainly of the 13th and 14th centuries, though much modified by a restoration in 1864 by Curzon. The nave is Early English, as are the south and north doorways. In the Decorated period, the chancel was lengthened and the stone porch was added. There are two instructive windows in the south wall: the more restrained is a typical Herefordshire window (p.78), with a little ball-flower adornment, dating from *c*.1310; the more florid, with complex tracery and a heavy encrustation of ball-flower, dates from 1864. In the chancel, a tomb recess, sedilia, piscina and doorway into the vestry are also from the early 14th century. The 16th-century screen is now under the tower. There are two further tomb recesses in the nave, and also an incised slab dating from the 15th century.

St. Mary Magdalene, Eardisley***

Eardisley today is the very epitome of the peaceful Herefordshire 'black-and-white' village, but this serene appearance hides a violent past. It looks a very English village, and this is unusual for one so far west in the county. So it is not surprising to find that it was a bulwark against the Welsh, and the site in the 11th and later centuries of a castle, located just to the west of the church. The conjunction of church and castle was particularly common in Herefordshire, and examples are seen all over the county.[3] At the time of the Domesday survey, the manor and castle were held by Roger de Lacy on behalf of the king; later the castle was held by the Bohuns and the Baskervilles. In 1263, Walter de Baskerville seized Peter of Savoy, the unpopular bishop of Hereford, in his cathedral and confined him at his castle for three months because he had made himself 'odious to the realm by his intolerable exactions on behalf' of the king. The castle, though by then probably only a gatehouse, appears to have survived until the Civil War, when it was burnt to the ground.

The church (Fig. 215) next door has fared slightly better—which is just as well, considering that it houses what has been described as the finest font in England. The original Norman church in the 12th century had a nave without aisles. It will immediately be seen that the south arcade is Norman, with round arches, and the north arcade is Early English, with pointed arches. The first

Fig. 215 Eardisley church

111

three bays of the south arcade are followed by a short length of solid wall which the Royal Commission on Historic Monuments interpreted as the remains of the wall or impost between the old Norman nave and chancel;[4] in this 'wall' is a (later) 14th-century recess of unknown significance. To the east is the fourth bay which was an opening of the original chancel into a south chapel. In the 13th century, the Early English north arcade was built, again with three bays; in the early 14th century, the north side of the chancel was opened beyond the third pier into two chapels. The tower was not built until 1708, following the destruction by fire of the previous detached wooden bell-tower.

The font (Figs. 46, 47) is one of the most outstanding works of the Herefordshire School, and is described in detail on p.19.

St. Thomas à Becket, Huntington

For rusticity and remoteness of situation, few churches can compare with Huntington. It is quite a small medieval church, nave and chancel without division, with a timbered bell-turret at the west end. The interior is noteworthy because of the very rude benches, and a series of memorial slate tablets from the early 19th century—more evidence of naïve rusticity, perhaps, but charming nonetheless.

St. Mary the Virgin, Kington**

Kington is the smallest Herefordshire market-town, with most shops plying their wares in the traditional manner. The town stands strategically at the confluence of two valleys, and above it presides the parish church of St. Mary.

Kington first appears in the Domesday survey (1086) as *Chingtun*, meaning 'royal manor', and a castle was built north of the church at the end of the 11th century. Not long after, the Honour of Kington was created by Henry I (1100-35) for Adam de Port, but by 1173 his descendant Roger de Port forfeited the Lordship by rebelling against Henry II. The Honour of Kington then seems to have become absorbed into a new lordship of Huntington, but this borough failed to prosper, and a new settlement called Kington-in-the-Fields (the present town) eventually thrived. Kington castle seems to have been abandoned quite early (before 1230).

The church (Fig. 216) is an impressive building, of many styles, but knit together to form an harmonious whole. The oldest part, fittingly enough in this troubled border region, is the late Norman tower, built around 1200. The walls are six feet thick, and originally it was detached from the church and provided a safe haven for the people. The tower now abuts onto the south aisle, opening into it through a round-arched doorway which appears to be Norman. The external staircase to the ringers' chamber is a 19th-century addition. Above the tower are two truncated pyramids and a broach spire—these date from 1794, following the destruction by lightning of the earlier spire. Double pyramids on the tower are a feature of several churches in the Marches, both English and Welsh. In the south aisle is the Norman font, with zigzag patterning around the rim and cable moulding around the base. Near the font is a baptismal tank sunk into the

Fig. 216 Kington church

floor, dating from the 17th or 18th centuries; it was used for the baptism of persons of 'riper years', as the Book of Common Prayer directs.

The Early English period contributed the very fine chancel, with three large lancet windows in the east wall, and six smaller lancets on the north wall; apparently these were originally balanced by a similar series on the south wall, but later alterations have drastically modified appearances. There is now a larger lancet with Y-tracery in the south wall, dating from the late 13th century. The arcades of the nave are Early English, with octagonal columns and steeply-pointed arches. The west window of the nave has four stepped lancets under a common hood-mould. To the south of the chancel is a 14th-century Decorated chapel, its east window showing reticulated tracery. This chapel houses the Vaughan monument (Fig. 122, p.49), commemorating Thomas Vaughan who was killed in 1469 at the battle of Banbury, during the Wars of the Roses. The fine, though much restored, alabaster effigies of Thomas and his wife lie on a tomb-chest, on the sides of which are a series of angels with shields.

The church was much modified in Victorian times—the north aisle was widened to become in effect a second nave, and a further north arcade was added providing a new, narrow north aisle.

St. James, Kinnersley***

St. James' church (Fig. 57, p.24), with the fine Elizabethan (and part medieval) castle behind, presents an attractive spectacle when seen from the A4112: on the left is the tower with a saddleback roof dating from the 14th century, with small ogee-headed windows; and to the right is the west façade of the church with a blocked Norman doorway and, above, an unusually tall Perpendicular window. Round the corner is a medieval timbered porch (Fig. 71, p.29).

The spacious interior has differing arcades—the north Early English, with octagonal piers (Fig. 217), the south Perpendicular, with thin piers consisting of four shafts with hollows between; to the Early English period belong also the south doorway, the chancel and the north aisle. The excellent painted decoration of the nave and chancel was designed by the Victorian architect, G.F. Bodley. There is some good woodwork: the pulpit is adorned with Flemish allegorical figures dating from c.1530, and there is Jacobean panelling behind the altar (Fig. 175, p.74).

Fig. 217 The Early English north arcade with decoration above by Bodley

Some fine monuments complete the attractions of Kinnersley church: high up on the north wall of the chancel is an alabaster and marble monument to Francis Smalman and his wife (d.1635) with two kneeling figures facing each other under a canopy, and six kneeling children beneath—a typical early Stuart piece of exceptional quality (Fig. 131, p.53. Below this is a small brass to William Leviot, rector of Kinnersley, who died in 1421. By way of contrast, at the west end of the nave is the classical angel monument (Fig. 142, p.56) to Lady Ann Morgan (d.1764) by Nicholas Read who worked from c.1749 till his death in 1787. The angel, with large wings, points to the medallion bust of the deceased. At the east end of the north aisle is the monument to John Parkinson (d. 1804) in the Greek style then coming into vogue (Fig. 147, p.58).

St. Michael and All Angels, Knill

This remote and little-known church is situated in lovely country in the valley of the Hindwell Brook (a tributary of the Lugg) on the extreme western edge of Herefordshire between Presteigne and Kington. The church is medieval, and consists of a low west tower, nave and chancel; one Norman window survives in the chancel. The Early English octagonal font (Fig. 99, p.40) is very good.

St. Michael and All Angels, Lyonshall*

In Domesday, Lyonshall is *Lenehalle*; the first element is the same as in Kingsland, Monkland and Eardisland (p.96) although Lyonshall is just south of the river Arrow rather than between it and the river Lugg; the second element is from OE *halh* which means nook or hollow.[5] Offa's dyke runs south-west of the church, and the village was a place of some moment in the Middle Ages: it was the seat of a substantial castle, probably built by Roger de Lacy whose family held the manor—the remains of the castle lie just north-east of the church and can be seen from the churchyard. In later centuries, Lyonshall ranked as a borough.

St. Michael's church stands above the A44 at the northern end of the current settlement, imposingly on a hillside; since medieval times the village has moved half-a-mile or so to the south. Surviving from the earlier Norman building are two Norman windows, a small window in the west wall of the north aisle, and a larger one high in the west wall of the nave above the tower arch; this was originally in the west wall of a former tower, but now opens into the present tower. Apart from these surviving vestiges, the church is Early English to Decorated (late 13th to early 14th centuries). The elegant and unusual north arcade is Early English, with piers which are quatrefoil in cross-section with shafts in the diagonals, some of which have some stiff-leaf carving. The south arcade is Decorated, with plain octagonal piers. Most of the windows are cusped lancets, but the east window in the chancel is a typical Herefordshire window.

The font consists of a 13th-century bowl on a Victorian stem of eight shafts, and has stiff-leaf carving similar to that in the north arcade. At the east end of the south aisle is a 13th-century decapitated stone effigy. There is an excellent Victorian timber porch.

St. Mary, Pembridge***

In the Middle Ages, Pembridge in the north-west of the county was a place of some moment, being a borough, with several fortified sites and a distinguished parish church. It is famous now as one of the prettiest 'black-and-white' villages in the county, but even more for its parish church with its outstanding detached bell-tower.

A Norman church has left few vestiges, and St. Mary's is now a large cruciform church of the 14th century. It 'stands for the arrival of mature Decorated architecture in Herefordshire',[6] with consistent employment of curvilinear tracery visible in 16 windows, including the four-light windows dominating the west and east ends. The nave is tall and well-lit, the arcades of octagonal piers, the capitals plain; Morris compares the interior elevation of the nave to that at Weobley, thought to be the prototype of Pembridge. Above the arcades the windows of the clerestory consist of a cinquefoil set in a roundel, each foil assuming an ogee shape—a pattern which Morris traces to Tewkesbury. Above the chancel arch are two further clerestory windows, and in the angle between the chancel and the south transept is a turret within which a spiral staircase gave access to the former rood loft. The only other tracery pattern at Pembridge is in the three stepped lancets in the lateral windows of the chancel; these do not show the ogee pattern and are earlier than the windows with reticulated tracery.

Pembridge church has some fine furnishings. Below the great west window is the 13th-century font, with a stem of four short pillars attached to a central square shaft; these expand upwards to form the bowl of the same shape in outline. There is an octagonal Jacobean pulpit (Fig. 168, p.72), with two tiers of carved panels, the upper arcaded, the lower with grotesque monsters. The reader's desk, lectern, and communion-rails come from the same period. The finest monument is the tomb-chest in the north side of the chancel, with two pairs of effigies from the 14th century. The earlier pair is of a civilian and lady, the later of a knight or priest and lady; these have been identified as the Gour family, Lords of Marston, a hamlet in Pembridge parish. The original west door bears the marks of bullets believed locally to be from Cromwell's soldiers.

The spectacular bell-tower (Fig. 58, p.24) is Pembridge's most famous landmark. From the outside it appears as a single-storey stone structure, with a series of truncated pyramidal roofs above, separated by vertical weather-boarding. The fantastic internal timber construction is based on a square of eight oak pillars which rise to the bell-chamber. Timber-framed buildings are notoriously hard to date, and previously the tower was dated to the later 14th century; since a complete restoration by the Department of the Environment in 1983-84, it is now thought that the original structure belongs to the early 13th century (i.e. it antedates the present church), though with substantial later additions.

St. Mary, Sarnesfield**

'Sarn' is Welsh for a road, and the church stands alone by the winding A4112, to the east of the junction with the A480; there is room for just one visitor's car at the entrance to the churchyard. St. Mary's (Fig. 218) is a very attractive church, both inside and out. The nave is late Norman (Transitional), separated from the narrow south aisle by an arcade of slightly pointed arches supported by short circular columns with scalloped capitals. A Norman west window now looks into the tower, which is later, being built around 1300. A chapel was added to the south of the chancel in the 14th century and contains several inscribed coffin-lids from the 13th and 14th centuries. In the east window of the chapel are some attractive fragments of medieval stained glass.

Fig. 218 Sarnesfield church.
There is Y-tracery in the east window

Perhaps the finest feature of the church is the roof of the nave, a 14th-century structure with tie-beams and trefoiled wind-braces (Fig. 80, p.33). Attractive also is the wooden porch of the same period. To the west of the porch is the tomb of John Abel (1577-1674), restored in Victorian times by a worthy group called the National Society for Preserving the Memorials of the Dead. John Abel is thought to be the architect of market houses at Brecon, Kington, Leominster, the screen and roof at Abbey Dore (Fig. 165, p.70) and the grammar school at Kington. His tomb's now illegible inscription is preserved in typescript inside the church.

St. Peter and St. Paul, Weobley***

Weobley, lying to the south of the A4112 Leominster to Brecon road, is one of the most popular of the black-and-white villages of Herefordshire. Its present tranquillity belies its former importance as a borough returning at times two members to parliament. At the time of Domesday, the manor was in the hands of Roger de Lacy, and in 1140 at the time of Hugh de Lacy Weobley became a borough. Church

Fig. 219 The nave looking west at Weobley

and castle were at opposite ends of the main street, church to the north, castle to the south. The castle was built around 1190, but little now remains. The church, too, goes back to the 12th century, though most of the present building came 200 years later.

The large church consists of nave with north and south aisles and south porch, a spacious chancel, and a tower curiously placed at an angle at the north-west corner. Of the Norman church, only the south doorway remains: the arch is rounded and decorated with zigzag. The chancel is Early English, with stepped lancet windows on the south side; the east window of the chancel is much later, being Perpendicular (Fig. 188, p.79). In the north wall is the 14th-century alabaster effigy of Sir William Devereux (k.1402 at the battle of Pilleth) on a tomb-chest (Fig. 121, p.49); in the south wall are effigies of Sir William's widow Agnes and her second husband, Sir John Marbury (d.1437). In the sanctuary is the statue of Colonel John Birch (Fig. 137, p.55), one of Cromwell's commanders in the Civil War, and M.P. for Weobley (d.1691) (see p.54).

Most of the rest of the church is Decorated, and it is this work which gives Weobley its distinction. Morris relates the design to that at Pembridge. The arcades are of five bays, the piers octagonal (Fig. 219). There is ball-flower embellishment on the north-east arch and the west doorway. Note the beautiful rose window in the south aisle. Near to it is a lovely stone coffin-lid (Fig. 112, p.46), carved with a foliated cross, commemorating Hugo Bissop of Norton Canon; the church guide points out that the carving of a bishop's mitre on the coffin-lid is a pun on the deceased's surname. Also in the south aisle, look up and see the corbels carved with grotesque heads. To the north of the chancel arch is the staircase leading to the former rood-loft. In the north aisle are parts of the medieval screen. The east window of the north aisle has fragments of grisaille glass from the 14th century; in the middle window of the north aisle are figures of six seraphim holding instruments of the Passion (15th century). At the west end of the church is the fine 14th-century octagonal sandstone font, the faces of which show varying patterns of window tracery.

The tower stands at an angle to the north aisle, and rises with clasping buttresses. There are, remarkably, no belfry windows. It supports the most spectacular spire (Fig. 70, p.28) in Herefordshire—a graceful stone edifice connected by flying buttresses with the pinnacles at the corners of the tower. To compensate for the absence of belfry windows, a series of lucarnes (small openings) starts at the base of the spire.

The Upper Wye Valley

St. Andrew, Allensmore

St. Andrew's is an attractive church with a Norman south doorway, Early English and Decorated windows, and a stumpy Perpendicular tower. There are several monuments, of which the most interesting is the incised slab to Sir Andrew Herl and his wife; this is one of the small group of such slabs dating from the end of the 14th century, in which the inlay is said to be of cement (the others are at Canon Pyon, Dilwyn and Hereford Cathedral). It is very rare for medieval inlays to consist of anything but brass.[1] The pulpit is Jacobean.

St. Lawrence, Bishopstone*

The village of Bishopstone is only a mile distant from the Roman town of *Magnis* (Kenchester), and Roman foundations and a mosaic pavement were discovered here when the rectory was being built in 1812. Wordsworth had connections with Bishopstone and wrote a sonnet on the local Roman antiquities. St. Lawrence's church is a mile from the village, close to the moated house of Bishopstone Court. Sir Stephen Glynne visited the church in 1867, and found it 'much modernised in a liberal and expensive manner, yet not wholly up to the mark of the present day'. To find it, take the A438 west from Hereford as far as Bridge Sollers; here turn right and at the next cross-roads ignore the sign to Bishopstone and proceed straight ahead to the next lane on the right which leads to the Court and the church.

It is a cruciform building, with nave, chancel, and transepts and a south porch; there is no tower but a Victorian bell-turret. Most of the church is Early English, but there is a blocked Norman window in the south wall of the nave, and what Pevsner called 'suspicious' Norman windows in the west wall; the main window in this wall, however, is Decorated. The best of the church is in the roof (Fig. 79, p.32)—a wagon-roof over the nave, and a complex construction over the chancel, with tie-beams, king-posts and struts—this is said to be Jacobean. There is a good Jacobean pulpit, and more 17th-century carving in the reredos and stalls. Of the same period is a monument to John Berinton and his wife (d.1614)—two recumbent effigies, very conservative for their date. There are roundels of foreign glass (?Flemish) in the south window of the chancel. The distinguished organ was built by Father Smith for Eton College in 1700, and was brought here in 1844. Smith also built the organ for Wren's St. Paul's Cathedral. Glynne found the organ 'rather too much for the church'. The 14th-century, timbered porch was transferred here from the old church at Yazor.

St. Leonard, Blakemere

St. Leonard's is a small church, just nave, chancel and bellcote, and it was largely rebuilt in 1877 by G. Truefitt. Fortunately, he made use of much of the fabric of the preceding church: for Sir Stephen Glynne had visited Blakemere seven years previously and his description tallies with many of the features that are seen today. Thus he commented on and illustrated the east wall of the chancel where there are three windows, the central one much higher than the outer two; he also mentioned the trefoil-headed and straight-headed windows in the south wall of the chancel; and he described the Early English chancel arch supported by trumpet-scalloped corbels and the 14th-century west window of two cinquefoiled ogee lights. The pulpit is Jacobean.

St. Andrew, Bredwardine**

Bredwardine on the river Wye some 12 miles north-west of Hereford is famous now for its links with the diarist Francis Kilvert, who was rector here from 1877 until his death two years later, and who is buried in the churchyard. But in truth, Kilvert's heart was really in Clyro, a few miles away, just over the Welsh border next to Hay-on-Wye; there he was curate from 1865 to 1872, and these were probably the happiest years of his short life. His heart-warming diary is a loveable account of his ministry, and has been compared, rather unfairly, with the diaries of Pepys and Evelyn: but they were mostly dealing with national events on a grand scale—Kilvert's diary is much more intimate, more human—and his picture of mid-Victorian country life is authentic and moving.

Kilvert's church stands in a circular churchyard above the Wye, with commanding views across the valley, and as so often in Herefordshire, immediately to the east of the churchyard is a motte and bailey indicating the presence of a Norman castle. Bredwardine has always been a river crossing, by ford or ferry,[2] and now by a bridge, the first brick-built bridge in Britain. The meaning of the place-name is unclear: the second element is derived from OE *worbign* (an enclosure), but 'bred' is probably from OE *brerd* (brim or bank);[3] an alternative derivation from OE *bred* (board or plank) has been suggested.

St. Andrew's church is of early Norman origin; the north wall has herringbone masonry, seen both internally and externally, indicating late 11th- or early 12th-century work, and there is a great deal of tufa, as at Letton. The herringbone pattern is interrupted by a blocked doorway and above it is a sandstone lintel with cable-moulding above and below. The lintel over the north doorway is carved with two central figures flanked by large rosettes (Fig. 17, p.8). The figures are crude and somewhat worn, and interpretation is difficult. Above the south doorway is a similar lintel (Fig. 18, p.8) carved with rosettes, comparable with those at nearby Letton and Willersley. These are all dated to the early 12th century, and are discussed on p.8.

There are original Norman windows in both north and south walls of the nave, framed with tufa. Around 1300, the nave was lengthened, and the large window on the south wall of the nave shows intersecting tracery. In the south wall of the chancel is an alabaster effigy of a knight wearing the SS collar, dating from around 1450; on the north wall is a mutilated effigy from the previous century. The identity of these effigies is uncertain: the former may represent Sir Roger Vaughan, Lord of the Manor, who died at Agincourt in 1415; the latter may be Walter Baskerville, an earlier Lord of the Manor (d.1369). The large Norman font (Fig. 92, p.38) is virtually identical with those at Kilpeck and Madley, and it is thought that all three were made by the same mason using breccia limestone from the Golden Valley. The north-western tower was added in 1790.

St. Andrew, Bridge Sollers*

The derivation of the name of the parish is uncertain: Sollers is certainly a Norman family name (cf. Sollers Hope); but 'bridge' refers not to the nearby bridge over the Wye (which dates only from 1896) but to another Norman family called Brygge. The church is strategically placed on a knoll beside the river about 6 miles north-west of Hereford along the A438; in Anglo-Saxon times, Offa's Dyke ran nearby, surprisingly far east considering the English place-names which lie some miles further west.[4]

Fig. 220 *The interior at Bridge Sollers. Note the Norman north arcade, the Herefordshire east window and the trussed-rafter roof with tie-beams*

The church consists of a Norman tower and nave, with north aisle, and an Early English chancel. There is some tufa in the wall of the nave. The most interesting feature is the south doorway—a 12th-century structure with carvings on the imposts, one consisting of a cat's head flanked by two dragons, the other of a dragon in profile (Fig. 50, p.20). The quality is good, and the work is probably related to the Herefordshire School.[5] There is a blocked Norman doorway in the north aisle. The roof over the nave (Fig. 220) is of the trussed-rafter type, with two tie-beams, and is probably medieval. The arcade separating the nave and aisle is late 12th-century, but the aisle itself was not built until *c*.1330. The chancel dates from around 1300 and the east (Herefordshire) window contains some good Victorian glass.

St. Mary, Brilley

Brilley church is set in lonely countryside to the north of the Wye, very close to the Welsh border. It is a plain building, dating from the 13th or 14th centuries, but restored in 1865. The chancel was rebuilt in 1888, and the tower in 1912 (replacing a wooden structure which was burnt down in 1910). The 14th-century roof over the nave has trussed rafters, collar-beams and tie-beams. The north transept is now the vestry, and in its south wall is a medieval ogee-headed recess which is probably the blocked doorway to the staircase to the former rood-loft. On the south wall of the nave is a cast-iron slab to Guilbert Hare and his daughter (d.1669); the church guide states that he married the daughter of an iron founder from Burrington, where there are similar iron slabs to his wife and second daughter (p.195). There is a plain 12th-century font.

St. John the Baptist, Byford*

The name appears to mean 'ford by the bend of the river', from the OE *byge* (bend). The church is situated on a knoll between the A438 and the Wye about 8 miles north-west of Hereford, and consists of a western tower (which looks medieval, but in fact dates from 1717), Norman nave and aisles and Early English chancel.

The eastern part of the nave is Norman, with a small round-headed window above a blocked doorway. The rest of the church is mostly of the 13th century, the chancel dating from *c*.1300. The south arcade is interesting: the eastern bays have pointed arches, but with Norman columns and trumpet-scallop capitals indicating a Transitional date towards the end of the 12th century (Fig. 180, p.77); the western bays are later (Early English), with moulded capitals. The respond at the west end was reset on an earlier corbel showing stiff-leaf carving.[6] The south transept is divided from the chancel by an Early English arcade, the capitals also showing stiff-leaf. The east window of the chancel is of the usual three-light Herefordshire pattern. Finally, the south transept has Perpendicular windows. It also has remarkable wall-paintings (p.65) dating from the 14th century, showing figures of St. Margaret and an unidentified lady. The rather plain font is dated 1638.

All Saints, Clehonger**

The OE name of the village, some 3 miles west of Hereford, means 'clay sloping wood'. The church of All Saints dates from the 12th to the 14th centuries, and is notable especially for its monuments. The south doorway is Norman, with water-leaf capitals on the columns on either side. Most of the rest of the church is 13th-century—the tower early with lancet windows, the south arcade somewhat later, with circular piers and octagonal capitals, the chancel and south aisle windows later still (with Y-tracery in the south aisle). The north transept was built as a chantry chapel in 1341 by Sir Richard Pembrugge; it has Decorated ogee-arched windows and a double-chamfered arch to the nave.

The monuments span 400 years, from the 13th to the 17th centuries. There are several 13th-century coffin-lids, including one with an excellent foliated cross. The finest monument is that of Sir Richard Pembrugge (Fig. 120, p.49). He is depicted in 14th-century armour, a dog at his feet, and bearing a large shield. Nearby is the altar tomb of a lady, probably Sir Richard's wife, with a jewelled band around her head and two angels holding her pillow. There are fine 15th-century brasses to Sir John Barre (d.1483) and his wife; he is in armour, she with a butterfly head-dress, two dogs at her feet. On the north wall of the chapel is a wall-monument to Herbert Aubrey and his wife (d.1671), with scrolls, cherubs and a broken pediment above.

St. Mary, Clifford*

The village, situated on the south bank of the Wye in the north-west of the county, was the seat of a powerful castle built by William fitz Osbern between 1069 and 1071.[7] St. Mary's church is situated high up above the village (take the turning opposite the castle to reach it), surrounded by trees. It comprises an 18th-century west tower, and an Early English or Decorated nave and chancel, with a Victorian north aisle. There is a superb oaken effigy of a priest, dating from about 1300, one of only two wooden effigies in the county (p.46). In the tower is a coffin-lid with an enriched foliated cross, dating from *c*.1300. The roofs over the nave and chancel are early sixteenth-century, the former with collar-beams and tie-beams, the latter has trussed rafters with two moulded tie-beams.

St. Michael and All Angels, Eaton Bishop***

This church (Fig. 221) possesses the finest stained glass in Herefordshire, that is nationally and indeed internationally famous. But the church itself is interesting, and has several unusual features. To find the church, take the A465 west from Hereford towards Abergavenny and after two miles fork right onto the B4349; after just over one mile, fork right again in Clehonger onto the B4352, and in less than a mile a lane on the right leads to Eaton Bishop; the church is at the end of the village, on the left.

The tower is Norman, and for some unknown reason is longer from east to west than from north to south; above is a broach spire at the foot of which are some dormer windows of uncertain age; they were not mentioned by Sir Stephen Glynne who visited the church in 1870, so possibly they are later than that date. The tower opens to the nave by a round

Fig. 221 Eaton Bishop church. Note the five-light window high in the east wall of the nave repeating the pattern of the east window of the chancel

Norman tower arch. The arcades are Early English, with circular piers and octagonal capitals. There is some stiff-leaf carving on the capital of the third pier of the south arcade. The most unusual feature of the nave is the tall five-light window in the east wall, above the chancel arch, which repeats the pattern of the east window of the chancel. In the south wall of the chancel are a good set of level sedilia dating from the 14th century.

The early glass is described in detail on p.62.

St. Michael, Kenchester

The church consists of nave and chancel only, built in late Norman times. The bell-cote is of the 13th century, and there is a typical Herefordshire east window (p.78). The best feature is the chancel roof, which has arched braces and collar-beams; the north post of the western truss is probably the former rood-beam, and it shows a length of vine-scroll decoration.[8] The unusual font is illustrated and described on p.42.

St. Michael and All Angels, Kingstone*

The earliest part of the church, some 5 miles west of Hereford, (Fig. 222) is the south doorway, which is Norman and plain, and dates from c.1160-70. Around 1200, a north aisle was built, and the first three bays of the arcade separate the nave from this. These piers are solid and circular, with scalloped capitals like Norman piers, but with pointed arches — features of Transitional architecture. Later the east bay of the arcade and the north chapel were added, and the chancel was rebuilt, all in the Early English style;

Fig. 222 Kingstone church

the capitals of the piers here are different and show stiff-leaf foliage. At the same time, the north-west tower was built.

The plain font is early Norman (but see p.38); like Kilpeck and Madley it is fashioned out of breccia limestone. Note also the 13th-century dugout chest by the north wall of the north chapel.

St. John the Baptist, Letton**

Letton is a little-known church in the north-west of the county, containing much of interest. The village lies astride the A438,and the church is in the grounds of Letton Court, on the west of the main road. The parish obtained some diocesan notoriety in the 14th century when the patron complained to Adam de Orleton, bishop of Hereford, that the rector, one Milo, had 'from old age and ill-health been absent from his church during many years without licence for non-residence, though often admonished to reside'.[9] A commission found that the church had fallen into extreme decay, and many parishioners had died without either confession or the last rites; so an assistant priest was appointed to help the ailing rector.

The church consists of a Norman nave and 13th-century chancel; the south transept and north tower were added in the 14th century. It is one of a small group of churches in the west of the county which exhibit both herringbone masonry and the extensive use of tufa; the herringbone masonry is in the north wall of the nave while tufa is found especially in the west Norman doorway and tympanum. The south doorway is even more notable and dates from the early 12th century. There is chevron decoration in the jambs, extending up through the red sandstone lintel to the arch above the plain tympanum. The lintel (Fig. 20, p.9) is adorned with rosettes and in small circles on the right there are two crudely carved heads; below, two other circles contain small figures which may be animals. The door itself is probably also 12th-century, and is a notable example of medieval iron-work: it is studded with nails, the hinges with curved arms and scrolls.

The chancel is 13th-century, the east window of three lights showing the typical Herefordshire pattern. Inside the chancel is a cusped tomb-recess. The south transept and tower were added in the 14th century; the timber-framed upper storey is 17th-century. In the south transept are further tomb-recesses, one showing ball-flower embellishment. There is a very fine 18th-century pulpit.

The Nativity of the Blessed Virgin Mary, Madley***

Three of the most famous village parish churches in Herefordshire are at Kilpeck, Abbey Dore and Madley; Kilpeck wins renown by its fantastic carvings, Abbey Dore by the splendour of its monastic remains, but Madley is known purely because of the quality of its architecture. Put quite simply, Madley is just the finest church *as a building* in the county.

Madley, some 6 miles west of Hereford has never been a large village, and yet it has a very substantial church (Fig. 223). Its name derives from Old Welsh and means 'good place'; and here in the late 5th or early 6th century is supposed to have been the birth-place of St. Dubricius (p.2).

Like many English parish churches, Madley contains work from each period of medieval architecture. The story begins with the small Norman round-headed windows, splayed internally, on each side of the north porch. These were the windows of the north transept of a 12th-century Norman church. In the walls above the middle of the arcades is a vertical joint where the east walls of the Norman transept met the Norman chancel. Early in the 13th century, the Early English period, the tower was built, with lancet windows above the west doorway. The six-bay arcades (Fig. 224) are also of this period, and lancet windows may be seen in the western ends of both the north and south aisles.

In the next century (the Decorated period), the spacious chancel was built (*c*.1320-40), terminating in a polygonal apse (rare in England); the east window shows reticulated tracery, and on either side the windows show geometrical tracery—both characteristic of Decorated windows. Note the ball-flower

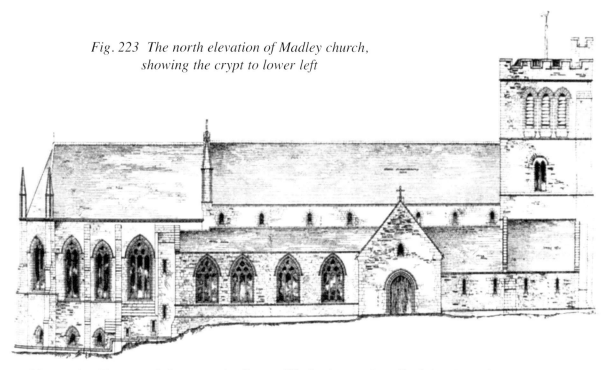

*Fig. 223 The north elevation of Madley church,
showing the crypt to lower left*

motif—another Decorated sign—on the fine sedilia in the south wall of the chancel. To the north of the chancel are some steps leading down to the crypt which lies beneath the eastern part of the chancel, taking advantage of the sloping ground. The crypt, said to be the last built in medieval England, is vaulted and supported by a single octagonal column (Fig. 225).

Just after the chancel, but still in the Decorated era, came the magnificent south chapel (the Chilstone chapel), divided from the inner aisle by a Decorated arcade, so Madley church has three arcades in all; this gives the whole building a breadth and grace most unusual in parish churches. The large windows in the south chapel have reticulated tracery, and similar windows were also inserted in the north wall, east of the porch. The west wall of this chapel is the west wall of the former Norman south transept. Finally, Perpendicular is represented by a single window in the south wall, west of the Chilstone chapel.

At the west end is an Elizabethan tomb-chest of Richard Willison and his wife (*c*.1575); the muti-

Fig. 224 The interior looking east at Madley

lated effigies are of stone, and on the sides of the chest are blank arches with shields, and kneeling figures. The monument is by the same John Gildon who was responsible for at least one of the monuments at Bosbury.

There are some further treasures to see. Above the chancel arch are some excellent medieval wall-paintings depicting the flagellation, crucifixion and resurrection of Christ; these can be illuminated by a timed switch on the north wall. At the east end of the north aisle is a 17th-century family pew, incorporating some older woodwork probably from the former rood-screen. In the chancel east window are some very beautiful stained-glass roundels dating from the 13th century, some of which depict the life of St. John the Evangelist; also some 14th-century figures from a former Jesse window which came from the same workshop that made the marvellous glass at Eaton Bishop, just two miles away. Further fragments of medieval glass are jumbled together in windows on either side.

At the west end of the church is the plain 12th-century font—the bowl is 49 inches in diameter, one of the largest in England, the stone probably coming from the same local quarry that provided the font at Kilpeck. Some carved Iberian 17th-century woodwork with panels and columns is next to the tower, having previously been behind the altar in the Chilstone chapel.

Fig. 225 The crypt at Madley

St. Michael, Mansel Lacy

St. Michael's is an attractive church set in an attractive village. The nave is Norman, with a blocked north doorway and the south aisle and chancel Early English; some of the windows are trefoil-headed lancets, but the east window of the chancel is a typical Herefordshire window of *c.*1310, with a little ball-flower adornment. The tower is 14th-century, and has a pyramid roof. There are two 17th-century memorials in the chancel to members of the Traunter family.

St. Michael and All Angels, Moccas**

The unusual place-name is Welsh, being derived from Mochros (*moch* = swine, and *rhos* = moor);[10] it cannot be a coincidence that about seven miles further down the valley of the Wye is the hamlet with the English name of Swinmoor. The church is said to have been founded by St. Dubricius, son of king Pepiau of Archenfield. He was born in Madley and founded a religious school at Hentland, near Ross, and then moved to Moccas. The later history of the church (or abbey) at Moccas is shrouded in uncertainty; but by the time of the Domesday survey, the manor was owned jointly by St. Guthlac's Priory, Hereford (a dependency of St. Peter's, Gloucester) and by Ansfrid from 'Nigel the physician'.

The church is beautifully situated in parkland surrounding Moccas Court, to the east of the B4352, one mile north of Blakemere, and is basically a simple Norman building, made distinctive by a rounded apse—rare in England, but frequent on the continent. The building, much restored, consists simply of a nave, chancel and apse, with a small bell-turret at the western end. It is largely built of tufa, commonly used in this part of the county (cf. Letton). It has been generally supposed that the building dates from the 12th century, but Gethyn-Jones argued for a late 11th-century date, largely because of the extensive use of tufa, which, he pointed out, was declining in the 12th century.[11]

There are two Norman doorways, north and south, and two Norman windows, north and west. The other windows are Decorated, impairing the purity of this perfect Norman church perhaps, but admitting

Fig. 226 The two Norman arches opening into the chancel and apse respectively at Moccas

some much-needed light. The tympana above the Norman doorways are now plain, but until 50 or so years ago they were carved. Keyser said that on the north was a lion with interlacing foliage;[12] and on the south a Tree of Life flanked by animals in the act of swallowing a human being who is head downwards, with head and one hand on the ground and the other hand against the tree. The Royal Commission on Historical Monuments described the lost tympana as showing, on the north, 'much-decayed carving of scrolled ornament and a beast', and on the south, 'human figures and beasts flanking a central stem from which spread crude scrolls' (Figs. 227 & 228).[13]

The interior is notable for the lovely vista of the two Norman arches opening into the chancel and the apse respectively (Fig. 226); the chancel arch is adorned with saltire crosses and stars (another indicator of an early Norman date), the motifs being continued laterally in string-courses; the arch to the apse is plainer. Centrally placed in the chancel is the tomb-chest of a 14th-century knight, with a stone effigy (Fig. 117, p.48). His identity is uncertain, but it is believed that he belonged to the de Fresnes family who held the manor from the 13th century. The same

The two Norman doorways at Moccas as drawn in 1850 showing the now missing tympana.
Fig. 227 (left) The north doorway; Fig. 228 (right) The south doorway

family installed the fine series of stained-glass windows in the 14th century; the glass came from the same workshops as that of Eaton Bishop and Madley, and the canopies are similar to those in Eaton Bishop, Tewkesbury and Wells.[14]

St. Lawrence, Preston-on-Wye

This church must have been in an unfortunate condition when Sir Stephen Glynne saw it in 1870, for he described it as 'in a neglected and dirty state'. Fortunately, this was put right long ago, for the church was restored (Pevsner says 'over-restored') by Nicholson in 1883, but it retains several old features. There are Norman doorways, both north and south, the latter with chevron decoration and trumpet-scallop capitals. There is a Decorated west tower, and a Decorated north chapel or transept. The pulpit is Jacobean, and there are also some 16th-century benches.

St. Mary the Virgin, Staunton-on-Wye

St. Mary's commands a wide view across the Wye valley. There is a Norman south doorway, and also a blocked north doorway. The Early English tower is divided into three stages by string-courses and at the base of the pyramidal roof is a 'cornice' of billet ornament.[15] The tower arch is triple-chamfered. The north side of the nave formerly had a two-bay arcade, remains of which can still be seen. The chancel was rebuilt in the 18th century, and later was given Victorian windows.

St. Michael and All Angels, Winforton

The exterior is striking because of the timber-framing of the bell-chamber of the tower, which was added in the 16th century. There was extensive restoration of the church in 1895. The finest artefact is the early 18th-century organ-case. The Jacobean pulpit, communion table and communion-rails are also notable.

The City and Environs of Hereford

Amberley Chapel

This little church, of no known dedication, is attractively situated about two miles north-east of Marden. It dates from the early 14th century, with some windows showing Y-tracery and others early reticulated tracery. The east window is of the Herefordshire type (p.78). In the chancel is a reset Norman trumpet-scallop capital.

St. George, Brinsop*

The outstanding quality of Brinsop's treasures, combined with its situation, make a visit to this church a memorable experience. The latter part of the village name is derived from 'hope', meaning valley, the prefix coming from the name of the family to whom the manor was sub-let after the Norman conquest.

The little church (Fig. 229) lies to the east of the A480 north of Credenhill, reached down a short lane. The building consists of a nave, chancel and north aisle, and dates from the Decorated period—the

Fig. 229 The interior at Brinsop, showing a Decorated arcade, a Herefordshire east window and a mainly late Perpendicular screen. The tympanum can be seen on the far left

first half of the 14th century. To the right of the south doorway is a holy water stoup, and above the door the remains of a medieval wall-painting of the Crucifixion can be traced. The screen separating nave and chancel extends across the nave and north aisle; it is originally 15th-century, the upper panels showing cinquefoiled ogee heads of varying design, though there is much later restoration.

Brinsop is famous, however, for the tympanum and the voussoirs over the vestry door, the work of the Herefordshire School (Figs. 41, 42 pp.17, 18). However, there is, further Romanesque carving to be seen at Brinsop: in the north chapel is a small section of an interlaced frieze, and near the south doorway is a panel built into the wall showing doves enclosed by rings, with the heads of beasts between.[1] This panel, at least, is likely to be the work of the Herefordshire School—doves being a frequent theme of that school. On the floor of the chapel is a 13th-century coffin-lid.

St. George, the patron saint of the church, is shown again in the east window: here is some excellent 14th-century glass, with the saint depicted wearing armour, his red cross on the shield, with a ground of lattice-work as at Eaton Bishop. Above St. George is Mary with the infant Jesus, and below St. John the Evangelist. The glass in the outer panels is not medieval.

In the 1920s, Sir Ninian Comper took Brinsop church in hand, and designed a ceilure, rood and gilt angels above the screen—not, perhaps, his happiest work. Better are the stained-glass windows in memory of the poet William Wordsworth and his sister Dorothy, who were frequent visitors at Brinsop Court. Also by Comper is the window in the south wall in memory of Hubert Astley, an ornithologist, depicting St. Francis surrounded by birds.

St. Mary, Burghill**

Burghill is a large village north of Hereford whose church has some excellent furnishings, the building itself being part 12th-, part 14th-century, with much Victorian restoration. To the earliest period belong the Norman window and door in the north wall of the chancel; a little later is the north arcade—the arches are pointed (Early English), the piers circular, with simple capitals and rounded abaci. In the early 14th century came the south arcade, which has octagonal piers, and the south wall of the nave and chancel—the windows here show trefoil-headed paired lancets, the largest in the chancel with early reticulated tracery. There is the head of a bishop in the south wall of the nave externally. The tower dates from 1812, the previous edifice having collapsed.

But the visitor to Burghill will be most rewarded by the furnishings. The font (Fig. 97, p.40) is outstanding, because it consists of a lead bowl standing on an intricately carved Norman stone stem. There is some excellent woodwork: the hexagonal pulpit is mainly Jacobean—the screen, however, is earlier, dating from the 15th to 16th centuries, although it was restored at the end of the 19th century. There is much delicate carving, with deep coving with ribs and bosses above, the canopy being supported by four

Jacobean posts. In 1867 Sir Stephen Glynne noted the presence of a piscina on a level with the previous loft over the rood screen, proving that there was once an altar there (cf. Wigmore and Little Hereford). The screen was moved eastward in 1880.

Finally, the monuments: in the chancel is an elegant alabaster tomb-chest of Sir John Milbourne and his wife (d.1440), with effigies; below the heads of the effigies are figures of angels, and below the feet more angels with a figure of the Virgin Mary. On the north wall of the chancel are two brasses—to Robert Masters (1619) and to John Awbrey and his wife (1617). On the Masters brass is depicted a globe on a stand—referring to the travels at that early date of Robert Masters to Virginia. The Awbreys are shown kneeling at a prayer-desk.

St. Lawrence, Canon Pyon**

The good inhabitants of Canon Pyon and King's Pyon would not be amused to learn that Pyon may come from Old English *peona eg*, meaning 'gnat island';[2] they would probably prefer the alternative explanation that Pyon comes from the Welsh *pen* meaning 'hill'. The Domesday survey records that King's Pyon belonged to Edward the Confessor, and Canon Pyon to Hereford Cathedral. Notwithstanding the possibly unflattering origin of the name, Canon Pyon church now stands graciously apart from the village to the west of the old Roman road (the A4110), in an idyllic and secluded situation. The south tower forms the porch to the church, and is early 14th-century, with Decorated belfry windows.

Fig. 230 Early English arcades at Canon Pyon; the south arcade leans to the right

The interior (Fig. 230) is older and strikes the visitor as quaint because of the pronounced outward lean of the walls, and especially of the south arcade; the latter is propped by flying buttresses spanning the south aisle, and dating from the 14th or 15th centuries. The arcades themselves are Early English (13th century), and some of the capitals show stiff-leaf carving (Fig. 183, p.78). The octagonal font is Perpendicular, with a band of quatrefoil decoration around the rim.

Separating nave and chancel is the screen which was originally 15th-century, but much modified in Victorian times; the frieze of grapes and vine leaves with dragons at each end is said to be original. In the chancel is a notable set of old choir-stalls, which probably (like the screen) came from Wormsley Priory. There are two poppy-heads in the stalls (one showing two bishops back to back between monkeys!). The misericords are excellent (Fig. 172, p.73); one shows a Catherine-wheel with sharp blades,[3] and other portrayals include a fox and goose, the pelican feeding her young, and a chained antelope—a badge of Richard II—which probably dates the stalls to 1380-1400. Also in the chancel are some good 17th-century communion rails and an unusual Early English piscina with a carved head below the basin. At the east end of the south aisle is a classical draped urn by Louis François Roubiliac (1702/5-62), commemorating George Sawyer, who died in 1753. Note also the 14th-century slab in the nave; this has indents of figures of a gentleman in civil dress with his wife, with inlays of a cement composition.

St. Mary, Credenhill**

The hill behind the church was the site of one of the largest Iron Age hill-forts in the county, covering an area of 50 acres and a population of perhaps 4,000 to 5,000 people.[4] The name of the parish means 'Creoda's Hill', Creoda being an Anglo-Saxon personal name.

St. Mary's church stands attractively above the village and is distinguished by a somewhat stunted palm-tree which grows near the fine 15th-century porch. The church has the usual hotchpotch of styles: a Norman doorway in the chancel, Early English chancel arch with lancet windows in the nave, Decorated windows in both chancel and nave. The chancel arch is flanked by two further arches which are said to be

Fig. 231 Reticulated tracery in the east window. The Early English chancel arch is flanked by two later arches, probably Victorian

Victorian; the effect is unusual and attractive (Fig. 231). The east window in the chancel shows reticulated tracery. The tower dates from the 14th century, and carries a concave-sided pyramidal roof. The font is dated 1667, and carries rosettes around a fluted bowl. But St. Mary's greatest treasure is undoubtedly the stained glass in the south chancel window described on p.61 (see back cover).

Mention must be made of Thomas Traherne, rector of Credenhill from 1657-69. He has now belatedly achieved recognition as one of the greatest of the 17th-century poets, along with George Herbert and John Donne. He was born in Hereford in 1637 and died in London in 1674. 'He is among the first English writers to respond imaginatively to new ideas about infinite space ... The boundless potential of man's mind is his recurrent theme, as is the need for adult man to regain the wonder and simplicity of the child.'[5]

St. Peter, Dormington

I visited this simple but attractive church (four miles east of Hereford) in February when the churchyard was a mass of snowdrops. It is a late 13th-century church, with trefoil-headed lancet windows, restored in 1877. There is an attractive shingled bell-turret with leaden spire. The roof is of the trussed-rafter type. The finest artefact is a singular Norman door-knocker, representing the head of a cat; the original is now in the museum at Hereford Cathedral (having been stolen and later recovered), and the one now on the door is a replica. The font is late Norman, plain with a roll moulding round the middle of the bowl. There is a handsome wall-tablet to John Brydges (d.1669), flanked by twisted Ionic columns, with a broken pediment above. Pevsner quoted the following poem from this memorial, and I cannot refrain from doing the same:

> Blest soul, whose happy mention is above
> In that quire where they only sing and love
> If Saints view humane actions then shalt see
> A griefe as great as thy loved memory
> Divided thus I'll mourn till Heaven prove just
> And once more match my body to thy dust.

St. Andrew, Hampton Bishop*

Hampton Bishop lies close to Hereford, just north of the B4224 east of the city, yet it has a rural atmosphere and a parish church that is full of interest. Much of the church is Norman (12th century), and most of the rest is Early English. From the road, the aspect is a little disconcerting, as the half-timbered upper part of the tower rises from the middle of the north side of the church.

The south doorway is Norman, and the lintel above the door is carved with scales above and saltire crosses below. There is zigzag decoration in the arch. Gethyn-Jones argued that the lintel probably dates from very early in the 12th century (before 1115), and that the chevron decoration in the arch was added later.[6] Opposite to the south doorway is the base of the tower, which is also Norman; there are small round-headed Norman windows in the north wall of the nave near the west end, and also in the tower itself. The chancel arch is Norman, and so is the arch leading from the chancel into the north chapel (though this arch is probably reset).[7]

In the 13th century, the north aisle was added, and is divided from the east end of the nave by a short arcade of two bays with a single pier between, the arches being pointed (Early English). The tower opens in two directions into the church—into the north wall of the nave and into the west end of the north aisle; both these arches are pointed, and presumably are later than the tower itself.

An unusual feature is the Perpendicular stone reredos of seven bays behind the altar in the north chapel (cf. Leintwardine). It is arranged in two tiers, and though mutilated, it remains impressive. Possibly it was brought to Hampton Bishop from some other church.

All Saints, Hereford**

The church presents an impressive exterior at the head of Broad Street. The tower is at the north-west corner of the church; it is late Early English (i.e. towards the end of the 13th century) and the belfry has on each face triple lancet windows under a common arch. Above is a battlemented parapet, from within which rises a recessed spire. The present church is also mainly Early English, with some evidence of transition to Decorated. There was, however, an earlier building: evidence of this can be seen almost hidden from view in the pier separating the north arcade from the north chancel/chapel arcade and in the corresponding pier on the south side, where remnants of earlier 13th-century piers can be seen, with capitals decorated with stiff-leaf foliage.

Fig. 232 View of the interior of All Saints from the steps leading up to the raised eating area of the café, showing the north arcade and early Perpendicular east window

The arcades are Early English (late 13th-century), the capitals of the south piers being octagonal, the slightly later north capitals being round (Fig. 232). Most of the windows of the south aisle are Decorated, with reticulated tracery, while those of the north are triple stepped lancets. The east chancel window is early Perpendicular. The roofs are interesting: tie-beams and arched braces over the nave, hammer-beams over the north aisle and a wagon-roof over the chancel. The interior has been radically transformed at the west end by the provision of a modern café with gallery; the design by Roderick Robinson has recently

Fig. 233 The old St. Nicholas church, Hereford, in 1827. This was demolished in 1842 when the church was built on a site that now lies just outside the inner ring road. The church stood at the junction of King Street and Bridge Street

won an award from the Royal Institute of British Architects. It has contributed greatly to the social value of the church without detracting from acts of worship, though it does impart a rather secular air to the building which all may not welcome.

There are some notable furnishings from the 14th to the 18th centuries. The Jacobean pulpit (1621) is a grand affair, decorated with blank arches and above is an imposing tester or sounding-board. The stalls in the chancel are of excellent 14th-century workmanship, with much fine carving and a full set of ten entertaining misericords under the choir-seats (Fig. 171, p.73). Grossinger comments that the misericords in All Saints are cruder in execution than those in Hereford Cathedral: 'they show a predilection for symmetrical arrangements of animals and mermaids facing each other, of beasts back to back, or of a face between two leaves.'[8] In the south chapel is a fine Queen Anne reredos, though it is plainer than those found in Wren's or Hawksmoor's churches in London. Above is some excellent stained glass by M.E.R. Rope (1933). Also in this chapel is a 14th-century chest.

St. Peter, Hereford*
Sir Stephen Glynne visited St. Peter's, at the western end of Hereford's old market area on 27 November, 1854, and was scathing in his comments: 'The interior suffers from frightful obstruction by pews and galleries in the most objectionable form. ... The chancel is entirely cut off from the nave by a large gallery containing the organ. There is also a double gallery at the west end of the nave' (Fig. 234). Fortunately all this has been put right, but Glynne's description is a reminder that Victorian restoration was not all bad!

The collegiate church of St. Peter was founded by Walter de Lacy *c.*1085, and in that year de Lacy was accidentally killed when he fell from the battlements of the church. There is nothing left of the Norman building, and the present church is mainly from the 13th and 14th centuries. The chancel is the

Fig. 236 The polygonal east end of the chancel at Marden

Marden church (Fig. 11, p.4) is attractively situated on the east bank of the river Lugg. Nothing remains of Offa's church, built presumably of wood, and the present church is mainly of the 13th and early 14th centuries. The exterior was largely rebuilt in Victorian times, but inside the arcades are 13th-century Early English, the circular piers of the north arcade being earlier than the octagonal piers of the south. The south doorway is also Early English. The 12-sided font, with blank trefoiled arches, is also from the late 13th or early 14th century. The 14th-century tower is sited north-west of the nave, and does not communicate with it; it has a parapet and within it rises a recessed spire.

But the most attractive and remarkable feature of St. Mary's is the polygonal east end of the chancel (Fig. 236), a rare feature of English parish churches, but seen also in Madley (p.122). This dates from the early 14th century, and the two-light windows exhibit Decorated features, with cusped cinquefoils.

Fig. 237 The interior of Marden church painted just before its restoration in 1858

Holy Rood, Mordiford

The Church of the Holy Rood is an interesting building, for it formerly had a central tower. This was adorned with a remarkable dragon, 12 feet long, probably painted in the 14th century. The site of the tower is revealed by the interpolation between the nave and the chancel of two arches, which were once the east and west arches at the base of the tower. The present south-west tower was built in 1811. The south doorway of the nave is Norman, with one order of shafts and scalloped capitals. The north aisle was added in the 19th century by F.R. Kempson; the capitals of the arcade are very florid (cf. Bishop's Frome). On the north wall of the chancel is a 13th-century coffin-lid, much embellished with foliage designs. In the south chapel is a monument to Mary Vaughan (d.1655) kneeling in prayer—a relatively late date for this motif.

St. James the Great, Ocle Pychard

'Ocle' is the same as 'Oakley', and means oak-wood, Pychard being a Norman family name.[13] The small church is medieval, of uncertain date—Pevsner thought it was from the early 14th century.[14] The west tower is small and projects into the nave. The east window is Perpendicular.

St. Mary Magdalene, Stretton Sugwas***

The village name is complex: Stretton refers to the Roman road nearby, while 'was' is from OE *waesse* meaning the flood-plain of the River Wye; it has been suggested that 'sug' is the name of a bird.[15] In the Middle Ages, the bishops of Hereford had a palace one mile to the east of the present church, and glass from its chapel can be seen in Ross-on-Wye. The medieval church, dating perhaps from the 13th century, had, by Victorian times, become seriously dilapidated; it was demolished, and the present church was built on a new site (just east of the present A438) in 1878-81, the architect being a gentleman called Cheiake who, Pevsner tells us, later emigrated to Canada.[16] Sir Stephen Glynne had visited the old church in 1854 and described the tower as being built wholly of wood-boards. Cheiake made use of a Norman doorway, which was inserted into the base of the new tower; and the upper stages of the tower were rebuilt from the old church, producing a remarkably pretty effect (Fig. 67, p.27).[17]

The church has two treasures: firstly, the superb tympanum, the work of the Herefordshire School which is described in detail on p.16, and secondly a very fine late 15th-century incised slab to Richard Greenway and his wife, now built into the south wall of the nave (Fig. 127, p.51); previously it lay over their tomb. A purse and dagger are at Richard's side and the couple are elegantly dressed. The lady is shown with a butterfly head-dress; this consisted of a single caul behind the head into which the hair was drawn back, and a wire framework on each side supported a large gauze veil, giving a diaphanous effect.[18] There is a plain Norman font.

Sutton St. Michael

St. Michael's is a small church, of Norman origin, standing almost alone at the western end of the village, and close to the Iron Age hill-fort of Sutton Walls. The plain chancel arch is Norman, and there are small Norman windows in the chancel. The font is a plain Norman tub, made remarkable by the four lions at the foot similar to those at Hereford Cathedral. There is also a very rare second font on a window-sill in the nave—a small classical urn dating from the 17th century, standing on the figure of an angel holding a book. This object dates from the Commonwealth period during which all fonts were abolished, and baptism was administered using a basin; during this time, the altar was sometimes placed longitudinally (east-west) to enable communicants to kneel in the Puritan fashion all round the altar; it is thought that the basin was placed on the shelf under the east window. Later the basin became separated from the angel, which remained in the centre of the east wall of the chancel, the basin subsequently being found under a pew in 1917.[19] Marshall conjectured that the memorial in the church to Elizabeth Cotton (d.1654) was by the same sculptor; this shows an inscription, with standing allegorical figures at the sides, a pediment with cherubs above and a shrouded corpse below.

Sutton St. Nicholas

In the village centre is the church of St. Nicholas, a building mainly of the 13th and 14th centuries. There is a south transept opening into the nave through a two-bay arcade supported by an octagonal Decorated pier. Of the same period are the piscinae with ball-flower decoration in the chancel, nave and south transept. There is a good 16th-century screen with linenfold panelling in the dado. The pulpit is Jacobean.

St. Philip and St. James, Tarrington*

The Norman church, situated to the south of the A438, originally consisted of a nave and chancel, with a semicircular apse projecting to the east; the southern part of this has been left exposed following excavation in 1931. The west tower was added soon after, but was largely rebuilt in the early part of the 16th century.[20] The north arcade and north aisle were built in 1836, and there was a later Victorian restoration resulting in the present appearance of the south wall.

From the exterior, the most interesting features are the two small Norman windows in the north wall of the chancel. Above these the arches are carved with varied geometrical designs, dated to the late 11th century by Gethyn Jones.[21] Internally, there is a frieze of round or vesica-shaped holes in the reararches above the windows. The south doorway is Norman, with one order of shafts and decorated capitals—on the west with scallops, and on the east with a crudely carved man and horse which Pevsner said was 'not to be trusted'.[22] The chancel arch is Victorian (Fig. 238) but the jambs are Norman, and their capitals are carved with scallops and heads. The abaci above are decorated. In the north wall of the chancel there is a beautiful 14th-century effigy of a lady in a tomb-recess decorated with dogtooth and ball-flower; it is a shame that it is hidden behind a pew. The 14th-century octagonal font is carved with cusped ogee-curved panels.

Fig. 238 The chancel arch and chancel, Tarrington

St. Margaret of Antioch, Wellington*

St. Margaret's is a substantial building, with a notable Norman west tower (Fig. 53, p.24). The buttresses on the faces of the tower are flanked in the first stage by shafts with Norman capitals, and small round-headed windows pierce the buttresses. There are further Norman windows higher in the tower. Inside, the chancel arch also is Norman. In the chancel are a 13th-century piscina and a Decorated tomb-recess. The stone porch is also Decorated, with ball-flower. The north aisle and arcade are Perpendicular, the arcade with octagonal piers. The roofs are especially good: over the south porch are cusped timbers and wind-braces; over the north aisle, more quatrefoiled wind-braces; and over the nave tie-beams and trussed rafters. The Jacobean pulpit is notable: the lower panels are moulded, the upper ones arcaded and embellished.

St. Bartholomew, Westhide

The oldest part of the church is the Norman west tower, low and massive, with a pyramidal roof. The chancel arch and south aisle and arcade were built in the early 14th century (Decorated), the pier of the arcade being octagonal, and the east window having geometrical tracery. The chancel and the north side of the nave were rebuilt in 1866-7. There are two interesting memorials: in the south wall of the aisle is an early 14th-century effigy in a tomb-recess of a man holding his heart in his hands, and there is an alabaster slab in memory of Richard Monyngton and his wife (d.1524), probably by the same workers responsible for the slab at Turnastone (Fig. 128, p.51).[23]

St. John the Baptist, Weston Beggard*

Apart from a farm and a cottage or two, the church stands alone in the Frome valley, remote from most of the parishioners who live in Shucknall nearly a mile away. The church was formerly subject to Stoke Edith (p.181), but later became an independent parish. To find the church, take the A438 east from Hereford towards Ledbury. One mile beyond Lugwardine, take a lane to the left signposted Weston Beggard, and the church is on the right.

The church consists of a western tower, with nave and chancel and south porch. Both the south doorway and the chancel arch are transitional from Norman to Early English. The chancel arch rests on corbelled shafts—the capital on the north side shows trumpet-scallops, that on the south upright leaves. The chancel itself is Decorated (early 14th century), though the east window is a Victorian restoration. The chancel is notable for its two tomb-recesses: that on the north is simple, though adorned with ball-flower; that on the south is surmounted by an elaborate canopy, with a multi-cusped arch, and a gable above decorated with leaves. The tower is 14th-century, with diagonal buttresses at the corners but no string course.

St. Peter, Withington

Like Pevsner,[24] Sir Stephen Glynne in 1867 was impressed by the late 13th-century tower and recessed spire: 'The steeple is a fair composition, has moulding round the summit, corner buttresses and no string-course, very good base mouldings, and a turret at the south-east. The spire (is) octagonal, (and) has at its base trefoil-headed lights set on the alternate sides.' The chancel and nave were probably built in the 12th century (two Norman doorways remain) but were much restored in 1858. The screen is described on p.68.

St. George, Woolhope

This was originally a Norman church, but there has been much later alteration. The finest part is the two-bay arcade separating the nave from the north aisle; the single pier is circular, with a scalloped capital. The first arch is semicircular; the second was changed to a pointed arch when the arcade was extended eastwards around 1300, and the piers in the north of the chancel are octagonal. The south arcade is Victorian. The roof over the nave and chancel is of the trussed-rafter type. The tower is early 14th-century. Also of this period is an effigy in the north aisle, under a canopy with ball-flower adornment; the effigy shows a frontal figure of a man with hands crossed and holding a book. Fragments of two impressive 13th-century coffin-lids are now embedded in the north wall.

St. Mary the Virgin, Wormsley

An Augustinian priory was founded near here early in the 13th century and the advowson and revenues of Wormsley church were given to it in 1262. The nave of the parish church dates from the 12th century, and the south doorway is original. The tympanum is carved with a trellis and lozenge pattern. The chancel was built in the 13th century, but was rebuilt in Victorian times. It retains its lancet windows. The pulpit and lectern have been made up of Jacobean panels (Fig. 167, p.71). After the dissolution in 1539, St. Mary's continued as a parish church until 1970; it was then closed and is now in the care of the Churches Conservation Trust. In the churchyard is the sarcophagus of Richard Payne Knight who built Downton Castle (p.195).

Around Ledbury

St. Bartholomew, Ashperton

Ashperton church is cruciform in shape, with nave, transepts and chancel dating mainly from the 14th century, and a west tower built in 1800. The windows are mostly lancets with cusped intersecting tracery, and the east window is of the Herefordshire type (Fig. 184, p.78).

Aylton*

Aylton is a small village west of Ledbury with church, farm and barn at its centre—the six-bay cruck barn dwarfing the tiny church. The little-known church of no known dedication is a real treasure. Originally it was a chapel of ease, and in 1528 it was annexed to Ledbury.

It is very small—nave and chancel in one, with a south porch and a western bell-turret. The porch has some 17th-century timbers and presents a quaint aspect. The nave is Norman, with a round-headed window in the north wall; the chancel was rebuilt in the 14th century, the east window being Decorated. The interior is mainly remarkable for the 15th-century screen which imparts a suitably rustic air to the building (p.67).

Holy Trinity, Bosbury**

In the Middle Ages, Bosbury was a place of some importance: the bishops of Hereford had a palace here, and the Knights Templars a preceptory. The village has several attractive black-and-white houses, of which the Crown Inn, the Old Court House, Hillhouse Farm and Temple Court are all worth seeing.

The church (Fig. 239) is remarkable externally for its formidable detached tower, and internally for some striking monuments and artefacts. Apart from the Morton chapel, the whole of the church dates from around 1200, with features of both Norman and Early English work. The south doorway has a round arch with scallop capitals (late Norman) on either side, and similar capitals crown the piers of the arcade; the arches here, however, are pointed, indicating that Early English has arrived (Fig. 240). The chancel arch also has scallop capitals. The trussed-rafter roof over the nave possibly dates from the 13th century.[1]

Fig. 239 Bosbury: the Perpendicular chapel is on the right

At the east end of the south aisle is the Morton chapel, built in late Perpendicular style in 1528; Thomas Morton was Archdeacon of Hereford, and was probably the nephew of the celebrated Cardinal John Morton (deviser in the reign of Henry VII of 'Morton's Fork'). He and his brother Sir Rowland had leased the manor-house of the bishops of Hereford at Bosbury, and the chapel was built as a chantry so that masses could be said for the soul of Sir Rowland's wife. The chapel has large Perpendicular windows, and fan-vaulting—a singular feature in a Herefordshire parish church (Fig. 90, p.36).

There are some impressive artefacts. The font, coeval with the church, stands on five legs; the bowl is square, with a circular lead-lined basin. The late Perpendicular oak screen has fan-vaulting on both sides—an unusual feature. The pulpit, reader's desk and lectern are largely Jacobean; the pulpit has carved panels of New Testament scenes, probably of Flemish origin—most exquisite is the Agony in the Garden.[2]

The chancel is dominated by the Harford memorials, for which the church is justly famous. John Harford (d.1559) and his son Richard (d.1578) were successive stewards of the bishop's manor, and their colossal monuments face each other across the chancel, John on the south wall and Richard on the north. The earlier monument is much the finer of the two (Fig. 129, p.52), and is the work of John Guldo (sometimes spelt Gildon or Guldon); he was also responsible for the Willison tomb (1575) at Madley. The memorials are full of north Italian influence, 'imitating terracotta work'.[3] Their quality has proved controversial: Pevsner found the earlier monument 'quite a metropolitan composition, even if executed with some homely touches' and confidently proclaimed that the later monument could not be by the same hand;[4] Whinney, however, thought that Guldo 'debased Renaissance ornament';[5] Esdaile noted that Guldo was steeped in North Italian tradition and described the works at Bosbury as 'among the most fantastic tombs in England'.[6] Their size alone justifies that comment. The figure of John Harford lies on a sarcoph-

agus supported by two lions, flanked by Corinthian columns supporting a pediment above. The figures of Richard Harford and his wife are on a sarcophagus held by two monsters, and on either side statues of Adam and Eve support the pediment.

The massive detached tower is a little later than the body of the church, dating from the 13th century. The doorway is Early English, not Norman (cf. the south doorway to the church). All the windows are lancets, and its appearance strongly suggests that originally it had a defensive function, providing a safe haven for parishioners in troubled times. The lower walls are nearly six feet thick. The tower houses five bells, one of which is more than four hundred years old.

Fig. 240 The interior of Bosbury. A Transitional arcade—the late Norman columns have scalloped capitals, but the arches are pointed

St. Michael, Castle Frome***

At the time of the Domesday survey, the manor was held by Roger de Lacy. The castle here stood about 400 yards east of the church, in an extremely strong position, now largely concealed by afforestation; it was probably from here that the de Lacy family controlled their estates in the Frome Valley.[7]

To reach the church, take the B4214 from Ledbury northwards towards Bromyard for about six and a half miles; the church is along a short lane on the right. The church, not mentioned in Domesday, is nevertheless at least in part very early Norman;[8] three plain doorways with blank tympana survive, together with a number of original windows. The round-headed chancel arch, with two plain square orders, has recessed jambs and stands on simple chamfered imposts. In the chancel stands an excellent alabaster monument to a gentleman, (? William Unett c.1630-40) and his wife (Fig. 133, p.53); they are shown recumbent, he with slashed sleeves, long hair, his right hand holding a book, the left hand on his breast, their children kneeling around the sides. Opposite, at the base of a window, is the bust of a knight in chain-mail, apparently holding his heart in his hands.

But of course it is the font that brings visitors from all over the world to Castle Frome, and this is described and illustrated on p.20.

All Saints, Coddington

This is a 13th-century church, though the doorways are still round-headed. The chancel arch is supported by corbels with stiff-leaf carving. The west tower and spire were added in 1865 to the design of F.R. Kempson. The best feature is the medieval roof with collar-beams on arched braces.

St. James, Colwall*

Colwall is pleasantly situated just to the west of the Malvern Hills; the parish church is not in the village, but a mile away to the west. St. James' is a substantial church, with a south-western tower, nave with north and south aisles, and chancel. The oldest part is the late Norman south doorway, which opens into the Early English south aisle. This is divided from the nave by a fine 13th-century arcade, the piers and abaci are circular, some of the capitals are carved with stiff-leaf foliage, and some also have human heads. Over the nave is the finest artefact in the church, the medieval roof (Fig. 83, p.34). The chancel was rebuilt in 1865 and the north aisle added in 1880. The Jacobean pulpit, complete with tester or sounding-board, is very handsome. In the chancel is a brass to Elizabeth Harford (d.1590). The south-west tower is Decorated, with a Perpendicular upper storey.

St. Mary, Donnington

St. Mary's is a small medieval church, heavily restored in the 19th century, when a wooden bell-turret was added. The only feature of note is the memorial to E.H. Webb, who died in 1655, with an inscription on drapery and surmounted by a military cap and trophy.

St. Michael and All Angels, Ledbury***

Ledbury takes its name from the river Leadon, a British river-name meaning 'broad'. By the time of the Norman Conquest, the interest of the bishops of Hereford was well-established here, for the Domesday survey records that King William restored the manor to the bishop after it had been appropriated by Earl Harold. Furthermore, a priest is stated to hold two and a half hides, which was more than any knight held. Ledbury, like Bosbury, was throughout the Middle Ages an important seat for the bishop.

The church appears to have evolved in Saxon times as a minster church on one of the estates of the bishop of Hereford; it was served by a body of priests who exercised pastoral care over a wide area. Aylton, Eastnor, and Pixley, for example, were originally chapels annexed to Ledbury.[9] Of the Saxon church no trace remains, but from Norman times onwards Ledbury exceeded in size and importance every other parish church in Herefordshire. By 1200, the college of priests had ceased to exist and Ledbury had become a portionist church, i.e. with two cathedral priests sharing the benefice, appropriating the revenues, and empowered to appoint a vicar. This arrangement lasted until the 16th century.

The church consists of a long nave, with north and south aisles, and a north porch and vestry; a chancel, with a north and south chancel chapel, and an additional outer chapel projecting on the north; the sanctuary extending to the east beyond the east ends of the north and south chancel chapels; and a detached north tower.

The history of the construction of the church is rather complex, and the best way to appreciate it is firstly to walk all round the outside,

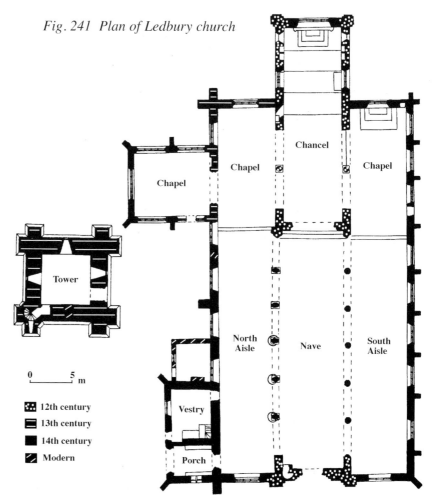

Fig. 241 Plan of Ledbury church

beginning with the west front. Here is a typical Norman doorway, with three orders of shafts and much chevron decoration in the arches. On either side and above the doorway are tall windows which appear to be Decorated: the one to the north (on the left) is indeed late 13th-century, with geometric tracing above the three lights; the corresponding window to the south is Victorian, while the one above the doorway is 13th-century but with Victorian tracery.

Moving round to the south aspect, there is a noble vista of windows in the south aisle, all with intersecting tracery of the Decorated era. Towards the east end, the three windows in the wall of the south chapel are different—these are a little earlier, and show Y-tracery of the late 13th century. In the chancel the easternmost pair of windows on both north and south are Norman and round-headed, proving that the 12th-century church was as long as the present one, though narrower, as is seen inside. The east window of the chancel is Perpendicular.

Walking round to the north, the visitor encounters the outer north chapel projecting from the north wall of the church. Here are five Decorated windows adorned with spectacular ball-flower. Nearby is the detached tower, one of the seven detached towers of Herefordshire; it was built in the 13th century, in the Early English era, and so has lancet windows throughout; the upper stage was added in 1733, together with the recessed spire (Fig. 63, p.26). After the tower, the 13th-century north porch is reached.

Inside, the nave is long, divided from the aisles by arcades of six arches with five tall octagonal piers built on the south side in the Decorated style and on the north a hundred years later; note however that

142

Fig. 242 Ledbury church showing the Norman arcade dividing the chancel from the south chapel, with round clerestory windows above, now functionless

the *bases* of the westernmost piers of the north arcade are Norman. Walk up the nave towards the chancel, and see the Norman arcades with rounded arches, circular piers with scallop capitals, dividing the chancel from the north and south chapels (Fig. 242). Above the arcades are round clerestory windows—these are now entirely internal and functionless, but originally they would have looked out to the exterior above the roofs of the lower Norman chancel aisles on each side. From the chancel, turn into the north chapel, and then walk through to the outer north chapel—the finest part of the church, with abundant ball-flower internally as well as externally.

St. Michael's has an excellent array of monuments, the best of which are as follows (in chronological order):

1) In the outer north chapel, standing upright against the wall, is the effigy of a priest in vestments, dated to the mid-13th century (Fig. 114, p.46); his face is sensitively portrayed, and above is a cusped canopy—the general opinion is that this is the finest monument in the church.

2) In the inner north chapel (next to the chancel) is the 14th-century effigy of a lady on a tomb-chest (Fig. 119, p.48), probably a member of the Pauncefoot and Carew families. As in the tomb of Blanche Mortimer at Much Marcle, 'an illusion of reality is fostered by drapery which flows over the tomb-chest and down its side'.[10]

3) In the south chapel, brasses to William Calwe, priest, early 15th century and to Thomas Capel, *c*.1490.

4) In the chancel, the huge monument to Edward Skynner and his wife (*c*.1631, Fig. 132, p.53). They are portrayed kneeling and facing each other, and between them is the effigy of a dead little girl, with ten kneeling children beneath. Note the hat of Mrs. Skynner, and her dress and ruff.

5) In the south aisle, the monuments to Anthony Biddulph (d.1718); Samuel Skynner (d.1725) by Thomas White (Fig. 145, p.56); Michael Biddulph (d.1800) by Charles Regnart; William Miles (d.1803) by John Flaxman (Fig. 149, p.58); Robert Biddulph (d.1814) by Sir Richard Westmacott (Fig. 150, p.59; according to Whinney this is 'a collection of isolated figures rather than an integrated design';[11] Daniel Saunders (d.1825) again by Westmacott; Edward Barrett (d.1857) by J.G. Lough. The best are those to Samuel Skynner, William Miles and Robert Biddulph.

6) In the chancel, the monument to John Hamilton, a child who died in 1851, is by Mary and Thomas Thornycroft (Fig. 153, p.60).

There are some fragments of medieval stained glass in the outer north chapel, and a series of windows by Charles Eamer Kempe in the south aisle. There is an ornate 17th-century font in the south aisle, and a heavy Victorian font by Sir George Gilbert Scott in the outer north chapel.

St. John the Baptist, Mathon*

From Ledbury, take the B4214 north towards Bromyard, and after four miles turn right into B4218; after three miles, turn right into a lane leading to Mathon; the church is on the left. The presence of herring-bone masonry in both the north and south walls of the nave betrays the very early Norman origin of the church, probably before 1100. The north and south doorways are also early Norman, with plain tympana; the south one has a rope moulding along the base. There is no chancel arch. The chancel was built later in the 12th century and at the east end are two Norman windows and a round window above. Foundations of an apse are said to have been found beneath the floor of the chancel.[12] The finest object in the church is the seven-bay roof of the nave with tie-beams, collar-beams and wind-braces (Fig. 84, p.34); this dates from the 14th century. The west tower and the porch are of the same date.

There is a good Jacobean pulpit, and an unusual carving of the same reign; this shows kneeling effigies of Jane Walweyn and her husband, she wearing a very striking hat.

St. Bartholomew, Munsley

This is a small church, just nave and chancel, and in part it is early Norman, for there is herringbone masonry in the east wall (p.75). Also Norman are the small round-headed windows in both chancel and nave, and the plain chancel arch. The rest of the church is largely Victorian.

St. Andrew, Pixley*

Motorists speeding along the A417 from Leominster towards Gloucester will pass the little church at Pixley unaware of the treasure that they have ignored. For St. Andrew's is tucked behind a farm, barely visible from the road, just half-a-mile south of the Trumpet cross-roads. Actually, the church is in the farmyard, and this farm (Pixley Court) was formerly a manorial centre;[13] over the centuries it has dwindled to its present status, but it retains a 16th-century cross-wing. It was a moated site, the moat probably surrounding the church as well as the house.[14] In 1528, Pixley was a chapel annexed to Ledbury.

It is a tiny church, just nave and chancel, with a Victorian bell-turret. The building is Early English, with lancet windows in the east wall of the chancel. The great attraction is the excellent woodwork, rude in construction no doubt, but very appealing. There are tie-beams in the roof, timber posts supporting the bell-turret, and above all the screen separating nave and chancel. The Royal Commission on Historical Monuments attributed the screen to the 14th century, with later additions, but Pevsner doubted whether the screen is 'early';[15] rustic it certainly is, and whether medieval or post-Reformation it imparts to the church a wonderful character. The screen has three bays with heavy moulded posts; the side bays are separated by chamfered posts carried to the upper part. The posts against the walls extend up to the tie-beam.

St. Lawrence, Stretton Grandison*

The first element of the name refers to the Roman roads which joined here, north-west of Ledbury (p.1); the second is the name of the great family of these parts (see Much Marcle). St. Lawrence's church stands on slightly higher ground overlooking the Frome valley, and makes a fine picture, with its elegant recessed spire reigning over the humbler dwellings around. It is an attractive church, built in the Decorated period, as shown by the ogee-headed lancet windows and others with reticulated tracery. In the north wall of the chancel there is a square recess, arched above, representing an Easter Sepulchre which has been cut into to provide access to a Victorian vestry. The hexagonal Perpendicular font has quatrefoils on each face. The pulpit is one of the few pre-Reformation pulpits in the county. There are good memorials to Sir Edward and Lady Hopton (d.1688), to John Taylor (d.1676) and William Jauncy (d.1797).

Ewyas and the Golden Valley

Holy Trinity and St. Mary, Abbey Dore***

Towards the southern end of the Golden Valley lies Abbey Dore, one of the most evocative monastic sites in all England. The abbey was begun by Robert, son of Harold of Ewyas, in 1147 as a Cistercian foundation, but no trace of the original church remains. Around 1180, the definitive church was started, the model being the Cistercian abbey at Cîteaux in Burgundy. Building continued for about 40 years, spanning the late Norman and Early English periods. The abbey suffered many vicissitudes during the Middle Ages, a particularly hard time being the early 14th century, when there was pestilence affecting cattle, and the soil had suffered from exhaustion. By the time of the Dissolution, in 1536, the abbey was in decline, and the property then passed to John Scudamore. The church and

Fig. 243 Abbey Dore church

accompanying monastic buildings fell into disrepair, but in 1633 Viscount Scudamore blocked off the former nave and aisles, rescued and re-roofed the presbytery, crossing and transepts, built a new tower over one of the south transept chapels, and refurnished the interior in a Laudian style. Laud was then Bishop of London, and his friend Matthew Wren (uncle of Christopher) became Bishop of Hereford at the time of the reopening of Abbey Dore church in 1634. Wren devised the form of consecration used at the service, and the church has remained a parish church ever since. So what the visitor sees today are the transepts and crossing, choir and retrochoir of the elegant medieval church furnished in an exuberant 17th-century style—an irresistible combination.

From the outside (Fig. 243), the building is decidedly odd, not to say somewhat ungainly—due to the rather featureless west front and the unusual position of the tower. The first pier of the north arcade of the ruined nave remains in solitary splendour—a massive Norman column with scallop decoration; one arch of the south arcade also survives.

Entry into the church is via a door into the south transept. Ahead, the four piers of the crossing belong to the 12th century, and beyond is the north transept, with the Royal Arms of Queen Anne on its north wall. On the walls of the transepts are a series of paintings and texts from the 17th and early 18th centuries (p.65). On the left is the wall built in 1633 blocking off the ruins of the medieval nave, and a 17th-century oak choir gallery on four classical columns. On the right, pointed arches of the 13th century pierce the east walls of both transepts; and between is a heavy 17th-century screen (Fig. 165, p.70), attributed to John Abel, the decoration mixing Gothic and classical detail; above it are the Royal Arms of Charles I, to the north the arms of Lord Scudamore and to the south those of the see of Canterbury impaling Archbishop Laud. John Abel (1577-1674) was a skilled Herefordshire woodworker and architect who was responsible for the old Town Hall at Leominster and the Grammar School at Kington; he is buried at Sarnesfield (p.115).

Passing through the screen into the chancel or choir, all the furnishings here belong to the 1630s—the stalls, communion rails and fine hexagonal oak pulpit, richly carved with arcades, Doric columns and arabesques, and with its sounding-board above. The altar is 12 feet long, still with its five consecration crosses; after the Reformation it was discarded and was later rescued from a farmyard. To the left of the altar are some relaid medieval tiles, some with heraldic shields. Behind are multi-shafted 13th-century columns of a complexity matched in England only, according to Pevsner, by Wells Cathedral.[1] This is Early English building at its very best. Above are three large lancet windows, filled with 17th-century glass (p.63): the central window depicts the Ascension, with two figures above, and in the lateral windows are the four Evangelists. Over the choir is the oaken roof, also the work of John Abel; elaborate carvings of foliage, monsters and caryatids may be seen.

On either side of the choir are the north and south aisles where there are two effigies of 13th-century knights in armour, and also a tomb-chest of John

Fig. 244 The ambulatory at the east end of Abbey Dore

Hoskins who died in 1638. Beyond the choir is perhaps the finest part of the church, the eastern ambulatory (Fig. 244)—a forest of vaults and clustered columns; here are stored some sculptured fragments and some superb roof bosses, including one with an abbot kneeling before the Virgin and child, (shown at the *Age of Chivalry* Exhibition in London in 1987), a representation of Christ in Majesty, and one of the Coronation of the Virgin.

St. Faith, Bacton*

Bacton church is well-sited, south of Abbey Dore and half a mile to the west of the B4347 in the Golden Valley, and it has some unexpected treasures for the visitor. It is a simple building—just nave and chancel, south porch and west tower. When Sir Stephen Glynne visited in 1872, he found it 'plain and rude', noting indeed the Blanche Parry memorial but not the altar frontal.

Fig. 245 The nave and chancel at Bacton

The nave and chancel are undivided, the boundary being marked by a slightly curved tie-beam (Fig. 245); there is a wagon-roof in the chancel, and a trussed-rafter roof with embattled cornice in the nave. The low tower with parapet is plain, and is apparently of post-Reformation date. In the chancel are some late-medieval stalls with poppy-heads. In the north wall of the nave is mounted a magnificent 17th-century altar frontal, with embroidered flowers, insects, birds and animals.

In the north wall of the chancel is the greatest treasure—the monument to Blanche Parry, maid of honour to Elizabeth I (Fig. 130, p.52). Blanche was born at New Court in Bacton and is depicted kneeling before her sovereign, who is shown facing the spectator. Over the figures is a canopy, with Corinthian columns on each side. A long inscription describes Blanche's years of devoted service to the Queen. In 1811, stained glass relating to Blanche was removed from Bacton to St. Eata's at Atcham, near Shrewsbury where it can still be seen. Good Victorian glass remains at Bacton.

On the south wall of the nave is the monument to Alexander Stanton (d.1620) and his wife, in the typical Jacobean posture of kneeling at prayer.

St. Clydog, Clodock***

This remote and little-known church nestling in superb scenery in the Monnow valley between the Black Mountains and Mynydd Merddin, just south of Longtown, is a real treasure because of the rarity and excellence of its furnishings.

The name of the patron saint is spelt in various ways, but is said to be one of the saints descended from King Brychan of Brecon. He was killed while out hunting by a jealous rival for a lady friend, and because of his godly life he became a martyr and later a saint. An enclosure built around his tomb later became the site of the church.

The church is built of red sandstone, and consists of a Norman nave, a slightly later chancel, and a plain late-medieval tower (Fig. 56, p.24). The exterior is austere, perfectly in keeping with its surroundings, and nothing outside prepares the visitor for the glories within. As so often in Herefordshire, the architecture is unremarkable—the treasure is all in the artefacts within, for Clodock is exceptionally rich in its array of furnishings of the 17th and 18th centuries. The church is spacious, and in the nave the box-pews are arranged in three series (Fig. 246); they mostly date from the second half of the 17th century, and some have lovely carv-

Fig. 246 The interior at Clodock from the west gallery, with the box pews arranged in three rows

ings. There is a fine three-decker pulpit with sounding-board above, also dating from the same period. Behind the pulpit is a funerary slab with inscription attributed to the 9th century. At the west end is the musicians' gallery and beneath it is the plain Norman font. There are remnants of medieval paintings on both the north and south walls of the nave (see pp.65, 66).

The chancel preserves the arrangements for Holy Communion during the 17th century (Fig. 174, p.73). The communion-table is enclosed on three sides by communion rails, and there is a very rare housel bench upon which the waiting communicants would sit. All these furnishings are of high quality, made locally from fine oak. It is very fortunate that the Victorians ignored Clodock, for these arrangements would then not have found favour: no wonder that Mark Chatfield included this out-of-the-way spot in his *Churches the Victorians Forgot*.

St. Mary, Craswall*

The parish of Craswall is set in wild, lonely country, high up on the north-east slope of the Black Mountains, at the head of the Monnow valley, and is most easily reached from Hay-on-Wye. To this remote area came the Grandmontine Order to establish one of their three priories in England (the others were at Alberbury, Shropshire and Grosmont in north Yorkshire). This Order had been founded in the later 1070s as a reaction against Cluniac magnificence—the Grandmontines advocated a life of toil and poverty and isolation from the world, and it is likely that they found all this at Craswall. The priory was founded about 1220-25, and remained poor throughout its life; it was suppressed as an alien establishment (being French) as early as 1462. Remains of the priory are preserved, about one mile north-west from the church.

Although so near the Welsh border, the name of Craswall is English, and was originally Cressewell—possibly a reference to a small spring at the Priory. St. Mary's church stands isolated (Fig. 3, p.*xii*), just beside the narrow road going to the head of the Monnow valley from Longtown over to Hay-on-Wye. It is a building of great romantic appeal, because of its isolation in this lonely countryside—an area that must once have supported a much larger population than now. It is a plain church—nave and chancel, the west end of the nave being now walled off to form a vestry. It has no great architectural merit, and is of indeterminate date, probably 14th-century. At the west end is a weather-boarded bell-turret. The interior is rustic and simple; a good roof of tie-beams and arched braces, a western choir-loft probably erected in the 17th or 18th century and an oak communion-table from the same period. There are original Perpendicular windows at the east end of the chancel and in the south walls; these are square-headed, with ogee-headed lights—the east window is said to have come from Craswall Priory. Around the exterior of the east end of the chancel and south wall of the nave is low stone seating.

My wife and I first came across Craswall church quite by chance, long before compiling this book, while driving along this lonely mountain road; on the spur of the moment, we stopped to explore and were enchanted—Craswall is a gem that should not be missed.

St. Mary, Cusop

Sir Stephen Glynne visited Cusop in 1851, finding 'a very small church in a lonely situation'; the situation is rather less lonely today, and the church was restored in 1857 but not enlarged. Of the old church, there remain a blocked Norman north doorway, a plain, semicircular chancel arch on imposts, and a lancet window in the chancel. The north vestry, the south porch and the west wall of the nave date from the restoration. The Norman font has above a frieze of saltire crosses, and the whole of the rest of the bowl is covered with a lozenge pattern.

St. Michael and All Angels, Ewyas Harold

Ewyas Harold was the site of one of the earliest Norman castles in England, built during the reign of Edward the Confessor. The parish church was granted to the Abbey of Gloucester (now the cathedral) early in the 12th century, and a Benedictine priory was established and lasted until it was suppressed in 1359. The massive western 13th-century tower, formerly detached from the church,[2] has walls 7 feet thick. The nave was rebuilt in 1868. In the early 14th-century chancel is a Decorated tomb-recess, with an effigy of a lady with her heart in her hand. The reredos includes some 16th- and 17th-century carvings from Holland and Germany.

St. Peter, Llancillo**

Where in England but in Herefordshire could such a treasure exist? And where else could there be a church so difficult to find, so tiny and yet so rewarding? When I finally tracked down Llancillo church, the congregation of eleven was just emerging from their Sunday afternoon service, and I wished I had joined them for it. To find it, take the Abergavenny road (A438) west from Hereford to Pontrilas. Look out for the Pontrilas Garden Centre, and 3.4 miles after this (still on the A438) turn right onto a bridge over the Monnow labelled 'Private'—but there is public access to the church. Having crossed the river, turn immediately right along a farm track. Follow this for one and a half miles, passing under the railway line through a gate, and finally entering a farmyard (Llancillo Court). Then turn left through a gate into a field and walk uphill for about 300 yards to the church. Between the farm and the church is a mound which is probably the remains of a motte and bailey castle.[3]

It seems remarkable that the redoubtable Sir Stephen Glynne found

Fig. 247 Llancillo church in 1896 after its restoration

Llancillo church in 1872. He wrote, 'It is impossible to conceive a church in a more secluded spot than this - so beautiful, yet so very difficult of access. It is in a retired vale, near the Monnow river, surrounded by hills and with scarcely any regular road to it.' Over a hundred years later, and all this is still true. What has changed, and changed for the better, is the state of the church: Glynne found it 'dirty and dilapidated'; and by 1896, the building had become unsafe. The bishop of Hereford advised closure; then the south wall fell in, the door was left open, the walls became cracked and crumbling; the roof tiles were blown off, sheep wandered in and out of the nave, the oak panelling was stolen. Undaunted, the Reverend Robert Whinney, vicar of Rowlstone, set up a restoration fund which prospered, and the result is the charming building that survives to this day.

The name Llancillo means 'Sulbiu's church', and it is mentioned in the *Book of Llandaff*, *c*.1150.[4] It is, unsurprisingly, a humble building (Fig. 247), consisting of just nave and chancel, with a western bell-turret. There is a deeply-splayed Norman window in the north wall of the chancel, and another in the east wall, the head of which has at some time been made pointed. The south window of the nave is rectangular and probably 16th-century. The interior is unpretentious; the main glory of the church is the panelled pulpit, dated 1632, and standing on four pedestals. It consists of two sides of an octagon carved with arabesques and other ornament. There is a plain 13th-century font: Marshall considers that the 'stem' under the bowl is really the base stone for the shaft of a churchyard cross.[5] From the same century is a 'dugout' chest. I found the simplicity of this church most evocative, and more impressive than many much grander structures—make the effort and go and see it!

St. Beuno and St. Peter, Llanveynoe*

Beuno was born in Powys *c*.560 and he is said to have built a monastery at Llanveynoe.[6] It is worth visiting this remote, beautifully situated little church in the Olchon valley, close to the Welsh border, to see the elementary but moving piece of Anglo-Saxon sculpture of the Crucifixion (Fig. 12, p.6). The church itself is not of great interest; it consists of nave, chancel and bell-cote, probably 13th-century in origin, but mostly restored. To find it, take the road south-east from Hay-on-Wye to Cusop and follow the narrow road going steeply uphill past Newforest Farm; pass over the watershed and go downhill past Craswall church and pub. Four miles further on, a lane on the right leads into the Olchon valley and Llanveynoe.

St. Michael, Michaelchurch Escley*

Herefordshire west of the Golden Valley is a world apart from the rest of the county. For here abounds the finest scenery: bare hills divided by deep valleys with their associated streams—Escley Brook, the upper Monnow, Olchon Brook—and then the flank of the Black Mountains. St. Michael's church stands almost alone in the Escley valley, a grey stone edifice more in keeping, perhaps, with Yorkshire or Cornwall than with Herefordshire. It is now a thinly populated area, but the abundance of graves in the churchyard indicates that this cannot always have been the case.

To reach the church, take the Abergavenny road (A465) west from Hereford, and after two miles fork right onto the B4349. Keep on this road until the T-junction with the B4348, then turn right and go down to the Golden Valley. Ignore the B4347 on the left, but shortly after turn left to Vowchurch and Turnastone. Then continue on this lane uphill and finally down into the Escley valley; turn left, and the church is shortly reached on the left.

The body of the church is medieval, of uncertain date, but the west tower was rebuilt in 1897. The nave and chancel are undivided, and over the nave is a wagon-roof (Fig. 88, p.35). There are two striking features: on the north wall is a rather worn medieval wall-painting of Christ of the Trades, in which a large-scale figure of Christ is surrounded by agricultural implements (p.65). The other feature is the wooden screen separating nave and chancel. Much of it looks Victorian, but the quality of the carving is good. Certainly, Michaelchurch Escley is a Herefordshire church with a difference—and must not be missed!

St. Peter, Peterchurch*

Peterchurch prides itself as the 'capital' of the Golden Valley, and its church has even been described as the 'cathedral' of the same. And indeed, old photographs showing the elegant Decorated spire soaring above the surrounding countryside give an impression of nobility. Alas!, it is no more: for some years ago the spire was dismantled and has now been replaced by a fibreglass structure which marries ill with the rest of the church and fails to enhance the beauty of the local scene. Some may feel that if the 20th century could not afford to rebuild what the 14th century accomplished, the tower ought to have been left without any spire. But the rest of St. Peter's church is impressive indeed.

Fig. 248 An unique perspective of three Norman arches at Peterchurch. The Norman font in the foreground

Entry into the church is via the north porch, a Decorated structure embellished with ball-flower (Fig. 74, p.30). The body of the church is Norman, divided into four cells—an arrangement that is, so far as I am aware, unique in England. The four compartments are, from west to east, nave; a square cell which was probably the base of a former tower; chancel; and semicircular apse. These are divided by a series of three Norman semicircular arches of diminishing height, yielding an unique perspective seen from the west end of the church (Fig. 246). The first and third arches are decorated with saltire crosses; the second (the richest, and the chancel arch proper) has chevron decoration in two planes. There is a lovely Norman south doorway (Fig. 22, p.9), with one order of shafts, scalloped capitals and chevron decoration. The tower, to the west of the nave, is late 13th or early 14th century. The font is a Norman tub, with rope moulding around the rim and the waist, with a frieze of zigzag below the upper moulding. It is very similar to that at Kington.[7]

Within the parish of Peterchurch is Urishay Chapel—a separate chapel built in the early 12th century within the bailey of the castle. The chapel became ruinous and has been partly restored by the Friends of Friendless Churches—the eastern part of the nave, the chancel arch and chancel have been re-roofed. To find the chapel, take the lane signposted to Urishay at the southern end of Peterchurch; the chapel is on the left after a mile or so.

St. Peter, Rowlstone***

St. Peter's is another Herefordshire church which, architecturally undistinguished in itself, is nevertheless famous because of the quality of its Norman carvings. It is set in glorious countryside in the south-west of the county, above the Monnow valley. A signposted lane leads off the A465 at Pontrilas. There is a motte and bailey 100 yards north-east of the church.

The church stands on a knoll above the roadside, and consists simply of a west tower, nave with south porch, and chancel. The nave and chancel are Norman, with round-headed windows surviving in each, though later Perpendicular windows have been inserted in the east wall of the chancel and the south wall of the nave. The semicircular chancel arch is of two orders, the inner roll-moulded, the outer square and enriched with saltire crosses. The tower is 13th- or 14th-century, and has a west window of plate tracery.

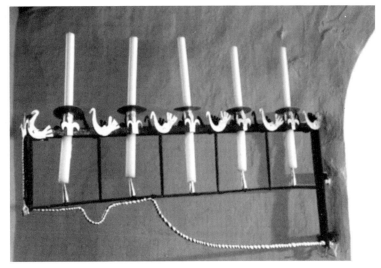

Fig. 249 Rowlstone: The south candle bracket

Interest, however, centres on the south doorway and the chancel arch— both notable examples of the Herefordshire School; these are described in detail on p.15.

There is another treasure in Rowlstone which is much less well-known, and may be unique in the country: this is the pair of 15th-century wrought-iron bracket candelabra extending from the north and south walls of the chancel. Each consists of two horizontal bars, divided into five compartments by twisted upright bars; in the middle of each division is a spike for a candle. Above these are six swans on the south bracket and six cocks with outspread tails on the north bracket, and in between each bird is a fleur-de-lis (Fig. 249).

St. Margaret, St. Margaret's***

St. Margaret's is propelled into fame by its single treasure, the rood-loft. The church is in remote countryside above the Golden Valley and it is not easy to find. From Hereford, take the A465 Abergavenny road to Pontrilas, and turn right into the B4347, passing through Ewyas Harold and Abbey Dore. One mile after the abbey, turn left to Bacton and continue up the hill to a T-junction; then turn right to Newton. In Newton turn right again for St. Margaret's; the church is found on the left.

It is the simplest of churches, consisting just of nave and chancel and weather-boarded bell-turret which projects precipitously over the west end (Fig. 250). As with other churches in this border area, it appears Welsh rather than English, and it was in the diocese of St. David's until 1852. There was once a Norman church here, proved by the existence of a Norman chancel

Fig. 250 St. Margaret's church

arch, now largely concealed by the loft. The south doorway has a pointed arch, of any date from the 13th century onwards; and it is believed that the nave was rebuilt in the 15th century. The roof has arched braces and collar-beams; one tie-beam is original, the other three being modern. Behind the chancel arch, stairs ascend to the rood-loft. Scattered around the nave and chancel, and contributing greatly to the atmosphere of the church, are a series of painted texts dating from the 18th century. These have now been meticulously restored, and shine out as though new.

But it is the rood-loft (Fig. 7, p.*xiii*, and Figs. 163, 164, pp.69, 70) which makes visitors exclaim with delight on entering the church. The loft is described in detail on p.70. Rood-lofts today are very rare in England, because they were nearly all destroyed following the Reformation. A number survive in Wales, the nearest to St. Margaret's being Patrishow just over the border in Breconshire. In the Middle Ages, the usual arrangements were a screen dividing nave and chancel, and above the screen, the loft on which would have been placed a large crucifix or rood, flanked by the figures of the Virgin Mary and St. John the Evangelist.

The 20th-century glass in the east window shows St. Margaret as a sheperdess carrying a representation of the church. It is by A.J. Davies.

St. Mary Magdalene, Turnastone*

This is a very small parish in the Golden Valley, south of Peterchurch and on the opposite bank of the Dore from Vowchurch. Why were two Norman churches built about 500 yards from each other? We must be glad that they were, for Turnastone is a little-known gem, well worth visiting; when I went there in March, the churchyard was a mass of wild daffodils, celandines and violets.

The building (Fig. 251) is quaint and rustic, just a nave and chancel, with south porch and a wooden bell-turret. Inside the porch, the south doorway is Norman. Above the nave is a

Fig. 251 Turnastone church

wagon-roof (Fig. 87, p.35). The showpiece of the church is on the north wall of the chancel, where there is an incised effigial slab to Thomas ap Harry and his wife (1522, Fig. 128, p.51), very similar to one at Westhide; both probably originated at the Burton upon Trent workshop, using Tutbury alabaster, and the workers involved may have been Henry Harpur and William Moorcock.[8] It depicts a man in armour and a lady with pedimental head-dress; to the left of the male effigy is a small satyr wearing a hat and playing the pipes. On the north wall of the nave is the memorial to Mary Traunter, who died aged 18 in 1685. There is a simple semi-octagonal Jacobean pulpit and a 12th-century font similar to that at Vowchurch (the stem of the font is modern).

St. Bartholomew, Vowchurch*

St. Bartholomew's has a lovely situation beside the river Dore south of Peterchurch in the Golden Valley, and is memorable for its Jacobean woodwork. It is a simple building, just nave and chancel undivided, a western bell-turret and south porch. Part of the south wall is Norman, where there is one round-headed window; the rest of the church was constructed in the 14th century, and on the south wall the junction between the 12th- and 14th-century work can clearly be seen.

The bell-turret was built in 1522, and was originally supported by beams resting on the lateral walls of the nave. In the early 17th century, the present oak structure supporting the turret was erected. The roofs of the nave and chancel form a veritable forest of beams (Fig. 82, p.33); in the nave, the tie-beams are supported by vertical posts, proving that the roof is later than the walls, dating from c.1613; above the tie-beams are collar-beams and queen-posts. The roof of the chancel is said to be medieval.

The wooden screen stretching across the church is a good example of rather crude local craftsmanship of the early 17th century; figures carved on the posts of the central arch are known as Adam and Eve. The screen is divided into compartments by balusters, and above the central arch is a pediment. Just behind the screen is a board inscribed, 'Heare below ly the body of Thomas Hill ande Marget his wife whose children made this skryne'. Also dating from the same century are the handsome communion-rails, two choir-stalls and the south porch; the latter has a fine array of balusters on each side.

St. Mary, Walterstone

This is a small medieval church, without specific features. There is stained glass from the 17th century in the chancel.

Archenfield

St. John the Baptist, Aconbury*
St. Dubricius, Ballingham
St. Michael, Dewsall* (p.197)
St. Mary, Foy*
St. Swithin, Ganarew (p.199)
St. Michael, Garway***
St. Giles, Goodrich*
St. Dubricius, Hentland**
St. Catherine, Hoarwithy*** (p.189)
St. Cuthbert, Holme Lacy**
St. Mary Kentchurch (p.195)
St. Mary and St. David†, Kilpeck***
St. Mary, Little Birch (p.199)
St. David†, Little Dewchurch (p.199)
St. Dinabo, Llandinabo* (p.198)
St. Deinst, Llangarron*
Christchurch, Llangrove* (p.186)

St. John the Baptist, Llanrothal*
St. John the Baptist, Llanwarne* (p.195)
St. Matthew, Marstow (p.199)
St. Michael, Michaelchurch*
St. Mary and St. Thomas à Becket, Much Birch (p.194)
St. David†, Much Dewchurch**
St. John the Baptist, Orcop*
St. Denys, Pencoyd
St. Peter, Peterstow
St. Dubricius, St. Devereux*
St. Weonard, St. Weonard's*
St. Tysilio, Sellack*
St. Bartholomew, Thruxton*
St. Mary, Tretire (p.199)
St. Mary, Welsh Newton*
St. Dubricius, Whitchurch
St. Peter, Wormbridge

Note the frequency of dedications to unusual Welsh saints. (†Welsh St. Dewi)

St. John the Baptist, Aconbury*

Aconbury is a tiny hamlet south of Hereford, signposted off the A49 some 3 miles south of Hereford. It nestles under the summit of Aconbury Hill, on which there are remains of an Iron Age fort. A priory of Austin nuns was founded here early in the 13th century by Margery, wife of William de Lacy (who founded Craswall Priory in the Black Mountains). The church that was built was never larger than it is today and is, therefore, an unusually unspoilt example of Early English architecture. Until the convent was closed at the Dissolution of the Monasteries in 1536, it educated the daughters of the gentry of the area; after the Dissolution, the conventual buildings were demolished, and the church became the local parish church.

The church (Fig. 252) is undivided, consisting of nave and chancel, with a timbered bell-turret added later. Over the west porch is a 13th-century window of three trefoiled lights, enclosed within a moulded order, in the tympanum of which are three moulded quatrefoils. The jambs of the outer door have attached

Fig. 252 Aconbury church

shafts with foliated capitals and moulded braces. Below the window is a doorway of the same period, with a moulded label and foliated stops. In the north wall are three windows, the easternmost a 13th-century lancet, the other two are two-light cinquefoiled windows, with a quatrefoil above. The partly restored and reset east window of the chancel has three lights with a moulded label and head-stops; the side-lights are pointed and the mullions carried up to the head on either side of the middle light—a common Herefordshire type. At the east end of the south wall are two lancets similar to those in the north wall, but these are higher to avoid the roof of the former cloister. On either side of these windows are two blocked 13th-century doorways. Near the west end of this wall, high above the ground, is a small chamber in the thickness of the wall—it must have been entered from the first floor of the western range of the conventual buildings by a doorway now blocked, but there is a quatrefoil set in the blocking.

The fine timbered porch (Fig. 72, p.29) dates from the 14th or 15th centuries and has an outer archway springing from attached shafts with plain moulded capitals. The side walls are two bays deep and each bay is subdivided into six lights with trefoiled ogee heads and tracery; the roof has three trusses with moulded wall-posts having attached shafts with moulded capitals or angels holding shields. The braces have carved traceried or panelled spandrels and the wall-plates are moulded.

Aconbury today has a somewhat forlorn aspect; the church is locked, and is no longer used for services. Yet it remains an excellent example of Early English work, and it ought to be opened to the public. Inside the church are said to be a medieval coffin-lid incised with a floriated cross, the burial vault of Lord Chandos (who used to own Aconbury Court), and the Royal Arms of Queen Victoria, with some wall-paintings of flowers from the same reign.

St. Dubricius, Ballingham

Ballingham church lies on relatively high ground overlooking a loop of the river Wye, and its 13th-century tower with recessed spire commands an extensive view. The roof over the nave is of the trussed-rafter single-frame type and is said to date from the 14th century. The Perpendicular porch, though plain, is handsome (Fig. 75, p.30). The monument to William Scudamore (d.1649) is in classical style, early for its date in Herefordshire.

St. Mary, Foy*

Foy stands towards the end of a great loop of the river Wye, ensuring that the busy world passes it by, for it is certainly a 'No through road'. To find it from Ross-on-Wye, cross the river and just after the round-about on the A49 turn right for Bridstow. Keep to the right at a T-junction and turn right at a cross-roads for Foy. In the *Book of Llandaff* the parish is recorded as *Llantimoi*, the church of St. Moi.[1]

The church has a commanding position above the Wye, and dates mainly from the Early English and Decorated eras. It consists of a western tower, nave and chancel; the latter has a lancet window in the north wall. The other windows are mostly Decorated, with the exception of the east window in the

156

chancel—this apparent Perpendicular window was not inserted until the 1640s under the will of John Abrahall; he expressly commanded that the window be built in the same manner as the east window at nearby Sellack. The glass in this window is a copy of the glass at Sellack.

The finest object in the church is probably the screen, parts of which date from the 16th and 17th centuries, though much restored; carved pillars rise from the linenfold panelling of the dado to the flat canopy above, with an intricately carved west border—is the canopy the surviving floor of the rood-loft? There is 17th-century woodwork in the pulpit, choir-stalls and communion rails.

Behind the pulpit is an altar-tomb with a cusped trefoiled canopy, small piscina, and a 13th-century effigy of a lady carved in low relief. A similar one is in the chancel. There are several wall-memorials of the 17th century and later to members of the Abrahall family, the best being to George Abrahall (d.1673) and Paul Abrahall (d.1675); the bust of the latter is shown holding a book in his left hand, flanked by twisted Ionic columns; above is a broken scrolled pediment, cherubs and a coat of arms.

St. Michael, Garway***

Garway is situated midst lovely scenery in the Monnow valley. To find the church, in the village of St. Weonard's on the A466 between Hereford and Monmouth, turn west onto a lane leading to Garway Common; at a T-junction there, turn right and go downhill for half a mile; then turn left down a smaller lane which leads to the church.

The church is one of the most exciting to visit in the county. The *Book of Llandaff* preserves charters for the foundation of monasteries at Bellimoor and Garway, in 610 and 615, so that the church here stands on ancient Christian ground indeed. The fate of these ancient foundations is not known, but it seems likely that they were succeeded by an Anglo-Saxon church; the next firm date is 1180, when the Knights Templar arrived having been given land in the area by Henry II.

The Knights Templar were founded during the reign of Baldwin II, King of Jerusalem (1118-31) to protect pilgrims on their way to the Holy Land, and in France they received the backing of Bernard of Clairvaux, who drew up their statutes in 1128. In England they built a number of churches with a round nave and square chancel to resemble the Holy Sepulchre in Jerusalem. The best known of these is the Temple Church in London. The foundations of the round church at Garway were excavated in 1927, and are still exposed to the north of the nave.[2] The Knights Templars continued in Garway for nearly 200 years. Their order was overthrown by King Philip IV of France in 1312 and their property then passed to the Knights Hospitaller (the knights of the Order of St. John of Jerusalem) until they were dispossessed by Henry VIII.

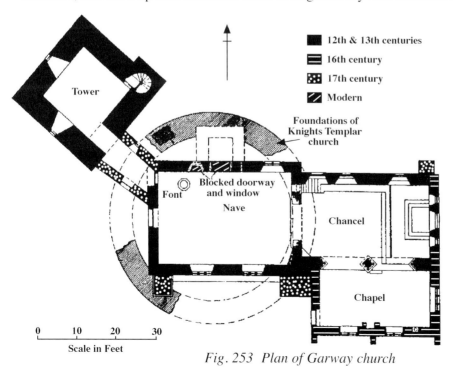

Fig. 253 Plan of Garway church

The round nave of the Templars' church was connected with the chancel by the chancel arch which survives, and which is the oldest part of the fabric of the present building. The solid later 13th-century tower (Fig. 60, p.26) is separate from the body of the church and is now connected to it by a passage built about 300 years ago. The present nave was also built in the 13th century, the round nave having been demolished. The existing chancel arch (Fig. 254) is a massive 12th-century structure, with three orders; the outer two have zigzag at right angles to each other, and the inner order consists of voussoirs, each moulded across the

Fig. 254 The Norman chancel arch and the Early English arcade into the south chapel at Garway

arch.[3] The inner order is supported on a plain impost, the two outer orders being carried on detached shafts with carved water-leaf capitals. One capital on the north side has a carved head. To the east of the chancel arch are the steps leading up to the former rood-loft. The chancel has an excellent roof, with tie-beams, collar-beams and two tiers of wind-braces laterally. It opens on the south to a chapel, through a two-bay Early English arcade. Outside the church are small sculptures of the Hand of God, the Lamb and the Cross, and others; these may be of 15th-century date, though Pevsner thought they were later.[4] Carved on the outside of the east and south walls are a series of symbols of uncertain age (Greek, Maltese and Lorraine crosses, and a reversed swastika), possibly connected with the Knights Templar.

St. Giles, Goodrich*

Situated high above Goodrich village, St. Giles impresses the visitor by its tall and remarkably elegant broach spire supported by a Decorated west tower (Fig. 68, p.27). Internally, the church consists of nave and chancel undivided, and a north aisle. The earliest part of the arcade is the central part, which is Early English, with circular piers and capitals. In the early Decorated period, the nave was extended westwards, and a north chapel was added to the chancel; the piers at both west and east ends of the arcade are octagonal. In the same period, a south porch was added. The east window of the chancel is Perpendicular.

In the north aisle are some wooden panels of the 17th century, both English and foreign. There is also a shrine similar to that at Bridstow with blind cusped arcades on the walls. In the east window of the north aisle there is some stained glass of the 15th century, depicting angels with shields.

St. Dubricius, Hentland**

Hentland (Fig. 9, p.2), south-east of Harewood End which straddles the A49, the very heart of Archenfield, is now a rural backwater—there is no village, and the church stands by itself except for a cottage, at the end of a lane which leads nowhere. Yet it was not always so, and the name of the parish gives the clue to an important past. For Hentland is derived from the Welsh 'henllan', meaning 'the old church', the name being first recorded in the *Book of Llandaff*, *c*.1150. But the parish goes back a long way before then, for it is thought to be at Hentland that St. Dubricius founded a monastic site in the 6th century (see p.2).

Hentland was a parish church until 1291, when it became a chapelry in the parish of Lugwardine; it did not become a parish church again until 1842. It underwent restoration by Seddon (who rebuilt Hoarwithy in the same parish) in 1853 and when Sir Stephen Glynne visited in 1861, he found that the church 'now put into nice order is in a retired situation amidst shady trees and orchards'. Though much has changed since 1861, Hentland's retired situation is still the same!

The church consists of a west tower, nave with north aisle, and chancel. The main body of the church is late 13th century; the north arcade has octagonal piers, and the east window of the chancel has three stepped lancets. The 15th-century roof over the nave and chancel is of the trussed-rafter type with, in the nave, scissor-braces also. In the north wall of the chancel is a stone credence table and in the window opposite is a piscina. The screen between nave and chancel is mostly Victorian, but contains some work dating from the end of the Middle Ages. Poppy-heads on the choir-stalls are 16th-century, and there is an excellent Jacobean chair and pulpit. The graceful octagonal font is Perpendicular, and is exceptionally well decorated with a man's and a woman's heads, fleurons and roses (Fig. 103, p.42). The tower is 14th-century, with Decorated windows.

Hentland's heyday in modern times was in the 19th century, and in recent decades it has been in decline. According to the church guide, the building had been badly neglected until about 15 years ago; but since then, a few energetic and dedicated people have laboured hard to restore both church and churchyard; they deserve to be supported, for this ancient place has much to offer.

St. Cuthbert, Holme Lacy**

St. Cuthbert's stands by itself at the end of a lane that leads south from the B4399, near to the river Wye, but over a mile from the present village. It is no longer used for services, and is in the care of the Churches Conservation Trust. The great attraction of the church, apart from its setting, is the fine array of monuments of the Scudamore family.

'Holme' comes from OE *hamm*, meaning 'land by a river bend', an apt description of the village site. At the time of the Domesday survey the manor was held by the Bishop of Hereford and tenanted by Roger de Laci, and it remained in the possession of that family until the 13th century, when it reverted to the Bishop of Hereford. The Scudamores settled at Holme Lacy in 1419, and remained there for over 400 years.

Fig. 255 Holme Lacy church

The church (Fig. 235) consists of a western tower, nave with chancel, and south aisle with a south chapel of the same length and almost the same width, with a south porch and north transept. The building is mainly of the 13th and 14th centuries. The plain tower is 14th-century, and has diagonal buttresses. The nave is divided from the south aisle by a rather nondescript arcade of square piers without capitals; the easternmost pier was added in 1924 to support the unusually wide arch here. Beyond is a typical elegant late 13th-century arcade of two bays, with a single pier of quatrefoil shape, dividing the south chapel from the chancel—making the main arcade (which is of uncertain date) seem rude indeed. There are some fragments of medieval stained glass in one of the north windows of the chancel. There are two sets of stalls with misericords, and an attractive late 17th-century font. This consists of a circular bowl with acanthus leaves and cherubs' heads, and a shaft with drapery and rosettes.

But it is the monuments that are the chief glory of Holme Lacy. The finest is that of John Scudamore and his wife (*c*.1571)—two alabaster effigies on a tomb-chest carved with shield and angels. The knight is armoured, with head resting on a helm and feet on a small lion, while his lady is fashionably attired with gown, collar, embroidered sleeves and head-dress - models of Elizabethan respectability and piety! Very different in the north wall of the chancel is the swaggering pose of the cavalier of the next century, James Scudamore (d.1668; Fig. 139, p.55). He is depicted leaning languidly on his tomb-chest, with cherubs above, framed by Corinthian pillars. Next to him is the monument to his wife Jane (d.1699), another marble monument with a central obelisk flanked by cherubs, with columns and a pediment behind. In the south chapel is the monument to John Scudamore, Viscount Sligo, who died in 1716 aged 33; there is no effigy but a central urn, with cherubs on each side, enclosed by tall fluted Ionic columns with a broken pediment above (Fig. 140, p.55). These last three monuments all date from the early 18th century. Of the later memorials, note the elegant tablet to the 12th Earl of Chesterfield (d.1935), by Mrs. Scudamore Stanhope.

St. Mary and St. David, Kilpeck***

The most celebrated Norman parish church in the whole of England is situated obscurely in a remote corner of Herefordshire, though with its own brown sign off the A465 Hereford to Abergavenny road some 9 miles south-west of Hereford. It is also a very small and humble building and it is famous not for the quality of its architecture but because of its outstanding carvings.

But Kilpeck existed before the Normans: it is in the kingdom of Erging (Archenfield) which evolved in post-Roman times, and where there is much evidence of the persistence of Christianity from an early date. The local saint was Dubricius, and the church at St. Devereux, less than a mile from Kilpeck, is dedicated to him.

Fig. 256 Kilpeck church showing the former porch (which may have helped preserve the doorway) and bell-tower, and the roof of the apse, now modified. This drawing was made sometime before the restoration of 1848

However, Saint David or Dewi also had a following, with dedications at Much and Little Dewchurch, as well as Kilpeck.[5] It is uncertain whether he is the same as the Welsh St. David.

Kilpeck is first mentioned in the 9th century; the first element in the name is the Welsh *cil* meaning 'retreat', the second is unexplained.[6] There was an Anglo-Saxon church here, for at the north-eastern corner of the nave of the present church the masonry has a different alignment. It leans towards the south, and the angle includes large stone quoins laid as long-and-short work extending almost to the existing eaves.[7] This was accepted by the Royal Commission and by Taylor and Taylor as of pre-Conquest date, though some doubt has recently been cast on this.[8] By the time of the Domesday survey (1086), the manor was held by William fitz Norman.

To the west of the present church is a Norman motte, with inner and outer baileys, the church being outside the bailey. Aerial photography reveals the outline of a massive rectangular enclosure, large enough to enclose a town, marked by a ditch and rampart, emphasised by modern roads which run outside its eastern and southern edges.[9] The 12th-century *Book of Llandaff* states that some form of religious community existed at Kilpeck long before the Conquest. It seems, therefore, that in the 12th century Kilpeck was not the obscure settlement that it has since become, but a centre of power and of wealth; and that the Norman lord, Hugh of Kilpeck, consciously financed the scheme of decoration for Kilpeck church.[10] This explains the extraordinary richness of its Norman carving.

In 1134, a Benedictine Priory was established at Kilpeck as a cell of St. Peter's Abbey in Gloucester, and the present church was probably built not long after, possibly incorporating in its fabric the earlier Anglo-Saxon work. It is a small three-cell building (Fig 256), nave, chancel, and semicircular domed apse, with arches between nave and chancel, and between chancel and apse. There is rib-vaulting in the apse, with zigzag on the ribs; and at the intersection, there is a boss of four beaked heads.[11] At the back of the church is a gallery, of uncertain date, but with a Jacobean rail and standing on pillars which are said to be Elizabethan. Below is the massive font—an enormous plain bowl of breccia (as at Madley), supported on five legs. Under the chancel arch is the holy-water stoup, with two hands gripping two heads on the bowl, and beneath four animal heads. The font is certainly Norman, the stoup possibly earlier. The building is of red sandstone, often not a durable medium for sculpture, but here of a hardness which has resisted 800 years of wear. The extraordinary carving, on which Kilpeck's distinction rests, is displayed in four sites: externally, the south doorway (Fig. 6, p.*xiii*), the west window, and the corbel-table, and internally, the chancel arch. These are described and illustrated on pp.13-15.

St. Deinst, Llangarron*

St. Deinst is a Welsh saint of whom, apparently, nothing is known; though another church dedicated to him is at Itton, Monmouthshire.[12] The church stands austerely over the village in the south-west of the county, and is dominated by the tall heavily-buttressed west tower, dating from the 14th century. The chancel also dates from this time, and one of the stones in the south-east buttress of the chancel bears a knot motif, similar to the tympanum at Byton (Fig. 16 p.8. Over the chancel is a single-frame scissor-braced roof. The nave, north arcade and north aisle date from 1841. Just to the west of the south porch, a two-light Decorated window has been apparently reset in a gable.

The octagonal Perpendicular font is excellent (Fig. 104, p.42). There are some attractive wall-monuments, including those to Rowland Scudamore (d.1697) and William Gwyllym (d.1698). In the south wall of the nave is mounted a small effigy of a civilian in high relief (*c.*1300). There is a tall Jacobean pulpit and some 17th-century communion rails.

St. John the Baptist, Llanrothal*

Llanrothal is another of Herefordshire's hidden gems, now in the hands of the Churches Conservation Trust. It is said to have been founded by a Celtic saint Rhyddol in the 6th or 7th century, and the *Book of Llandaff, c.*1150, refers to it as Lann Ridol. To find it, in Welsh Newton on the A466 Hereford to Monmouth road, turn to the west opposite the church and follow this lane into the Monnow valley, ignoring a later turning to the left. After about two miles, you will see the little church on the left. Park near Llanrothal farm and walk across the fields to the church.

The church now stands quite alone (Fig. 10, p.3), but in the Middle Ages it was surrounded by a village; this later became deserted, possibly because of the Black Death (1348-49). Services continued to be held at the church but became increasingly irregular in the 19th century. By the 1920s, dilapidation was becoming severe, and the nave was abandoned and its roof removed in 1948. The chancel was restored and preserved. In 1985, the church was taken over by the Redundant Churches Fund, and since then the nave has been re-roofed and its walls repaired.

The nave, at least in part, dates from the 12th century, for there are Norman windows in the north and west walls. The south wall of the nave is 13th century (Early English) with lancet windows and a south

Fig. 257 The chancel at Llanrothal

doorway of the same period. The chancel (Fig. 257) is also Early English, with a pointed chancel arch and an east window with paired lancets and a small circle above. A large square-headed Perpendicular window has been inserted in the south wall of the chancel. The altar-rails and pulpit are 17th-century; the altar itself is a massive stone slab still bearing its consecration crosses.

St. Michael the Archangel, Michaelchurch*

Nestling in its own private valley is the remote little church of Michaelchurch (known to the Welsh as Llanvihangel), now no longer used for services and in the care of the Churches Conservation Trust. To find it, take the little lane in the angle of the junction of the A49 and the A4137 south of Harewood End. Follow this lane past Gillow Manor to a T-junction; turn right and after half-a-mile, the church is found on the right side of the lane.

It is a humble building of great antiquity—the church is said to have been founded by Bishop Herwald of Llandaff in 1056, though none of the fabric of the present building dates from that time. The great attraction of Michaelchurch is that it was ignored by the Victorians and therefore retains furnishings and fittings from earlier eras.

It consists of nave and chancel only, with a timber bell-turret at the west end. The north and west walls are Norman (late 11th or early 12th century), and there is a blocked Norman doorway in the north wall with a small piece of tympanum carved with a lattice pattern, and a tiny Norman window high in the west wall. The remaining walls and most of the windows date from the 13th century. Much of the walls internally are covered with painting—on the east and south, medieval borders with chevron pattern etc., and elsewhere, post-Reformation biblical texts. Between nave and chancel is a rustic screen, partly old and partly restored. Some of the finials on the choir-stalls are good, and may at least in part be original.

There is a striking Norman font (Fig. 94, p.39), patterned with interlacing arches above, saltire crosses in the middle and a knot motif below. More unusual is the Roman altar in the blocked doorway in the north wall of the nave. The Latin inscription is translated 'Beccicus dedicated the altar to the god of the three ways', a phraseology used especially of deities worshipped at crossroads. The origin of this piece is not known, but its presence augments the feeling that here is a sacred site of pre-Christian origins.

162

St. David, Much Dewchurch**

Situated on the B4348, south-west of Hereford, Dewchurch (the church of St. Dewi i.e. St. David) originally had a Welsh name—Lann Deui Ros Cerion (later Llanddewi), indicating the long-lasting Welsh influence in this area. Although not mentioned in Domesday, both church and castle date from Norman times. The castle was a motte and bailey 300 yards north-east of the church standing on the summit of a low ridge.[13]

St. David's church has a Norman south doorway, with a plain tympanum; the lintel above the door is composed of three stones joggled together (cf. Hatfield)—suggesting a

Fig. 258 The plain Norman chancel arch at Much Dewchurch, flanked by monuments to members of the Pye and Symons families

date early in the 12th century.[14] The chancel arch is also plain Norman (Fig. 258), and there are 12th-century windows above the porch, and in the north aisle, chancel and nave (now looking into the vestry). The tower with its lancet windows is 13th-century, but the pyramidal roof and dormer windows are Victorian. Victorian also are the north arcade and aisle.

The finest attractions of the church, however, are the monuments to two families, the Pyes and the Symons, who were successively owners of the great house of the parish—The Mynde. In the north-east corner of the nave are two Pye monuments: the Elizabethan monument to John and Walter Pye (*c*.1570) with two recumbent effigies on a tomb-chest, the older man holding his beard with his finger, and the large Renaissance wall memorial to Walter Pye and his wife (*c*.1625). This is an impressive alabaster and black marble affair, with husband and wife kneeling before a prayer-desk, with their 13 children below. There are two Pye grave-slabs on the floor, dated 1680 and 1727. The Symons have four monuments in the church; to John Symons (d.1763), Thomas Symons (d.1818), Thomas Hampton Symons (d.1831) and, perhaps the best, the memorial to Richard Harcourt Symons (1850) described by Pevsner as 'a romantic conceit';[15] it depicts a seated lady below a weeping willow (Fig. 152, p.59).

St. John the Baptist, Orcop*

The most impressive aspect of Orcop church is the early 16th-century western tower: the lower stage is of stone, then there is a weatherboarded upper stage, a truncated pyramidal roof, the belfry, and finally a short spire (Fig. 64, p.26). The overall effect is not unlike the double pyramidal roof at Kington (Fig. 216, p.112). The tower is supported internally by a complex timber structure. There is an Early English arcade dividing the north aisle from the nave, and over the nave is an attractive wagon-roof.

St. Denys, Pencoyd

St. Denys was an Italian who became the first bishop of Paris in the 3rd century;[16] his cult spread far and wide in the Middle Ages. The church at Pencoyd dedicated to him was in a sad state in 1861—Glynne reported that it was forlorn and neglected. The church was restored and the chancel rebuilt in 1877-78. The west tower is from the 14th century.

St. Peter, Peterstow

The most interesting feature of the church is the north wall of the Norman nave, which incorporates part of an even earlier wall, presumably Anglo-Saxon.[17] A section of wall 24 feet long and 3 feet 6 inches tall comprises six large irregular stones, with smaller stones filling the spaces between. 'The western edge of the last of the large stones has been neatly dressed, as if to form the north-west quoin of the early wall. This quoin is vertically below the early Norman window of the present nave, thereby proving that the early Norman fabric is an adaptation of an even earlier building.' Inside the church is an Early English chancel arch and a Jacobean pulpit.

St. Dubricius, St. Devereux*

It is always amazing how close medieval churches can be to each other. Here is the tiny church of St. Devereux, less than a mile from Kilpeck and Wormbridge. It is mainly Early English, but with a Perpendicular east window in the chancel. The two monuments to Thomas Goode (d.1664) and Ann Goode (d.1668) are simple and appealing in their naivety (Fig. 141, p.56).

St. Weonard, St. Weonard's*

St. Weonard (pronounced 'Wonnard'), an obscure Celtic saint, was known in Welsh as St. Gwenarth; in the *Book of Llandaff*, St. Weonard's is called *Lann Sannguainerth*. The dedication is unique in England, though in Wales two miles west of Abergavenny there is the village of Llanwenarth. The church stands prominently on a hill on the A466 between Hereford and Monmouth. Just to the south of the church is a prehistoric burial mound, which may have later been re-used as a motte.[18]

Apart from two lancets in the south wall of the nave, the church is Perpendicular, an unusual style for Herefordshire. The tower has diagonal buttresses and is battlemented. The church consists of nave and chancel, each with its north aisle and chapel. The north chapel was built in 1521, and is known as the Mynors chapel (the Mynors still live at nearby Treago Castle). The arcade separating the nave and north aisle has octagonal piers and capitals), and there are good Perpendicular parclose screens enclosing the Mynors chapel (Fig. 159, p.68). In the east window of the chapel, there are some fragments of the original glass of 1521. In another window is a panel of Flemish glass of the late 15th century depicting the call of St. Peter (see p.62 and back cover). The north aisle and chapel have an attractive barrel-roof. The memorial to Anne Williams (d.1678) is rather plain. In the Victorian south porch is an ancient holy-water stoup carved with a man's head.

St. Tysilio, Sellack*

In the *Book of Llandaff, c*.1150, Sellack is known as *Lann Suluc*; Suluc is a diminutive form of Suliau or Tysilio, to whom the church is dedicated.[19] He is said to have been a Welsh prince of the 7th century, who became abbot of Meifod in Powys—the church in Meifod is dedicated to him; in Brittany at Saint-Suliac is a cult which may be of another person with the same name.[20] At any rate, the dedication to St. Tysilio is unique in England. Sellack is one of three Herefordshire

Fig. 259 The chancel and Victorian north arcade, Sellack

parishes (the others being Hentland and King's Caple) where for 300 years Pax cakes are distributed after morning service in Palm Sunday; these are flat round cakes, stamped with a lamb and flag, supposed to bring peace to disputatious people, given with the greeting 'Peace and Good Neighbourhood'.

The church, to the north-east of Peterstow, lies on the A49 north of Ross, and has a lovely situation beside the Wye, it consists of a western tower with spire, a nave with north transept, and chancel, with a north chapel. The tower is Decorated and bears one of the finest broach spires in the county. Originally, the Norman nave was divided from a north aisle by a Norman arcade, but only one bay at the west end survives. Proceeding eastwards, a Victorian arcade now separates the nave from a Victorian north transept, with very florid leaf carving in the capitals (Fig. 259). Beyond this, the chancel is divided from the north chapel by an Early English arcade of one bay. There is Perpendicular vaulting over the north chapel, and a Perpendicular window at the east end of the chancel. This window has some notable 17th-century stained glass, similar to that at Abbey Dore, together with some earlier fragments. There is a Jacobean pulpit with sounding-board, and altar panelling and west gallery of the same period. There are some interesting monumental tablets — the best to William Powell (d.1680) and Thomas Symonds (d.1760).

St. Bartholomew, Thruxton*

This church has just one superlative treasure which makes a visit worth while — the tiny Crucifixion in 14th-century stained glass in the south side of the chancel (Fig. 154, p.61). The church is mainly Decorated, though with an early Perpendicular east window. To find the church, take the A465 Abergavenney road from Hereford and after five miles, turn right at Tram Inn for Thruxton; the church is along a lane on the left.

St. Mary, Welsh Newton*

The church at Welsh Newton, in the deep south of the county on the A466, is known for two things: first, its unusual stone rood-screen; and second, as the burial place of a saint.

It is mainly a church of the 13th century (Early English), with lancet windows in the north and south walls of the nave. At the west end are two further lancets, between which is placed the slender west tower with a short spire above. The east window of the chancel is a little later, with two lights and a circle above. In the south of the nave is a gabled dormer window, which is Decorated, and which served

Fig. 260 Welsh Newton church

to light the rood and screen. There is an external corbel-table on the south of the chancel immediately above the windows, suggesting that at one time the roof may have been lower (Fig. 260).

Over the nave and chancel is a continuous, fine wagon-roof with ribs and bosses. Between nave and chancel is the stone screen (Fig. 158, p.68), consisting of a triple arcade stretching across the church. The piers are octagonal, and the arches are enriched with ball-flower decoration in the outer mouldings. Stone screens are quite rare, and this is a fine example of the early 14th century. Against the north wall of the chancel is a stone seat, with shaped arm-rests of the 13th century.

In the churchyard under the cross is buried St. John Kemble, one of the 40 martyrs of England and Wales canonised in 1970. He was a native of the county, and after ordination to the Catholic priesthood at Douai, he served in Monmouthshire and Herefordshire for 53 years. After the scare of the Titus Oates plot in 1678, he was apprehended at the age of 80 and hanged, drawn and quartered on Widemarsh Common in Hereford; his hand is preserved in St. Francis Xavier church in the city.

St. Dubricius, Whitchurch

The church has a lovely situation on the bank of the Wye. The north aisle was added to the medieval church in 1860, and there was considerable general restoration at this time. Sir Stephen Glynne visited in 1861 and commented that many of the original windows had been reinserted in the new south wall. The chancel is Decorated, with reticulated tracery in the east window; in the south wall is part of an earlier 13th-century column. The roofs of the nave and chancel are single-framed. The font is Norman, with arcading round the bowl.

St. Peter, Wormbridge

This church mostly derives from what Pevsner calls the 'violent' restoration of the 1850s. There is a late Norman north doorway, and the lower part of the tower is 13th-century. There are some fragments of 14th- and 15th-century glass in the chancel windows, including representations of the Virgin and Child and the Massacre of the Innocents. Beneath the tower and in the nave are extensive woodwork panels, both English and Dutch, dating from the 17th and 18th centuries. They were given to the church in 1870.

Around Ross-on-Wye

St. Michael, Brampton Abbotts*

Sir Stephen Glynne visited Brampton Abbotts in April, 1846, and was not impressed: 'A poor church; comprising only a chancel and nave with a mean belfry attic at the west end'. The 'mean belfry attic' was replaced later in the 19th century by a timbered bell-turret (Fig. 65, p.26) supported by a sophisticated and complex structure at the west end of the church. The largely Norman building has a round-headed south doorway with scallop capitals, a timber 14th-century porch and straight-headed Perpendicular windows in the south wall. Internally the wide and straight-sided chancel arch is unusual, and this also has scallop capitals. The font is Perpendicular (Fig. 102, p.41). On the north wall of the nave is a brass to Joan Rudhall (d.1507), showing her in pedimental head-dress and long girdle.

St. Bridget, Bridstow*

This church, a few miles north of Ross-on-Wye, has components of four different styles: a Norman chancel arch, an Early English north chapel, a Perpendicular tower, and Victorian nave and chancel. The chancel arch has two orders, enriched with

Fig. 261 Bridstow church

167

Fig. 262 The interior of Bridstow church in 1840

zigzag, the capitals being carved with foliage and volute similar to that found in several nearby churches, e.g. Fownhope and Yatton, and dated to *c*.1125-45.[1] From the north wall of the chancel, an Early English arcade of two bays opens into the chapel. The west tower is Perpendicular, but rather low. The south door has some good medieval woodwork.

The rest of the church is by the Victorian architect T. Nicholson, and was built in 1862. The windows are predominantly Decorated in style, and the arcade has varied capitals. The stone pulpit is ornate. There is a recess in the north wall of the chancel containing a small altar-tomb with cusped cinquefoiled arches, dating from *c*.1300.

St. Mary, Fownhope***
The village is prettily situated south-east of Hereford between the Wye and the Woolhope Dome on the B4224. Its original name, as recorded in the Domesday survey, was Hope, meaning valley, and a church there was recorded in Domesday. The first element of the name did not appear until the 13th century, and its meaning is uncertain: Gelling thinks it might mean 'multi-coloured', while others have held that it derives from the Anglo-Saxon *fana*, meaning 'flag'.[2] Through the ages, it has been a fairly substantial village, one of the largest in the eastern half of the county and this is reflected in the size of its parish church.[3] Outside the churchyard wall on the main road is the parish stocks.

St. Mary's is one of the few Herefordshire churches with a central tower, surmounted by a shingled broach spire. The church is not, however, cruciform: it consists of a nave with south aisle, the tower with south chapel, and chancel beyond. The tower is Norman, and there are twin Norman windows (three of them now blocked) on each face of the tower. The rest of the church (Fig. 263) is mainly Early English to Decorated, including the north doorway and the two eastern arches of the south arcade, the piers being rounded. Around 1300, the arcade was extended westwards, with one octagonal pier; the south chapel (on the south side of the tower) and the south aisle were built *c*.1330. All the windows of the south aisle are

Fig. 263 Fownhope church. The tower is between the nave and the chancel. The arch leading from the base of the tower to the nave is Norman, while the arch beyond to the chancel is Early English (pointed). There is intersecting tracery in the east window. The eastern column of the arcade is rounded, the nearer (western) column octagonal (see text)

early Decorated, with primitive reticulated tracery. The north windows of the nave show similar tracery, and were presumably renewed at about the same time. At the base of the tower are three arches of differing form: the western, opening to the nave, is Norman; the eastern and southern, opening to the chancel and south chapel respectively, are pointed. Towards the end of the 13th century, the chancel was rebuilt, the windows here showing Y- and intersecting tracery. On each side of the chancel is a Decorated sepulchral recess, replete with ball-flower. There is a fine piscina in the south wall of the chancel, and other piscinae are to be found at the east end of the south aisle, and in the south chapel. There are two fonts, dating from *c*.1670 and *c*.1760 respectively; the former, more solid, shows fleurs-de-lis and was dug up from some neighbouring ruins; the latter, more elegant, is a baluster font found in the vicarage garden![4] Near the font is a dugout chest, carved from a single block of oak, *c*.1325.

The greatest attraction of Fownhope church is, of course, the Norman tympanum, an outstanding work of the Herefordshire School, which is described on p.17.

St. Michael, Hope Mansell

This pleasing church lies in a sheltered valley on the edge of the Forest of Dean. It is quite small—nave, chancel and a Victorian bell-turret—but there is evidence that formerly there was a south aisle (the nave is wider than the chancel, the extra width being to the south). In the north wall of the nave is a Norman doorway. There is a large round-headed Georgian window in the south wall of the nave, and perhaps this was inserted when the south aisle was removed. In the south wall of the chancel are trefoil-headed lancets. Both chancel and nave are covered by a single-framed trussed-rafter roof.

St. John the Baptist, King's Caple*

To find the church, take the A49 south from Hereford at the first set of road traffic lights past the roundabout south of the river, turn left into the B4399 towards Holme Lacy; then at a mini-roundabout right onto the Hoarwithy Road, and follow this road to Hoarwithy. Here turn left over the bridge across the Wye, taking the first turning right on the opposite bank to Ruxton, and follow the lane round to the left to King's Caple.

This is another church built in close proximity to a Norman motte, for just across the road is Caple Tump, a mound some 15 feet high. Caple means 'chapel'; King's Caple is so called to distinguish it from Hugh's Caple about three miles away which became How Caple.[5] The people of this area owed direct allegiance to the Crown.

Most of the church belongs to the Decorated period (late 13th and early 14th centuries). The tower has a string-course adorned with that Decorated hallmark, the ball-flower, and in the south wall of the nave is a window with geometrical tracery. Unusually for Herefordshire, the finest parts of King's Caple church are Perpendicular—the south porch, and, especially, the north chapel (the Aramstone chapel). Both these have stone vaulting (Fig. 89, p.36), with ridge and diagonal ribs meeting at a rose in the centre. In the south wall of the nave is a plain tomb-recess without effigy. There is some excellent woodwork, notably the very tall Jacobean pulpit, with sounding-board above. There are also some Jacobean stalls in the chancel. The west gallery dates from the 18th century, and on the west wall of the church is a Benefactions board erected in 1796.

But the finest part of the church is undoubtedly the north chapel. Here are some fragments of medieval stained glass and two 17th-century box-pews. Also there are two excellent early 19th-century monuments: Mrs. Holcombe Ferguson is commemorated by a relief of her mourning husband and small boy (d.1814); this is by John Flaxman (1755-1826). Nearby is the monument of Eliza Woodhouse (d.1833), with a kneeling, weeping woman by Sir Richard Westmacott (1775-1856) . The two monuments side by side make an interesting study, and may be compared with two other monuments by the same sculptors at Ledbury (see pp.58-59).

St. John the Baptist, Lea*

The church is plain: a 14th-century tower with recessed spire; a 15th-century east window in the chancel; the rest mostly Victorian. Between the north aisle and the north chapel is part of the restored 15th-century screen, the lights having ogeed, sub-cusped, crocketed and traceried heads. There is an original Perpendicular north arcade, and the octagonal capitals are decorated with an entertaining variety of heads, both human and animal. In the nave is a 13th-century dugout chest. Even more interesting is the exotic Italian font (Fig. 107), described in detail on p.42.

St. Mary the Virgin, Linton-by-Ross*

Linton church, to the east of Ross, is interesting because of the building problems that it poses. The site may have been used in Roman times for heathen worship. The ridgeway by which the building is approached is deflected round the church's nearly circular precincts (as at Madley).[6] The oldest part of the church is the north aisle; the west end of this belonged to a Norman west tower, long since demolished - see the unusual string-course decorated with zigzag. Inside the church, the short north arcade is seen to be Norman, with semicircular arches, and one massive pier which is

Fig. 264 Norman arcade on the north (left) and Early English on the south (right) at Linton-by-Ross

much too large for the arch which it supports (Fig. 264). West of this arcade, and now forming the north wall of the west end of the nave, is a section of solid wall which was previously the south wall of the former Norman west tower. The south arcade is in marked contrast—it is Early English, with pointed arches. At the west end is the new tower, Perpendicular, with a very tall tower arch opening into the nave and carrying a short stone spire; it is rib-vaulted internally. The chancel is Early English, the east window being a little later.

St. Bartholomew, Much Marcle***

The village lies along the A449 Ledbury to Ross road;'Marcle' means 'boundary wood',[7] and this was originally well-wooded country. The church is mentioned in *Domesday Book*, and just to the north of the church is a motte and bailey. The present building (Fig. 2, p.*xi*) is largely Early English, dating from the 13th century. It is unusually shaped: proceeding from west to east, there are a nave and north and south aisles (with south porch), then a central tower, then the chancel with a north chapel and vestry leading from it. The arcades dividing the nave and aisles have circular piers and capitals (Fig. 265), some of which are carved with stiff-leaf foliage and heads etc. Above there is a clerestory of lancet windows. One window in the south aisle has intersecting tracery (early 14th century); other windows are later Decorated or Perpendicular. The chancel and north chapel are of the same date as the nave, and the east windows have three stepped lancet lights so commonly found in Herefordshire and dating from around 1300. The south doorway is Early English, but the porch is later, Decorated, with ogee-headed side-windows. Lastly, the central tower is Perpendicular, with battlements.

The earliest of the four monuments for which Much Marcle is famous is the wooden effigy in the nave; wooden effigies are rare—there are only two in Herefordshire, the other being at Clifford. The figure is over six feet long, carved from a single block of oak overlaid with gesso (plaster prepared as a ground for painting) and then painted. The facial expression is intense (Fig. 116, p.47), and the man, a civilian, is clothed in the costume of the mid-14th century. His identity is not known, but he may be Walter de Helyon, whose family later gave their name to Hellens, the large house near to the church.

On the north side of the chancel is the finest monument in Much Marcle—the tomb of Blanche Mortimer, Lady Grandison (*c*.1360-70). She was a daughter of Roger Mortimer of Wigmore, first Earl of March (p.91), and she married Sir Peter de Grandison, who is buried in the Lady Chapel of Hereford Cathedral. The canopied tomb is richly adorned with heraldic devices, the arms and shields of the Mortimers and Grandisons. The canopy has cusped arches, and above are the shields; the wavy crusting with cherubs' heads at the top is not original. But it is the effigy which is most beautiful: the face is realistic, the hands and fingers graceful, the drapery falls naturally over the tomb-chest (Figs. 8, p.*xiv* and 118, p.48, and compare Fig. 119). This work can stand comparison with any other 14th-century tomb in the country.

Another late 14th-century tomb is in the north chapel, with the effigies of a knight and lady of unknown identity. Angels support the lady's head, and

Fig. 265 Noble Early English arcades at Much Marcle.
The base of the tower is between the nave and chancel
(cf. Fownhope, Fig. 263) and two pointed arches are seen.
The east window is of the 'Herefordshire' type

dogs at her feet are biting her gown. Under the knight's head is a helmet, and at his feet a lion. Around the sides of the chest are angels and shields.

Also in the north chapel is the imposing 17th-century memorial to Sir John Kyrle and Sybil Scudamore, his wife (Fig. 134, p.54). Their sophisticated effigies rest on a tomb-chest of black and white marble; around the sides are cartouches with wreathes. The spirit is Jacobean, even though Sir John did not die until 1650. Around the chapel are some fine wall-monuments and hatchments.

Also in the church is a sculpture 'Musica Celestis' carved by Lady Feodora Gleichen, presented to the church in 1928; and a fine bucket-shaped font dating from the 12th century.

St. Mary the Virgin, Ross-on-Wye**

The spire of St. Mary's (Fig. 266) soars gracefully over Ross-on-Wye, as seen in the famous view from across the river. It is a fascinating church, elegant and enriched with many treasures.

The church consists of a western tower, spacious nave with north and south aisles, a south aisle chapel, and a long chancel with a south chancel chapel. The arcades were built in the early 13th century, the south first, the north a little later, but both were heightened in 1743 (Fig. 267). The piers of both arcades are circular; the abaci on the south are also circular, but on the north are octagonal. Around 1300, the aisles were rebuilt, resulting in some fine Decorated windows. The north and south porches, and the first part of the chancel are Decorated. High up in the east wall of the south aisle is a piscina for a former altar in the rood-loft (as at Little Hereford and Wigmore). The east end of the chancel, with its fine window containing stained glass (see p.62), is Perpendicular, and so are the windows of the south aisle chapel, which was built c.1510. The tower is Decorated, but its handsome spire was rebuilt in the 18th century.

There is a fine array of monuments covering three hundred years—the most interesting are: the alabaster effigies of Judge William Rudhall (d.1530) and his wife, with a row of saints along two sides (Fig. 124, p.50); at the west end is a remarkable Annunciation, with the Virgin Mary receiving the descent of the Holy Ghost in the form of a dove, followed by the Christ-child carrying his cross—the judge and his family kneeling before the Virgin. John Rudhall (d.1636)

Fig. 266 Ross-on-Wye church

Fig. 267 The heightened south arcade (Early English) at Ross. Beyond may be seen the Perpendicular arcade leading into the south chapel

172

and his wife lie on a further tomb-chest with a black marble top, the children being portrayed on the side (Fig. 135, p.54). But for swagger, few can compete with the alabaster statue of Col. William Rudhall (d.1651). He is sculpted in Roman armour, surveying the other monuments which crowd around his feet (Fig. 136, p.54). Then, in the north wall of the chancel, is the tablet erected in 1776 in memory of John Kyrle, known as the Man of Ross; it is by Marsh, a local sculptor and above the inscription are two oval medallions. Lastly, in the Greek style, is the bust of Thomas Westfaling (d.1817) by William Theed the elder; below is depicted a figure of Charity, teaching children (Fig. 151, p.59).

The font is a late 17th-century baluster, similar to that at Holme Lacy.

St. Michael, Sollers Hope

The church has a lovely situation in a valley (whence 'hope'); it dates mainly from the 14th century, with Decorated windows in the north and south of the chancel, and Perpendicular windows in the east of the chancel and in the nave. At the west end is a timbered bell-turret with a short spire.

The oldest monument is the 13th-century incised slab in the chancel, engraved with a knight in chain-mail; it is the only example in England of a great helm on a slab; the helm is flat-topped, and the head is shown in profile, partly turned to face the viewer.[8] There are further coffin-lids on the west wall of the nave. Fragments of medieval glass in the north and south windows of the chancel represent the arms of the Staunton and Whittington families; the Whittingtons were owners of the valley for over 200 years from c.1300, and construction of the church is believed to have been financed by Dick Whittington's elder brother, Robert. The pulpit is Jacobean.

St. John the Baptist, Upton Bishop*

This is a substantial church in the south-east of the county, with items of interest ranging from Roman to Victorian times. Embedded in the south wall of the chancel is part of a Roman tombstone, showing the head, shoulders and raised right hand of a man set in a recess. In the north wall of the nave is a blocked Norman doorway. Inside, the nave is divided from the south aisle by a Transitional arcade, with circular piers, scalloped capitals, square abaci but pointed arches—dating the arcade to the late 12th century. The chancel is Early English, with lancet windows; a later Decorated window has been inserted between the two lancets in the east wall, doubtless replacing the central lancet of a group of three.[9] Lastly, the west tower is Perpendicular, with diagonal buttresses.

In a tomb-recess in the south aisle is a fine 14th-century effigy under an ogee arch. The figure is a civilian holding a square object in his hands. The elegant Perpendicular font is octagonal, carved with quatrefoils. There is good Victorian glass by Clayton and Bell and Hardman. South of the chancel is a hexagonal vestry built in memory of the famous Victorian hymn-writer, Frances Ridley Havergal, sister of the then incumbent.

St. Michael and All Angels, Walford-on-Wye

St. Michael's is set graciously in a large churchyard, and is a building mainly of the 13th century. It is a large church, with nave and narrow north aisle, and chancel with a north chapel, from which projects the tower. The arcade of the north aisle is Norman/Early English (c.1200)—with trumpet-scallop in the westernmost capital and stiff-leaf in the others, the double-chamfered arches being pointed. Later in the 13th century were built the chancel arch, the arcade leading into the north chapel and the tower. Over the chancel arch are two hatchments of the Clark family of Hill Court, and a funeral helm of Col. Kyrle, c.1600. There is an excellent Perpendicular font (Fig. 105, p.42).

St. Lawrence, Weston-under-Penyard

The church is entered through a timbered porch of the 14th or 15th century. The nave is divided from the north aisle by a late Norman arcade (Fig. 76, p.31), with circular piers and scalloped capitals. Over the nave is a single-framed roof with tie-beams. The chancel is Early English, but much altered; in the east wall are three lancet windows. The tall and stately tower is Decorated, with a Perpendicular west window.

Yatton Chapel**

Yatton means 'settlement in a pass'—an accurate description of its situation. A short distance down from the col is the old chapel, now alone except for its neighbouring farm. It is cared for by the Churches Conservation Trust, which has happily replaced the corrugated iron roof mentioned in Pevsner. It is the most rewarding of all the Trust's churches in Herefordshire. To find the building, take the A449 from Ross towards Ledbury, and after three miles fork left onto the B4224 towards Hereford. Just before the left turning to How Caple, turn right into a narrow lane which climbs; at the first cross-roads, keep straight ahead, but when the lane next divides keep right, and after a short distance, right again. It is probably best to park here, and walk down the track to the farm and the chapel.

It is a humble church—a simple two-cell structure, with undivided nave and chancel. North, south and west walls contain windows of the 13th century; in the south wall there is also a square-headed window which was probably inserted in the 16th century. The east wall was rebuilt in 1704. There are two fonts—one has always been in the chapel, the other was brought here when the church at Brobury was closed.

The great treasure of Yatton is the elaborately carved south doorway (Fig. 23, p.9), which is discussed on p9. It cannot, of course, compare in quality with the doorway at Kilpeck—and it is more likely that this is a relatively accomplished work by a local sculptor rather than a minor work of the Herefordshire School itself. There is for instance at Yatton none of the amazing figure-carving seen at Kilpeck. But Yatton remains a little-known gem, well worth visiting.

Post-Reformation Churches

The 17th and 18th Centuries

The building of churches in Herefordshire, as in the rest of the country, came to an abrupt end at the Reformation, and for over 100 years no new churches were built. The first significant event in the seventeenth century was the rescue of Abbey Dore by Viscount Scudamore in 1633; this involved the conversion of the eastern part of the monastic church into a parish church, and the building of a new tower. A new tower was also built in 1680 at Canon Frome. In the second half of the 17th century, there were three new churches, all providing evidence of Gothic survival: Brampton Bryan was largely rebuilt in 1656 because the church had been severely damaged during the Civil War; and churches were built at Monnington-on-Wye in 1679 and at How Caple in 1693-95. In none of these buildings is there any trace of the classical architecture which was currently fashionable; at the time when Sir Christopher Wren was rebuilding St. Paul's Cathedral and the City churches in Renaissance style, Herefordshire was still wedded to outmoded late Perpendicular styles.

The county had to wait for the 18th century before Gothic was abandoned: in the second decade came new churches at Norton Canon (1716) and Tyberton (1719-21). In neither case is the architect known—the interior of Tyberton especially is pleasing. Preston Wynne followed in 1727, Whitney-on-Wye in 1740 and Stoke Edith in 1740-42. Then in 1752-56 Shobdon was created in the style of William Kent. This is the most celebrated Georgian church in Herefordshire, an amalgam of sham Gothick and rococo. At the end of the 18th century, the early Gothic Revival was in evidence at the new chapel at Brockhampton-by-Bromyard, designed by George Byfield (1798). And in 1819, but still Georgian in spirit, Acton Beauchamp was rebuilt.

St. Barnabas, Brampton Bryan*
St. Mary, Monnington-on-Wye**
St. Andrew and St. Mary, How Caple*
St. Nicholas, Norton Canon*
St. Mary, Tyberton**
Holy Trinity, Preston Wynne

St. Peter and St. Paul, Whitney
St. Mary, Stoke Edith**
St. John the Evangelist, Shobdon***
St. John the Baptist, Grendon Bishop
Brockhampton-by-Bromyard chapel**
St. Giles, Acton Beauchamp*

St. Barnabas, Brampton Bryan*
Brampton Bryan is in the far north of the county, on the A4113 to the east of Knighton, At the time of the Domesday survey, the manor was held by Ralph de Mortimer, but by 1172, when Wigmore Abbey was founded, Bryan de Brampton was associated with Hugh de Mortimer in the foundation of the abbey. The de Bramptons held the manor (and later the castle) under the Mortimers until the male line died out in

1294; in 1309, Margaret de Brampton married Robert Harley, and the Harleys have continued in Brampton to the present day. The family achieved their greatest renown in the 17th and early 18th centuries—in the Civil War, Lady Brilliana Harley, wife of Sir Robert Harley, MP, conducted a spirited defence of the castle on behalf of Parliament; and in the reign of Queen Anne, another Robert Harley became successively Speaker of the House of Commons, secretary of state, Chancellor of the Exchequer and head of the government, and later Earl of Oxford.

The Civil War led to the mutual destruction of both castle and parish church; the castle was never rebuilt, and remains as an attractive ruin; but the church was rebuilt in 1656—one of a small number in the country dating from the Commonwealth, and built by Sir Robert Harley, Lady Brilliana's widower, a man of Puritan sympathies.

The church is nicely situated in an attractive village, made distinctive by the yew topiary which extends around the hall and castle. As befits a Puritan church, it is really a preaching box—a rectangle with no real chancel, just a recess along the east wall in the 17th-century manner. The windows are Perpendicular in style—there is no trace of any Renaissance influence. The church has a notable double hammer-beam roof (Fig. 86, p.34), supported on wooden wall-posts like the roof at Vowchurch. The details of the roof are Jacobean, but the constructional system is Perpendicular.[1] At the south end of the sanctuary is the fine wall-monument to Robert Harley, Earl of Oxford, with a garlanded frame, and an urn above. The long epitaph chronicles his distinguished career, culminating in his appointment as Chancellor of the Exchequer and head of the government in 1710; five years later he fell from favour, was accused of high treason and sent to the Tower. After two years, he was acquitted by the House of Lords. In the south of the nave is an effigy of a lady holding her heart in her hands (Fig. 115, p.47). This dates from the early 14th century. (A similar effigy can be seen at Ewyas Harold.) The pulpit is Victorian, but has inlaid tarsia panels from the 17th century. The attractive reredos features the Lord's Prayer, the Ten Commandments and the Apostles' Creed.

St. Mary, Monnington-on-Wye**

There are two Monningtons in Herefordshire (the name meaning 'settlement of Manna's people')[2]—Monnington Straddel near Vowchurch (Straddel being the old name for the Golden Valley), and this one on the Wye, some 10 miles to the north-west of Hereford, and reached off the A438. The church is flanked by the elegant Monnington Court with its lake and wildfowl.

The church exhibits the unusual combination of a late medieval tower and a nave and chancel built in 1679. The tower is Perpendicular, with an embattled parapet. But it is the body of the church, especially the interior, that is so stunning. The reign of Charles II did not see the building of many churches in England outside London; some were rebuilt at this time to repair damage sustained during the Civil War, but just why Monnington church was rebuilt is obscure. It was built by Uvedale Tomkins, who had inherited the manor, and lived in the adjacent Court.

It is really a very late example of Gothic survival, later than Broughton (Staffordshire; 1630) and Foremark (Derbyshire; 1662). The nave and chancel are built more or less in Perpendicular style, with flat-headed 'Tudor' windows in the nave, and an east window of three lights, with a horizontal transom and surmounted by a round-headed hood-mould. Even at this late date, there is no hint of Classical architecture.

The interior is a delight: there is an array of 17th-century furnishings equalled in Herefordshire only by Clodock. The communion-table has heavy twisted legs, and the communion rail has elongated twisted balusters. The screen separating nave and chancel is of oak, with four bays on each side of the central opening. The open upper panels have twisted posts and rounded arches, and the lower closed panels have unusual mouldings. The hexagonal pulpit has twisted balusters at the angles, each face having two ranges of differing panelling; originally, there was a sounding-board above. There is 17th-century panelling in the reredos, and the benches have turned front legs and shaped arms. There is a very fine Royal Coat of Arms on the south wall of the nave. The font, dated 1680, is an octagonal bowl.

In the churchyard, contemporary with the body of the church, is an excellent timber-framed lychgate. There is an old tradition that Owain Glyndwr is buried in this churchyard.

St. Andrew and St. Mary, How Caple*

Next door to How Caple Court and its gardens to the south of Fownhope and just west of the B4224, stands the parish church in an enviable position above the river Wye. The church consists of tower, nave with south transept, and chancel (Fig. 268), but only the last is medieval, the rest being rebuilt in 1693-95. Even at this late date, there is no sign of classical styling, but for all that the church makes a very pretty picture.

It is helped, of course, by its wooded setting. The chancel is Decorated, and a Decorated window has been reset in the

Fig. 268 How Caple church

17th-century nave. The low-pitched chancel roof is 16th-century. In the north wall of the chancel is a German diptych presented to the church by Mr. Lennox Lee in 1920; it was restored by the Courtauld Institute in 1984. The panels are painted on both sides, and came from a south German altar-piece of the 16th century. The other great treasure of How Caple is the unusual screen dividing nave and chancel, surmounted by the Royal Coat of Arms of William III, to correspond with the rebuilding of the church. It is a most unusual structure of three bays with square posts, a moulded cornice and twisted pillars and arches. The octagonal font is late Norman, and has rather primitively carved geometrical and foliage patterns.

St. Nicholas, Norton Canon*

This church, which stands to the west of that part of the village that lies along the A480 north-west of Hereford, presents the unusual spectacle of a medieval tower combined with a brick nave, chancel and transepts built in 1716, but retaining many medieval windows. The north-west tower is Early English, and built of sandstone. The architect of the 18th-century building is unknown, but he incorporated in his work 13th-century windows in the chancel, nave and transepts—at a time when Gothic was deeply unfashionable. Sir Stephen Glynne, who did not like 18th-century churches, visited Norton Canon sometime before 1840, and wrote: 'The whole appears to be of late date and bad character'. Times and fashions have changed, and we now view 18th-century styles more favourably.

There are some attractive 17th- and 18th-century fittings. The pulpit contains some Jacobean work, including an arcaded panel and guilloche ornament. The communion-table has turned legs and the communion rails have turned balusters. There are some panelled pews in the nave and north transept. From the Middle Ages come the octagonal font (13th century) and the grisaille glass in two windows in the nave and north transept.

St. Mary, Tyberton**

This church, internally at least, is the finest 'traditional' Georgian church in Herefordshire—Shobdon, a work of the Gothick revival, is of course more celebrated, but would be difficult to describe as a typical Georgian church! Externally Tyberton has been marred by alteration of the windows which were changed to lancets in 1879. To find the church, take the A465 Abergavenny Road from Hereford, and after two miles fork right on to the B4349, and in another mile fork right again on to the B4352. Tyberton is on this road two miles beyond Madley.

By the early 18th century, the medieval church was in such a poor state of repair that William Brydges, who had taken over the Tyberton estate, decided to rebuild it. The nave and tower were built of red-brick in 1719, the chancel a year or so later; the architect is unknown. It cannot have been John Wood the elder, who would have been only 15 at the time. Wood (1704-54), however, certainly designed Tyberton Court (now demolished) in about 1728, and at the same time he was responsible for the *interior* design of the apse, which is the finest part of the structure at Tyberton. The church consists of a west tower, nave and chancel. The tower has round-headed windows, and at the top is an urn at each corner, with a pediment between. There is a south porch, and within is the Norman doorway preserved from the medieval church. This has one order of shafts and scalloped capitals.

Fig. 269 The apsidal sanctuary at Tyberton

The interior is remarkable for the furnishings and fittings and for the apsidal east end (Fig. 269). The latter, straight, severe, and windowless from the exterior, was converted by John Wood into an elegant apse covered by a half-dome, but the reredos is the *pièce de résistance*. Instead of the usual panels containing the Creed and Commandments the oak panelling behind the altar is carved in high relief with religious scenes, including the Emblems of the Passion—unexpected in the world of King George I. It 'is one of the most extraordinary examples of religious symbolism of the eighteenth century to be found in a parish church'.[3]

The font is a graceful bowl carved with heads standing on a fluted stem. It was designed by Steven Reeves, a member of a Gloucester family of masons and carvers and was made of oolitic stone, painted to resemble grey marble.[4] The Royal Arms of George I are dated 1720. The box-pews, pulpit, lectern and communion rails are all noteworthy examples of work of their time.

There are many memorials to the Brydges family, who lived at Tyberton Court; the best are those to William Brydges (d.1764), who had arranged and paid for the rebuilding of the church, and Francis Brydges (d.1793) by Thomas King of Bath (1741-1804).

Holy Trinity, Preston Wynne

The church stands alone in a field. A dignified building dating from 1727, it would be hard to guess this now, for the original Georgian windows were converted into small Gothic ones in the 19th century, as at Tyberton. The western tower has battlements and pinnacles.

St. Peter and St. Paul, Whitney

The medieval church was destroyed in 1740 when the river Wye flooded, and the present building was erected shortly afterwards, using old materials wherever possible. The west tower has a recessed pyramid roof. The interior has some good 17th- and 18th-century furnishings: a Jacobean reredos and pulpit, communion rails with turned balusters, and a west gallery.

St. Mary, Stoke Edith**

A certain air of melancholy seems to afflict Stoke Edith, which lies just south of the A438 between Hereford and Ledbury—the grandeur of the Foleys has gone, following the destruction by fire in 1927 of their great house; and the churchyard has a somewhat forlorn aspect. This is a shame, for there is much to admire in the church which is one of only a handful of Georgian churches in the county.

Before the Domesday survey, the manor had been held by Queen Edith, wife of Edward the Confessor. Stoke Edith church was originally founded as a minster on the royal Mercian estate of Yarkhill.[5] The neighbouring parishes of Westhide, Weston Beggard and Tarrington all belonged to Yarkhill, and thus were subject to Stoke Edith. By 1200, the college of priests had been replaced by two portioners, as at Ledbury (p.142); but in contrast to Ledbury which was protected by the interests of the bishops of Hereford, there was no powerful individual to look after Stoke Edith, which declined, losing Tarrington and Ashperton to Monmouth Priory and Weston Beggard and Yarkhill to St. Katherine's Hospital, Hereford.

Of the medieval church the tower and spire alone remain. The tower was built in the 14th century, the Decorated era, and has angle-buttresses. The spire may be a little later: it is an octagonal solid stone panelled structure on arched squinches.[6] The rest of the church was rebuilt by the Foleys in 1740-42. It is a plain rectangular hall, made memorable by the set of columns across the sanctuary (Fig. 270). The columns have caused some comment: for those who care about such things, Doric columns should have a metope frieze at the top of the column, between the capital or abacus and the cornice; plain columns without such a frieze are Tuscan, which of course Pevsner rightly calls them, and mentions the metope frieze along the wall.[7] According to Whiffen, the architect (unknown) was unable to fit Doric columns into the building, so the frieze was taken out and run along the wall instead.[8] This lack of academic correctness is doubtless very shocking, but will not disturb the ordinary visitor. At the west end of the church is a gallery.

Fig. 270 View from the west gallery, Stoke Edith

There is an elegant set of wrought-iron communion rails, and a complete set of box-pews. At the front is the squire's pew, comfortably furnished. The font is a small marble bowl. Behind iron railings is the effigy of a 15th-century lady wearing a butterfly head-dress and with dogs at her feet. There are two large monuments to the Foleys, of which the finer is that to Paul Foley, Speaker to the House of Commons (d.1699, Fig 138, p.55).

St. John the Evangelist, Shobdon***

I suspect that visitors to Shobdon may be sharply differentiated into two groups: those who weep at the spectacle of the 12th-century carvings now left to crumble in the park; and those who rejoice at the extravagance of the Strawberry Hill Gothick church which replaced them. But whether you would weep or rejoice (or perhaps both), Shobdon must not be missed: the work of both the 12th and 18th centuries must be seen by all who love parish churches.

Both the new church and the 'arches' formed of the Norman chancel arch and north and south door-ways, are located in the grounds of the Shobdon estate. From Mortimer's Cross on the A4110, turn west onto the B4362 for Shobdon and Presteigne. Before reaching Shobdon itself, turn right into a lane with its brown sign for 'Shobdon Arches', then turning left into the estate. There is ample parking at the Visitor Centre; the Arches are about 400 yards north of the church, reached by walking up a grassy ride.

Shobdon means 'Sceobba's hill', and the village lies on rising ground between the valleys of the Arrow and Lugg. At the time of Domesday, the manor was held by Ralph de Mortimer; and in the 12th century Hugh de Mortimer gave it to his steward Oliver de Merlimond, who built a castle, and founded the abbey and church. The story of de Merlimond's pilgrimage and the beginning of the Herefordshire School of Romanesque carving and the outstanding work in the 12th century church at Shobdon is told on pp.11-12.

The Shobdon estate was bought in 1705 by Sir James Bateman, who rebuilt Shobdon Court on a grand scale. His son, Sir William, married a grand-daughter of the Duke of Marlborough, and in 1725 he was created Viscount; he died in 1744. His son John became the second viscount; he died childless in 1802, and is commemorated in the church by the Nollekens monument; but it was John's younger brother Richard who was the motive force behind the rebuilding of Shobdon church. Richard was a friend of Horace Walpole (1717-97), then engaged in converting his former coachman's cottage near Twickenham into the stuccoed and battlemented Strawberry Hill. This influential building started a fashion for Gothick amongst some aristocrats, who delighted in building sham castles, follies, and sometimes more substantial edifices.

The architect of Shobdon church is unknown; it was not William Kent (who died in 1748), but the building is very much in his spirit, with the functionless ogee arches in which Kent delighted. It may have been Richard Bentley (1708-82), who at that time was gothicising Richard Bateman's villa at Windsor.[9] Rebuilding was first mentioned in a letter of Richard Bateman in April, 1746; the old church, apart from the tower, was demolished in 1752, and the new one completed by 1756. Whether the old church was in such an advanced state of dilapidation that entire rebuilding was unavoidable is uncertain: but that is what ensued, and, as already mentioned, the Norman chancel arch and doorways were re-erected in the parkland, a quarter of a mile from the church.

From the outside, a superficial glance might indicate a rather undistinguished medieval church; but

Fig. 271 The nave and chancel, Shobdon

close inspection will reveal definitely unmedieval touches, such as the cusped and ogee-headed window inserted into the 13th-century tower, and the even more elaborate windows of the 18th-century nave. Internally, the church is a combination of sham Gothic and rococo—to some, a lovely interior, with its blue and white furnishings; others may find it a little too cloying, the sweetness of confectionery.

The chancel and the two transepts are divided from the nave by triple pendant ogee arches, which arc, of course, purely for decorative effect (Fig.

271). The south transept is the Bateman family pew, comfortably furnished and with its own fantastic fireplace. Rather more spartan is the north transept (Fig. 4, p.*xii*), designed for the servants of the household. Both pews were entered directly from the outside. There is a lovely three-decker pulpit, complete with its hangings, together with the reader's desk and lectern. At the west end is a gallery which was not added until 1810. Quatrefoils and trefoils punctuate the bench-ends, giving a rhythm to the nave corresponding to the ogee arches above the windows. Note the monument to Viscount Bateman by Nollekens (1804, Fig. 146, p.56); Joseph Nollekens (1737-1823) was a prolific sculptor who achieved great renown in his time. Lord Bateman is shown in profile with a cavorting cherub above. The font, the work of the Herefordshire School, is described and illustrated on pp.18-19.

In considering the church and ruins at Shobdon, Harbison in a neat phrase wrote, 'So two distant realities have changed places: the church becomes a boudoir or a bower; its former decoration, still expounding solemn truths, is converted into a garden ornament.'[10] *Sic transit gloria mundi.*

St. John the Baptist, Grendon Bishop
St. John's stands alone in fields, and looks attractive, especially from the south. The tower with short spire and nave date from 1787-88, but the design was refashioned and an eastern apse added in 1870.

Brockhampton-by-Bromyard New Chapel**
At Lower Brockhampton, a ruined sandstone Norman chapel stands close to the moated house which dates from the 14th century. In 1798, a new church was designed for Brockhampton Park, the architect being George Byfield; this is his only church. With the exception of the Gothick rebuilding at Shobdon, this was the first church of the incipient Gothic Revival built in Herefordshire: and it is advanced for its date—after all, it was designed more than 20 years before Savage's St. Luke's in Chelsea, the first church of the Gothic Revival in London. And like Savage, Byfield chose the Perpendicular style.

Beware: the chapel is usually locked, but is open before and after Evensong held on the fourth Sunday afternoon of each month, and on afternoons on the three days of a Bank Holiday weekend. To reach it, take the A44 east from Bromyard, and after two miles, just at the beginning of the park, turn left down the drive with a National Trust sign, and the church is about 400 yards along on the left.

The church is attractively sited in the grounds of the park, which is now a National Trust estate. There is a handsome west tower, with battlements and pinnacles, and four pairs of perhaps too symmetrical Perpendicular windows in the nave, each consisting of two lights. The interior (Fig. 272) is strikingly beautiful: the pews are arranged in a collegiate fashion and there is a small west gallery. There is excellent glass: in the south-west window is a striking representation of the Transfiguration (later altered to portray the risen Christ by adding the wounds of the Crucifixion) by the Birmingham glass painter, William Eginton (1773-1834). This was probably painted c.1810-15, using stains and enamels on clear glass with the aim of imitating oil-painting. In the east window is some lovely more conventional late Victorian glass

Fig. 272 The nave and chancel, Brockhampton-by-Bromyard

depicting Faith, Hope and Charity. There are several wall-memorials, the best being that to Lydia Bulkeley (d.1812) by John Bacon junior (1787-1859, Fig 148, p.58). There is an excellent mosaic reredos and some modern woodwork by local craftsmen.

St. Giles, Acton Beauchamp*

The church has a lovely setting, alone on a knoll above a small valley. From the Worcester road out of Bromyard, at the edge of the town, immediately after crossing the infant river Frome, a lane on the right follows the river, winding down the valley; after three miles, turn left and then again left into a cul-de-sac leading to Acton Beauchamp.

The west tower is medieval, the rest of the church being rebuilt in the Georgian manner in 1819 (Fig. 273)—it is the last Georgian church in the county. The tower is notable for the lintel set above the south doorway, which is a section of an Anglo-Saxon cross-shaft,

Fig. 273 Medieval tower and Georgian church at Acton Beauchamp

dating probably from the 9th century (Fig. 13, p.7). The doorway itself has one order of shafts, the west capital is scalloped, the east carved with three heads. The nave and chancel have large round-headed windows, and the interior is peaceful and fitted out in the Georgian style. The octagonal font is Perpendicular.

The 19th and 20th Centuries

After the Napoleonic Wars, the Greek and Gothic Revivals disputed for supremacy in London and elsewhere, but by 1830 the Greek Revival was a spent force, and from then until the First World War Gothic was again triumphant. During this period 70 churches were built or rebuilt in Herefordshire, most of them by local architects, notably F.R. Kempson (e.g. Bishop's Frome) and T. Nicholson (Bridstow). Architects with a national reputation also participated: Sir George Gilbert Scott (Eastnor, Edvin Loach and Cradley); G.E. Street (Monkland); and above all G.F. Bodley. He built two churches very early in his career (Llangrove, 1854-56, and Canon Frome, 1860), and one at the end (Hom Green, 1905-06); he also was responsible for much of the internal decoration at Kingsland and Kinnersley, and is buried in the latter churchyard.

Other notable Victorian churches are at Moreton-on-Lugg and Welsh Bicknor. But the greatest post-Reformation churches in the county are St. Catherine's, Hoarwithy, by J.P. Seddon (1885) and All Saints, Brockhampton-by-Ross by W.R. Lethaby (1901-02). Hoarwithy is outstanding for its period because it is not Gothic but Italian-Byzantine in character; and at Brockhampton we can glimpse the beginnings of modern architecture.

Space does not permit a full description of the 70 Victorian and Edwardian churches. Four (Bishop's Frome, Bridstow, Hope-under-Dinmore and Stretton Sugwas) have been included amongst the medieval churches, for although the buildings are Victorian, the main interest is in their medieval or 18th-century treasures. The remaining 66 have been divided into three groups: 11 of the most interesting buildings are described in some detail; shorter notes are provided for 32 churches which have features of interest; and, for the sake of completeness, the remaining 23 churches are simply listed.

St. John the Baptist, Eastnor*   St. Andrew, Moreton-on-Lugg*
St. Mary, Edvin Loach*   St. Andrew, Adforton*
Christchurch, Llangrove*   St. Catherine, Hoarwithy***
St. Lawrence, Canon Frome*   All Saints, Brockhampton-by-Ross***
St. Margaret, Welsh Bicknor*   Hom Green church*
All Saints, Monkland*

St. John the Baptist, Eastnor*

Eastnor Castle, east of Ledbury on the A438, was built for the first Earl Somers by Sir Robert Smirke in 1812, and the Somers family have left a large mark on the parish church. In 1852, Sir George Gilbert Scott (1811-78) was commissioned to rebuild the church. He was the most prolific, if not the most original, of the great architects then practising at the height of the Gothic Revival; he was capable of great designs, but also of much more routine work. The church as we see it today is basically his work, but he retained the 14th-century west tower with diagonal buttresses and the Norman south doorway and north arcade. Scott designed the rest of the church in the then fashionable Decorated style, complete with ball-flower embellishment of some of the windows.

There are a number of monuments: under the tower are three designed by James Stuart (p.57) and executed by Thomas Scheemakers—Joseph Cocks, d.1778, Mary Cocks, d.1779 and the Reverend John Fletcher, d.1793. In the Somers chapel are the monuments to the first and third Earls Somers, designed by Scott (1855) and Sir J.E. Boehm (1883) respectively.

St. Mary, Edvin Loach*

In the Domesday survey, the manor of Edvin (meaning 'Gedda's fen') was one of the far-flung holdings of Leominster. Edvin Loach was held by John de Loges in 1212, while Edwyn Ralph was held by one Ralph in 1176.[11] The medieval church now lies in ruins, but it is nonetheless interesting and instructive. To find the church, take the B4214 north from Bromyard towards Tenbury Wells, and half a mile after passing through Edvin Ralph, turn right into a narrow lane; after another half a mile or so, turn right, and then turn right again into a short track leading to the church.

The surviving walls show extensive use of herringbone masonry, and above and by the side of the doorway can be seen blocks of tufa. Taken together, these features almost certainly mean that the Norman church was built towards the end of the 11th century. A further point of interest is that both the

Fig. 274 The church by Sir Goerge Gilbert Scott (1859) at Edvin Loach

old church and the new stand within the confines of a motte and bailey; Shoesmith comments that the bailey defences more or less follow the edges of the churchyard.[12]

By the middle of the 19th century, old St. Mary's was showing unmistakable signs of decay, and a new church was commissioned from Sir George Gilbert Scott in 1859. He designed a small church, not grand but intimate, not fussy but restrained, sitting appropriately on its remote hilltop.

The exterior is attractive (Fig. 274), with an embraced tower carrying a broach spire, and a polygonal apse. The style is Early English, the windows single or paired lancets. Inside, the tower arch is tall, and rests on sturdy columns. The chancel is divided from the nave by a timber arch. The roofs are good, and there is good Victorian glass in the chancel windows.[13]

Christchurch, Llangrove (Long-grove)*

This church lies to the north of Whitchurch, which itself is on the A40 to the west of Ross-on-Wye. George Frederick Bodley (1827-1907) was the architect of this unpretentious building and it is almost certainly his earliest church. It was built in 1854-56; afterwards he went on to achieve great works, and became one of the most celebrated of later Victorian architects, building such churches as Hoar Cross, Staffordshire and Pendlebury, Lancashire. He developed a restrained style of architecture, less fussy than some of his predecessors; in his earlier days he favoured the Decorated style, as enjoined by Pugin and *The Ecclesiologist*; later, as at Holy Trinity, Prince Consort Road, Kensington, he preferred Perpendicular. He built three churches in Herefordshire—Llangrove and Canon Frome

Fig. 275 *The elegant interior, Llangrove. Note especially the simplicity of the arcade*

at the beginning of his career, and Hom Green near Ross-on-Wye shortly before his death. His greatest work was done when High Victorian architecture had lost much of its earlier exuberance, and his clean lines and cool spacious effects combine to lead towards the architecture of the 20th century.

The church at Llangrove consists of a nave with south aisle, chancel, and a western bell-turret. The window tracery of the chancel is attractive, and based on the English Decorated style; a little later, (certainly at France Lynch, Gloucestershire, his next church, and perhaps at Canon Frome in 1860) like many of his contemporaries, Bodley expressed himself in French Gothic, but there is no sign of this at Llangrove. The interior (Fig. 275) is cool and elegant: especially notable is the simplicity of the arcade, the piers rising without any capitals to the arches—something which would never have been done in the 14th century. Here Bodley is showing his originality—he is never content slavishly to copy Gothic building, but introduces his own vital touches which distinguish his churches from the routine mid-Victorian run-of-the-mill church. The roofs of both nave and chancel are fine. The church is exceptionally well cared for and is a delight to visit.

St. Lawrence, Canon Frome*

The church stands next to Canon Frome Court, a mansion built by the Hoptons in 1786. From Ledbury, take the A438 east, and at the Trumpet Inn junction turn right onto the A417. One mile after Ashperton, turn into a lane on the right, and after about 200 yards fork left and go along the drive to Canon Frome Court; the church is behind the house.

There is a simple red-brick tower, dating from 1686, but the rest of the church was built by George Frederick Bodley (1827-1907) in 1860. St. Lawrence's is one of his earlier churches, following his work at Llangrove and France Lynch in Gloucestershire. The south window of the nave, next to the porch, is striking, the east window of the chancel more conventionally Decorated. The roof over the nave is single-framed. The two-bay arcade leading into the north chapel is clean, where many of his contemporaries would have indulged themselves with fancy overblown capitals (cf. Bishop's Frome, Fig. 205, p.103); the rose window in the east of the chapel is excellent (Fig. 276) and filled with very good Victorian glass by Clayton and Bell.[14] Perhaps one should not be surprised

Fig. 276 The rose window, Canon Frome

that an architect who could design like this aged 33 should go on to achieve greatness.

St. Margaret, Welsh Bicknor*

The villages of English Bicknor and Welsh Bicknor lie on opposite banks of the river Wye—the former in Gloucestershire, the latter in Herefordshire. The original settlement of Bicknor is the English one, entered in *Domesday Book* as *Bicanofre*; the second element of the nave comes from OE *ofer*, meaning hill or ridge; the first element is conjectured to be *bica*, point or hill, referring to the prolongation of the ridge at English Bicknor above the Wye.[15] But to the Welsh, Welsh Bicknor was known as Garth Benni, and there is mention of a church here in the 6th century in the 12th-century *Book of Llandaff*.[16] Davies also discussed the possibility that a bishopric was established in this unlikely place between the late 6th and early 10th centuries.

The church at English Bicknor is situated high on the ridge, but at Welsh Bicknor it rests in woody seclusion on the bank of the Wye, and the journey to it is not for the faint-hearted! Unfortunately, the church is usually locked, but hopeful visitors should proceed from Ross-on-Wye along the A40 towards Monmouth; after three miles, fork left along a lane to Goodrich. After passing through Goodrich village, cross the B4229 along the lane signposted to Welsh Bicknor, and proceed without flinching to the very end of this road, ignoring all warning notices. The end of the road is steeply downhill, with a hairpin bend. It is best to park here, and walk the remaining hundred yards or so to the church which stands on the river bank, next to the youth hostel.

Fig. 277 Welsh Bicknor church
by T.H. Rushforth (1858)

There was a very small medieval church here, but when Sir Stephen Glynne visited on 14 October, 1858, he wrote 'the whole of the body [of the church] has recently been taken down and is being rebuilt'—and the result is what we see today.

St. Margaret's is, indeed, a little-known Victorian treasure built, as Pevsner remarks, without regard to expense. The architect was T.H. Rushforth of London. It consists of a south-west tower, nave and chancel, and south chapel (Fig. 277). The tower has round-headed windows in the Norman style, with four lights on each face at the belfry level. The porch is mainly Early English; some of the masonry here is in urgent need of renewal. There are four neo-Norman windows in the west wall of the nave; other windows are mainly lancets. Both the chancel arch and the arcade dividing the south chapel from the nave are richly decorated. The enormous capital of the solitary pier is carved with heads at each corner and foliage. Equally impressive are the pulpit (Fig. 170, p.72), reading desk and font (Fig. 110, p.43), all lavishly enriched. In the south chapel is the sole survivor from the medieval church, the late 13th-century effigy of a lady said to represent Margaret wife of Sir John de Montacute, who helped to establish Edward III on the throne, thus leading to the downfall of Roger Mortimer. She lies clad in a heavily draped gown, holding a ribbon in her left hand.

All Saints, Monkland*

As with Kingsland and Eardisland, 'land' here is really *lene*, the area around the rivers Lugg and Arrow. This is monk's land, a couple of miles west along the A44 from Leominster, because the ancient church here began life as a cell of Benedictine monks founded by Ralph de Todeni, standard-bearer to William the Conqueror at the Battle of Hastings. The cell was subject to the Abbey of Conches in Normandy, and was one of the alien priories suppressed by Henry V in 1414. The medieval church was demolished in the 1860s and rebuilt under the direction of one of the most eminent Victorian architects, G.E. Street. However, one looks in vain at the exterior of Monkland, however, for signs of the brilliance which Street showed, for example, in the church of St. James the Less, Westminster; for here Street largely rebuilt the former church, putting the original stones back in their old position. The medieval church, in effect, was re-erected, not redesigned, by Street, and Norman and Early English windows are preserved in the nave, some of them still with their tufa surrounds. From the outside, therefore, All Saints still seems a medieval church, but within, the Victorian era takes over. Street's design was acclaimed by *The Ecclesiologist* (the nearly all-powerful arbiter of High-Church taste in the mid-Victorian era). So when Sir Stephen Glynne visited Monkland, in September, 1865, he was able to write with approval, 'This church has been lately partially rebuilt, and has undergone a complete and very satisfactory restoration in true ecclesiastical spirit'.

The interior (Fig. 278) is Victorian art of the highest order, for Street was a stickler in his attention to detail in every aspect of the furnishings. Outstanding at Monkland is the reredos by Goodhart-Rendel, consisting of a crucifix sculpted in alabaster under a canopy of Purbeck marble, with a background of Salviati's mosaic. The roof of the

Fig. 278 The interior of Monkland church by G.E. Street (c.1863)

chancel is painted, and there is good Victorian glass in the east and south windows. Also notable are the low stone screen, the wrought-iron gates and the pulpit. The plain Norman font has been retained, though the stem and foundation date from Street's restoration.[17]

Outside the church, the lych-gate, also designed by Street, is a memorial to the most famous vicar of Monkland, the Reverend Sir Henry Baker (1821-77); he became the first chairman of the compilers of *Hymns Ancient and Modern*, and his best known hymn is 'The King of Love my Shepherd is'.

St. Andrew, Moreton-on-Lugg*

When Sir Stephen Glynne visited St. Andrew's in 1856, he found it 'a poor church having a nave with small south aisle and chancel, a north porch and mean low steeple at the west of the aisle—stuccoed with pointed tiled roof'. I therefore entered the church expecting little of interest: none of my other background reading had forewarned me of great things—and inside, I found a Victorian gem! The church was rebuilt in 1867 in the then fashionable Decorated style, the architect being W.H. Knight, and the building is competent, certainly not distinguished, though perhaps the spire crowning the south-western tower should have alerted me to the possibility of excellence within. A Norman window survives in the south wall of the chancel, and a 15th-century arcade still separates the south aisle from the nave. There is a very good Perpendicular screen now enclosing the organ; the upper panels display cinquefoiled, ogeed and traceried heads and the cornice is enriched with running vine-ornament.

But it is the decoration of the chancel which confers distinction on St. Andrew's. Outstanding are the mosaics of the north, east and south walls, especially the angels with the lute and pipes, all by Salviati's of Venice (1887), donated by the Evans family of Moreton Court. (Mosaics by Salviati's are present in the reredos of the chancel at Westminster Abbey, no less!) The mosaics in the north wall of the nave are later (1899) and less impressive. The chancel also contains a low brass screen and painted roof—indeed, the whole of the chancel is Victorian art of rare quality.

St. Andrew, Adforton*

This little-known church on the A4110 between Wigmore and Leintwardine is worth visiting for its own sake, and also as a prelude to a visit to the much more impressive church by the same architect at Hoarwithy. J.P. Seddon (1827-1906) 'was a diligent student of mediaeval architecture, and developed a style of his own, which owed something to his love and study of Venetian Gothic'.[18] As a young man, he was articled to Professor T.L. Donaldson (who built Holy Trinity, Brompton), and from 1852 onwards he restored and built many churches in England and Wales. In his restoration work, it was noted that 'he showed a greater willingness to retain old material than many of his contemporaries'.[19] Eastlake, in *A History of the Gothic Revival*, written in 1870, picked him out as one of the rising architects of the next generation.

At Adforton in 1875 he designed a small church on a rising knoll above the village, making the most of the vantage-point of the land given to the trustees. It consists of a nave and apsed chancel, with a bell-cote at the eastern end of the nave. All around is a series of windows of varying design. The interior is simple, the chancel arch plain and unadorned. There are wagon-roofs over both nave and chancel. The font, designed by the architect, is excellent (Fig. 111, p.44). The building is satisfying in its own right, and to architectural students interesting as a forerunner of Hoarwithy.

St. Catherine, Hoarwithy***

Without a doubt, this is the most exciting Victorian church in Herefordshire; it lies above the west bank of the Wye between Hereford and Ross. It was originally built as a chapelry to Hentland church in 1840. This building was apparently an ugly brick structure with round-headed windows on a steep hillside above the river Wye, and at the request of the vicar, Prebendary Poole, it was transformed by the architect, J.P. Seddon. It was Seddon's partiality for Italian and Byzantine styles that was given free rein at Hoarwithy and the result is astonishing. He did not destroy the earlier church but encased it in sandstone and transformed the building both within and without.

Fig. 279 *The south colonnade at Hoarwithy*

The visitor will probably first see the church from below, noting the tall Italian campanile (Fig. 5, p.*xiii*) and a low colonnade in front of the south side of the church. The building is approached up steep steps; then turn around to the north side where the apsidal east end can be admired with its half-apses to north and south. Walk through the open base of the tower, and then round the corner where there is the most entrancing vista along the colonnade. This consists of twin columns with intricately carved capitals (Fig. 279), between which are glorious views of the Herefordshire countryside. Some of the carving is reminiscent of the work of the Herefordshire School at Kilpeck. Proceed along the arcade, turn right at the end and enter the church via a west porch which opens into a narthex. Over the doorway is a tympanum of Christ in Majesty—another reminder of the Herefordshire School.

With all this architectural excitement, the visitor might well wonder whether the interior will prove an anticlimax; not so! The old nave has been radically altered by the addition of windows on the north, south and west walls, but all the interior drama is really concentrated at the east end. The chancel, raised on steps, is apsidal, with a half-apse on each side (Fig. 280). There is a continuous array of round-headed

windows and above the altar is a mosaic of Christ in glory, holding an orb, the other hand raised in benediction. The domed ceiling of the chancel is supported by four marble columns, resting on solid bases of porphyry. The enormous Byzantine capitals of the columns would look entirely out of place in an ordinary English parish church, but here they are impressive indeed. The richness of the fittings is extraordinary: the altar is of white marble inlaid with lapis lazuli, the central cross being of chrysolite. The pulpit, also of white marble, has panels of green marble and porphyry. There are mosaic floors throughout, even in

Fig. 280 *The raised apsidal chancel with a half-apse on each side at Hoarwithy. The dome's ceiling is supported by four marble columns. Designed by J.P. Seddon*

the cloister. The oak stalls and prayer-desk were carved by H. Hems. The overall decorative scheme was the work of George Fox. There is some impressive stained glass (see back cover); that in the five east windows was designed by the architect in memory of Prebendary Poole, though perhaps the best glass is in a north window designed by H.A. Kennedy. In the west wall are a further series of stained-glass windows; but high up, and almost concealed by the roof timbers, is quite a different window which has been thought to be the work of Burne-Jones.

How was it that a work of such startling originality should have been built at that time in an obscure corner of an obscure county? Seddon's work at Hoarwithy lasted from 1874 to about 1903, with most of it dating to the 1880s. At this date, Gothic was supreme—almost the only precedent amongst Anglican parish churches for a building in the Byzantine or Romanesque style was James Wild's Christchurch Streatham in south London, built in 1841. Hoarwithy precedes J.D. Sedding's great church of the Holy Redeemer, Exmouth Market, Clerkenwell (1887-88) and it looks forward to Sir Edwin Lutyens' St. Jude-on-the-Hill, Hampstead Garden Suburb (1909)—perhaps this is a measure of the greatness of Seddon's achievement.

All Saints, Brockhampton-by-Ross***

William Lethaby (1857-1931) was a pupil of the Victorian architect Norman Shaw and, as a friend of

William Morris, was actively involved in the work of the Arts and Crafts Movement. He was primarily an architectural scholar, and this is his only church. By the beginning of the 20th century, the Gothic Revival begun some 70 or 80 years earlier was losing some of its force; and at Brockhampton Gothic is reduced to its essentials—a sort of stripped Gothic that persisted with diminishing vigour until the outbreak of the Second World War. Brockhampton was truly a pioneering building. The church is found to the west of the B4224 north of Ross.

The new church was funded by Mrs. Alice Foster of Brockhampton Court in memory of her parents. Lethaby was chosen as architect on the recommendation of her husband's aunt, who ten years previously had employed Norman Shaw to design an outstanding church at Batchcott, Shropshire. Mrs. Foster laid the foundation stone on 21 June, 1901 and the church was completed by the next year.

The setting, opposite the main entrance to Brockhampton Court, is lovely and the church, with its thatched

Fig. 281 (top) The old church of St. Michael at Brockhampton, sketched in 1851

Fig. 282 (below) All Saints, Brockhampton by William Lethaby (1901-02)

roof, pink sandstone, creeper-mantled walls and twin towers, presents a striking appearance (Fig. 282). It is cruciform in shape, with shallow transepts, one tower over the crossing and another over the porch. East of the porch, the southern aspect is dominated by the large vertical window in the transept, criss-crossed by bold intersecting concrete bars.

Entering by the porch one sees six doves of peace carved above the semicircular door arch; above is the oak-framed belfry. The interior is astonishing (Fig. 283): steep concrete arches punctuate the nave at intervals, and similar arches outline the entrance to each transept. The arches have no capitals, the arcades simply flowing down into the walls. One can only guess the effect this interior must have had in 1902—even now, it has lost none of its emotional impact. And within a very few years, E.S. Prior, another pupil of Norman Shaw, had built a church (St. Andrew, Roker, Sunderland) with arches very similar to those at Brockhampton. At the west end of the nave is the font designed by Lethaby, with a frieze of vine-leaves and grapes.

Passing from the nave into the crossing, the visitor is confronted by the interior of the tower, illuminated by eight high windows of varied tracery. The exquisite chancel has a fine east window with glass by Christopher Whall portraying six saints and angels. On either side of the altar are tapestries

Fig. 283 The interior at Brockhampton

designed by Sir Edward Burne-Jones and made in the William Morris workshops. On the south wall is a piscina set in a window-sill with the window beyond consisting of two quatrefoils in a rectangle.

The wild flowers carved in the choir-stalls inspired an anonymous lady to embroider an altar cloth (now mounted on the west wall), a series of six seat-cushions, and many hymn-book covers. Also on the west wall is a 16th-century triptych with Flemish side-panels.

Hom Green Church*

The last significant church to be built in Herefordshire is that at Hom Green (1905-06). It was built in memory of Major Lionel James Trafford, who lived nearby at Hill Court, an early 18th-century mansion. The church was designed by G.F. Bodley, and was one of his last works. Unfortunately by the 1970s the congregation had declined, and the church was closed. It was bought in 1997 by REHAU Ltd., who had taken over Hill Court as their UK headquarters. Their refurbishment of the mansion has been widely praised, and the same painstaking and sensitive approach is evident in the church, though there is no public access to the building.

Fig. 284 The nave looking west at Hom Green church by G.F. Bodley

It is a small church, built of brick with dressings of stone; it consists of nave with chancel, and a western bell-turret. The west front has three blind windows below the bell-turret, separated by a pair of buttresses; at the east end is a tall chimney for the vestry fireplace and a buttress in the centre of the east wall, which is without windows. The windows in the north and south walls are all straight-headed.

The interior is more striking (Fig. 284): it is divided into twin naves by a tall arcade, with plain capitals, and above is a wagon-roof. The delicately carved screen which originally divided nave and chancel has now been moved to the west end. Modern grey marble floors and light wood panelling give lightness to the building. There is some good glass in the south window, erected as a memorial to local victims of the First World War. The transformation of the building from church into an informal conference centre for symposia, training courses and music recitals has been most sympathetically undertaken; it is an imaginative use for a redundant building and a credit to the company concerned.

*The five Victorian churches of the city of Hereford may conveniently be described together.
Between them, they illustrate well the three phases of the Victorian Gothic Revival.*

St. Nicholas (1842) (See Fig. 233, p.132)

This church was rebuilt on its present site in 1842, before the High-Church revival initiated by Pugin and the Tractarians really got into its stride. St. Nicholas' is a plain preaching box, with a shallow chancel, Early English windows and a west tower. The architect was Thomas Duckham.

St. Martin (1845)*

St. Martin's is an ancient foundation, dating back to the 12th century, and originally it stood just south of the old Wye bridge. The medieval church was severely damaged in the Civil War and subsequently demolished. For two hundred years, the parishioners worshipped at All Saints'; then, in the first half of the 19th century, Hereford south of the Wye expanded considerably and a new St. Martin's was built to the design of R.W. Jearrad.

It has a rather bleak Early English exterior, with a thin spire reminiscent of many of the Commissioners' churches of the 1820s and 1830s. Inside, however, it is light and airy. The chancel was deepened in accordance with contemporary practice later in the 19th century, and the effect of the blind arcading in the east wall is striking. In the south transept is the attractive St. Martin window, the earliest stained glass in the church.

St. Martin's has in recent years achieved some fame because of its links with the SAS, and after the Falklands conflict a fine memorial window was placed in the north transept. This is a fitting tribute; it avoids triumphalism, and is perfectly in tune with the post-imperial attitudes of the late 20th century. It is pleasing to record that this church is open daily.

St. Paul, Tupsley (1865)

This suburban parish was created out of the parish of Hampton Bishop in the 1860s to provide for the needs of Hereford's expanding population. The architect was F.R. Kempson, who here was able to indulge his fondness for ornate exuberant capitals to the full (cf. Bishop's Frome). There is a substantial south-western tower with a broach spire. The most remarkable feature of St. Paul's are the four stained glass windows executed in the style of the pre-Raphaelites. These were installed between 1924 and 1931, and were the work of Henry Dearle, who had taken over the management of the William Morris firm after the death of Morris in 1896. The two windows in the north aisle show Peter and John healing the lame, and Christ healing the woman with an issue of blood; and in the south aisle, the empty sepulchre, and Christ preaching from the boat and the miraculous draught of fishes. The last window was made to a design by Sir Edward Burne-Jones.

St. James (1869)

This is a substantial and attractive stone church by Thomas Nicholson, largely rebuilt after a disastrous fire in 1901. Entry is through a stone porch, with pillars on each side surmounted by ornate capitals, and a cusped arch above. The arcades have round piers with elaborate stiff-leaf capitals. Above, the clerestory windows are sexfoiled. There is some good 20th-century glass, including the east window of the chancel which is a memorial to the fallen in the Great War, and an excellent representation of the parable of the sower in the south transept, in memory of a former vicar, the Reverend Frederick Lansdell (d.1933).

Holy Trinity (1883)

This is a large new church built by F.R. Kempson. By the 1880s, the extravagancies of High Victorian architecture seen twenty years earlier were beginning to sober down and Kempson's earlier exuberance appears to have lessened; for here the capitals are restrained, without the floridity of his earlier churches. The whole church is quite plain: windows are lancets in the clerestory, and groups of three lancets in the aisles. The chancel is deep. There is no tower.

The following 27 churches are arranged approximately in chronological order.

St. Mary and St. Thomas à Becket, Much Birch

This church was built in 1837, that is to say, early in the Gothic Revival, but before the writings of Pugin and the polemics of *The Ecclesiologist* had imposed an iron grip on most church architects. Thus the chancel is not deep, the building is light and not plunged into reverential dimness, and the windows are Early English lancets; ten years later, and all this would have changed! The chancel ceiling is vaulted and painted with cherubs' heads. The architect was Thomas Foster.

St. Mary the Virgin, Yazor*

This church is in the care of the Churches Conservation Trust. It was built by George Moore, commencing in 1843, on land given by Uvedale Price who lived nearby at Foxley, and was a well-known apostle of the Picturesque movement in landscaping. The church, which lies alongside the A438 north-west of Hereford, has nave, transepts, and a polygonal apse. The sanctuary fittings are a good example of Victorian art (Fig. 177, p.74), and the glass in the apse windows by Warrington is also good.

Sir Stephen Glynne visited the old church, 300 yards away, in 1846, and left a full description of the building,

Fig. 285 The old church at Yazor,
now an ivy-clad ruin by a farmyard

which now lies in ruins (Fig. 285). It consisted of a nave and chancel, south aisle and south transept, a pretty north porch (now at Bishopstone, p.118) and a west tower with a saddleback roof as at Kinnersley (Fig. 57, p.24). The arcade is Perpendicular, with octagonal piers. The building is now without a roof, except the south transept.

Holy Trinity, Hardwick

The church is attractively situated in the Wye valley, 2½ miles from Hay-on-Wye. It was consecrated in 1853, the architect being Thomas Tudor of Monmouth. The church is built in Early English and Decorated styles; the best feature is the hammer-beam roof with flying angels carved on the ends of the hammer-beams. When we visited in May, there were purple orchids, cowslips, milkwort and lousewort in flower in the churchyard.

St. George, Burrington

The church was rebuilt between 1855 and 1864, the architect being Pountney Smith. Externally, it is pretty, with a timber-framed upper storey to the west tower. Churchyard monuments are generally outside the scope of this book, but mention must be made of the six cast-iron slabs (Fig. 286) now situated to the east of the church. These used to be in the old chancel and date from 1619 to 1754; they are the work of the ironmasters of Bringewood, close to Downton Castle (see below). There are two similar slabs at Brilley (p.119).

Fig. 286 One of the six cast-iron slabs in the churchyard at Burrington. This one is in memory of Maria Hare, d.1674

St. Mary, Collington

The church was built in 1856 by A.E. Perkins; it consists of nave and chancel only. The most interesting feature is the 13th-century octagonal font showing pointed arches on colonnettes (Fig. 106, p.40)

St. Mary, Byton*

The church was built in 1859-60 by an architect called Bannister; Pevsner described it as 'rather a disorderly design'.[20] The church is worth visiting for the Norman tympanum which is now set in the south wall (Fig. 16, p.8).

St. Mary, Kentchurch

Situated attractively in the Monnow valley, this church was built in the Decorated style in 1859. Surviving from the previous church is the remarkable memorial to John Scudamore (d.1616) and his wife; two semi-reclining effigies lie one above the other, the gentleman of alabaster above, the lady of free-stone below, flanked by their ten children.

St. Giles, Downton-on-the-Rock

The medieval church now lies in ruins in the village. It was replaced in 1861 by an elegant Early English structure designed by Pountney Smith. There is a south-western tower with broach spire. This church is in the grounds of Downton Castle, built by Richard Payne Knight in the 1770s (p.138). In the estate are the original iron-works of Bringewood (see above).

St. Peter and St. Paul, Stoke Lacy

The church was rebuilt in 1863 by F.R. Kempson in the Early English style. Kempson was based in Hereford, built ten churches in the county and restored others. Perhaps his most striking work was the neo-Norman church at Bishop's Frome. Stoke Lacy is not so impressive, but he left the original Norman chancel arch, and the very good 16th-century screen. There is quite a striking Victorian stone pulpit.

St. John, Pencombe

When Sir Stephen Glynne came here in 1856, he found a church of mixed Norman and Early English features, and the chancel remarkable for its division into chancel proper and apse. The new church was built by Thomas Nicholson (1823-95). He was the diocesan surveyor and architect at Hereford, and designed seven churches in the county, and several others in Wales. At Pencombe, he consciously replicated the features that Glynne had noted, even if he strayed from historical accuracy in detail (Pevsner pointed out that the south doorway has a neo-Norman arch but Early English stiff-leaf capitals).[21]

St. John the Baptist and Christchurch, Llanwarne*

Sir Stephen Glynne visited Llanwarne, south of the junction between the A49 and A466 south of Hereford, in 1861, and he described the old church of St. John the Baptist which he thought resembled the churches of Hentland and Holme Lacy. Not long afterwards, this church was abandoned because of repeated trouble with the foundations, and its ruins now stand picturesquely in the valley (Fig. 287). The four-bay Decorated arcade with circular piers and capitals, and reticulated east and south windows in the south aisle survive. The tower is Perpendicular. There are some 13th-century cross-slabs.

Fig. 287 The ruins of the medieval church at Llanwarne

Three years after Glynne's visit, Christchurch was built a short distance to the west to the design of Messrs Elmslie. It is an unusual plan, cruciform with a polygonal apse, and a north porch with short spire above. The bowl of the late 17th-century font is decorated with acanthus leaves and the stem with drapery; it is very similar to that at Holme Lacy.[22] There is some Flemish stained glass from the 16th and 17th centuries in the apse.

St. Michael, Dulas

The old church was visited by Sir Stephen Glynne in 1864; he described a simple building with a Norman west doorway; outside the east window ran 'a rude stone projecting ledge or seat' such as may be seen today at Craswall (p.149). In 1865 this church was demolished and the new one built in the Early English style by G.C. Haddon. The notable features are the 17th-century woodwork (pulpit, lectern, desk etc).

St. Silas, Bollingham

This small church was rebuilt in Victorian times; there is really nothing of interest except for the roof, which is original—the RCHM said 14th- or 15th-century—and rather interesting.[23] On display are the principal and common rafters, the purlins, the wall-plates, tie-beams, collar-beams, king-posts and foiled wind-braces at the sides.

St. Michael, Breinton

This is a small Victorian church, built by F.R. Kempson in 1866-70, and he incorporated in its structure several small Norman windows. Quite why it was rebuilt at that time is unclear—for only eight years previously Sir Stephen Glynne had visited Breinton and found the church in good order, noting its rural and secluded situation. The Elizabethan communion-table has richly carved bulbous legs with Ionic capitals. There is a painted and framed oak panel to Capt. Rudhall Booth (d.1685).

St. Andrew, Dinedor

Dinedor (meaning 'fortified hill') is the site of an Iron Age hill-fort. Of the medieval church, only the tower with its pyramidal roof survives. Sir Stephen Glynne noted in 1851 that the church was 'small and rather mean'; and by 1867 the building 'had fallen into such decay and was so dilapidated, that the only wonder is how it had held together at all' (church guide). So the church was rebuilt by F.R. Kempson, whose instructions were to retain as much as possible of the old material and architectural features. There is a plain octagonal font dating from the 15th century. In the tower is a memorial to the Reverend Francis Brickenden, rector here for 33 years, consisting of a tablet surmounted by an urn.

St. Michael, Dewsall

St. Michael's church looks attractive as the visitor walks over a little bridge from Dewsall Court; it is a small building, just nave and chancel and bell-turret with shingled spire, and a timbered porch dating from the 14th century. The south doorway and the priest's doorway are both round-headed, attributed by the RCHM to the 13th or 14th century; but Pevsner wondered whether they could be earlier.[24] Most of the rest of the building dates from 1868. The finest artefact is the font; this has a circular bowl, with its underside trimmed to an octagon, embellished with a little ball-flower. Marshall thought that the font was originally Norman, cut down and embellished in the early 14th century.[25] The place-name means St. Dewi's well or spring.

St. James, Cradley

This large church is substantially Victorian, the chancel being the work of Sir George Gilbert Scott in 1868, the north aisle and general restoration being done by A.E. Perkins. Surviving from the previous church, however, is the Norman south doorway with chevron decoration, and the Early English chancel arch. There is a Norman window in the south wall of the tower; in the north wall is a section of an Anglo-Saxon frieze, one of the few Saxon fragments surviving in Herefordshire. The upper part of the tower is Perpendicular, with an embattled parapet. The font (Fig. 109, p.43) is dated 1722.

St. Michael and All Angels, Little Marcle

The architect, J.W. Hugall, is called by Pevsner 'one of the naughtier High Victorians';[26] by which I presume he means that Hugall was not bound by the edicts of *The Ecclesiologist* to design in a liturgically correct, High-Church fashion, and was therefore free to follow his fancy—which is what he did in Little Marcle in 1870. The little church, just nave and chancel, has a lively west front facing the road. Between two idiosyncratic windows, a buttress is carried up to support a polygonal bell-turret with colonnettes bearing a short spire. There are crosses on the nave, chancel and porch. It is an unconventional design, bearing some resemblance to the west front of Street's church at Milton-under-Wychwood, Oxfordshire.[27]

St. Guthlac, Little Cowarne

This is a Victorian church built by F.R. Kempson in 1870. The unusual, and attractive, feature is the west tower, which is a saddleback, with in addition a south gable. There is one Norman window in the chancel, and an Early English lancet in the nave. The unusual dedication refers to the probability that Little Cowarne was given to St. Guthlac's Priory, Hereford in the 11th century; the dedication was revived in 1992.

St. Mary, Kenderchurch

The church stands alone on a knoll above the Hereford-Abergavenny road. Sir Stephen Glynne saw it in 1867, and found it in bad condition, with mutilated windows. He noted, without describing, the sculpture of the Norman tympanum above the south doorway; this has now vanished. He was impressed by the rood-screen and loft, which he said was in a pretty complete state.

Four years later, the restoration was drastic; surviving from the old church are the Norman font, the pulpit, and the screen. The latter is mostly Victorian, but incorporates late medieval work, including the moulded top-rail, the cross-beam at the head of the cove, and the moulded side-post on the south. The Jacobean pulpit is excellent, and is carved with guilloche enrichment.

St. Peter, Pipe and Lyde*

Both elements of the name refer to streams in the neighbourhood.[28] In 1856 Sir Stephen Glynne described this church as being in 'rather a lonely site adjoining the turnpike road'; the turnpike road has now become the busy A49 north of Hereford, and the situation is far from lonely. The nave was rebuilt in the Early English style by F.R. Kempson in 1874, and he also added a broach spire to the original Early English tower. The late Norman south doorway was reset at its original level, but the floor appears to have been lowered, leaving an unusually tall doorway. The chancel was also substantially modified, but it retains the Herefordshire east window and the south window with Y-tracery described by Glynne. He also found the rood-beam 'a fine horizontal cornice of foliage with vineleaf and grapes'; the stone staircase to the former rood-loft survives against the north wall of the nave. The medieval chancel roof has collar-beams supported by arched braces.[29] The Victorian font is mounted on a 13th-century shaft; the original bowl is on the floor beside it, and was brought in from the churchyard.

Putley church*

Putley church, which lies behind Putley Court to the west of Ledbury, was largely rebuilt by Thomas Blashill in 1875; in the foundations of the north wall he found a large collection of Roman bricks, tiles etc, which were shown to the British Archaeological Association in 1876.[30] In the chancel is a fine 13th-century piscina. The pulpit and low screen is of 17th-century workmanship, made up from panelling from the Putley Court pew. But the show-piece of the church is the wonderful Victorian reredos of alabaster and mosaic (Fig. 176, p.74).

St. Bartholomew, Docklow

Sir Stephen Glynne visited Docklow in 1873, and was not impressed: 'the windows are modern and wretched ... the exterior is so finely mantled with luxuriant ivy as to conceal its deformities'. Seven years later, the nave and chancel were largely rebuilt and now look attractive, with the medieval tower capped with a shingled pyramidal roof and short spire.

St. Dinabo, Llandinabo*

The church dedicated to this unknown Welsh saint (sometimes known as St. Junabius)[31] was built in 1881 by A. Lloyd Oswell. The church is easily missed: from Hereford, take the A49 south. Llandinabo church is by the farm of the same name (where there is a key to the church) on the left side of the A49 two miles beyond Much Birch.

Lloyd Oswell encased the outer walls of the previous building, plastered the inner walls, rebuilt the west wall and added the north vestry and aisle, the south porch and the pretty half-timbered bell-turret. Inside, there are several items of interest. The greatest treasure is the rood-screen (Fig. 161, p.69); it is one of the best in Herefordshire. The chancel is roofed by medieval braced collar-beams; the nave roof also has arched braces, probably medieval. In addition, there is a Jacobean pulpit, a brass to Thomas Tompkins (d.1629), a child who was drowned, shown standing in a pool, and glass in the east window by Kempe.

St. Faith, Dorstone

This church at the head of the Golden Valley has much of interest. It is believed that the medieval church was founded by a descendant of Richard de Brito, one of the murderers of St. Thomas à Becket. In 1827 the medieval church was demolished and a poor building substituted. This was visited by Sir Stephen Glynne in 1864; he was not favourably impressed. In 1889, this church was in turn demolished, and the present structure built. During the rebuilding, a tomb two feet below the floor was accidentally broken into; inside was a male skeleton, with a pewter chalice and paten dating from the 13th century.

The architects of the present church were Messrs Nicholson and Son. The 13th-century tower arch survives, and in the tower is a coffin-lid from the same period. There is a medieval double piscina on the south wall of the chancel; one of the drains is carved in an octofoiled pattern. Also in the chancel are three original windows—the east of four lights (in contrast to the usual Herefordshire three) and on the south a window with Y-tracery and another with Perpendicular tracery.

St. Michael and All Angels, Lingen

This is a very pretty, if undistinguished, Victorian church of 1891, the architect being H. Curzon. The tower is older, perhaps 16th century, and above it is a timbered belfry and shingled spire. Inside there are some 16th-century benches, and a monument to John Downes (d. 1687).

St. John the Baptist, Aston Ingham

This church is not of any great interest in itself, but it possesses one great treasure, the lead font dating from the reign of William and Mary (Fig. 108, p.43). The medieval church was rebuilt in 1891 by Nicholson and

Fig. 288 The old church at Lingen

Son, but the architects retained the medieval chancel arch and the 16th-century west tower. There are two damaged effigies from the 13th century on either side of the altar; one of these shows in high relief the head and shoulders of a priest within a trefoil-headed recess, with a foliated cross below.

The following churches were also built during the Victorian and Edwardian eras:
St. John, Ivington, 1842
St. John the Baptist, Newton, 1842
All Saints, Bishopswood, 1843; architect John Plowman
St. Swithin, Ganarew, 1849; J. Pritchard
St. Mary Magdalene, Huntington, near Hereford, 1859; B. Cranstoun
St. John of Jerusalem, Ford, 1851
St. Michael the Archangel, Felton, 1853
St. Matthew, Marstow, 1855; Thomas Nicholson
St. Mary, Tretire, 1856

St. Peter, Staunton-on-Arrow, 1856; Thomas Nicholson
St. John the Evangelist, Storridge, 1856; Frederick Preedy
St. Peter, Titley, 1856; E. Haycock
St. John, Howle Hill, c.1860
St. John the Baptist, Yarkhill, 1862; Ainslie and Blashill
St. Luke, Stoke Prior, 1863; F.R. Kempson
St. Matthew, Frome's Hill, 1864; F.R. Kempson
St. Mary, Little Birch, 1869; W. Chick
St. David, Little Dewchurch, 1869; F. Preedy
St. Andrew, Bredenbury, 1877; T.H. Wyatt
St. Peter, Grafton (Bullinghope), 1889; F.R. Kempson
St. Mary, Moorcourt, c.1890 (a timber-framed structure formerly a private chapel)
St. Dubricius, Hamnish Clifford, 1909; W.J. Weatherley
Christ Church, Wellington Heath, rebuilding 1951 of an 1840 church

Finally, the post-war expansion of Hereford has necessitated the building of two new churches.

Hereford St. Francis of Assisi*

This church on the Abergavenny road, opposite Macdonald's, was built in 1966-67, the architect being Peter Besanquet. It is an imaginative design, with a steeply sloping roof over the church. Inside, the sanctuary (Fig. 289) is bathed in light from concealed windows above the nave and also from another concealed window by the side of the organ. To the right of the altar is a stained glass window celebrating the praise of Creation by Jim Budd (1997). Behind the altar is a plain cross on the wall, draped in a linen cloth. To the left, high on the wall, are the organ pipes, acting as a foil to the cross. Beneath the altar is space for a display, which, when

Fig. 289 The interior of St. Francis of Assisi, Hereford

we visited, was a depiction of the Resurrection. The Norman font, carved with arcades, came originally from the church of Chardstock, Devon.

This is a lovely modrn church, with an appeal of moving simplicity. It is very much a church of the 1960s, with a design reminiscent of the celebrated church of St. John Peckham by David Bush, built in 1965. Next to the church is a large hall and rooms for community activities.

Hereford St. Bamabas

A modrn church and community centre, in Venns Lane, one mile north-east from the city centre. It was built in 1983, to the design of Roderick Robinson of Hereford. The premises comprise a suite of community rooms, well-built, and in one corner is a fairly small chapel, plainly furnished. There is some attractive modern glass along one side. The church acts as a centre for services to the deaf, and is linked to All Saints Church.

GLOSSARY

Abacus: a flat slab above a capital.

Acanthus: a prickly-leafed plant whose leaves are represented in Corinthian capitals.

Advowson: the right of presentation of a priest to a church.

Agnus Dei: a figure of a lamb, representing Christ, bearing the banner of the Cross.

Alabaster: a compact marble-like form of gypsum (calcium sulphate) long favoured for memorial effigies.

Ambulatory: an enclosed walkway.

Apse: the semicircular or rectangular end of the chancel.

Arabesque: decoration using fanciful combinations of flowing lines, foliage and intertwined tendrils etc.

Arcade: a range of arches supported by piers or columns.

Arched braces: see Roof.

Architrave: the lowest of the parts of the entablature above a column.

Ashlar: blocks of masonry fashioned to even faces and square edges.

Augustinian canons: members of an order whose rule is based on the teachings of St. Augustine.

Aumbry: a recess or cupboard to hold the vessels for Mass or Holy Communion.

Austin canons: see Augustinian.

Ball-flower: an ornament resembling a ball within a globular flower, a motif used in Decorated architecture *c.*1300 – 1350.

Baluster: a small pillar or column of artistic outline.

Balustrade: a series of short columns, usually supporting a railing.

Barge-boards: projecting boarding along the edge of a gable to cover the rafters and to keep out rain.

Baroque: a vigorous, exuberant style of architecture prevalent in the 17th century in Europe, and in a modified form from about 1700 - 1720 in England.

Bay: the space between the columns of an arcade.

Beakhead: a Norman ornamental motif consisting of a row of birds' or beasts' heads with beaks biting into a moulding.

Benedictine: a monk or nun of the order founded by St. Benedict.

Billet: a Norman ornamental motif consisting of raised rectangles or cylinders with spaces between.

Blind arcade: an arcade of piers or columns attached to a wall.

Boss: a projection at the intersection of the ribs of a vault or roof.

Box-pew: a pew with a tall wooden enclosure.

Breccia: a lithified sedimentary rock composed of angular fragments.

Bressummer: a transverse beam supporting the superstructure.

Broach spire: a spire at the base of which sloping half-pyramids of stone effect the transition from a square tower to an octagonal spire.

Buttress: a mass of masonry projecting from or built against a wall to give extra strength.

Buttress, flying: an arch, or half-arch, transmitting the thrust from the upper part of a wall to an outer support.

Cable: a Norman moulding imitating a twisted rope.

Campanile: an isolated bell-tower.

Capital: the top part of a pier or column.

Caryatid: a female figure supporting an entablature.

Ceilure: an embellished part of the roof above the rood.

Censer: a vessel for the burning of incense.

Centaur: a mythical monster, half man, half horse.

Chamfer: a bevel or slope made by paring the edge of a right-angled block of stone.

Chancel: the east end of the church containing the altar.

Chancel arch: an arch at the east end of the nave opening into the chancel.

Chantry chapel: a chapel endowed for the saying of Masses for the soul(s) of the founder(s) after death.

Chevron: Norman zigzag moulding on arches or windows.

Cinquefoil: an ornament divided by cusps into five lobes.

Clerestory: an upper storey of the walls of the nave pierced by windows.

Coif: a covering for the head worn by women.

Collar-beam: see Roof.

Common rafter: see Roof.

Consecration cross: five crosses incised on a stone altar, symbolising the Five Wounds of Christ; a set of 12 crosses marked on the inside and outside walls during the consecration of a church.

Console: a projecting bracket, often S-shaped, to support a cornice or decorative objects (vases, urns etc.)

Corbel: a block of stone projecting from a wall, often supporting roof beams.

Corbel-table: a series of corbels below the eaves.

Corinthian columns: one of the order of classical architecture.

Cornice: the top section of the entablature.

Cosmati work: a type of mosaic technique used by Roman decorators in the 12th and 13th centuries.

Coving: a concave moulding on the under-surface of a ceiling or screen etc.

Credence: a shelf over a piscina; a table beside the altar on which the bread and wine are placed.

Crenellated: notched or embattled (as in a parapet).

Cresting: ornamentation along the top of a screen etc.

Crocket: decorative projections on the sloping sides of spires, pinnacles, etc.

Crossing: in a cruciform church, the space at the intersection of the nave, chancel and transepts.

Cupola: a domed or polygonal turret crowning a roof.

Curvilinear: see Tracery.

Cushion: in Norman architecture, the rounding-off of the lower angles of the square capital to the cylindrical pier below.

Cusp: a projecting point between the foils in a Gothic arch.

Dado: decorative covering of the lower part of a wall or screen.

Decorated: historical division of English Gothic architecture, from c.1300 - 1350.

Diaper: a low-relief pattern, often composed of square or lozenge shapes.

Dogtooth: Early English ornamental motif consisting of a series of raised pyramids.

Doom: a picture of the Last Judgment.

Doric: one of the orders of classical architecture.

Double-framed: see Roof.

Drip-stone: a projecting moulding over doorways or windows to throw off the rain, usually ending in a carved stop.

Dugout: a hollowed log made into a chest.

Early English: historical division of English Gothic architecture from c.1200 - 1300.

Easter sepulchre: a recess in the north wall of the chancel used to house the consecrated Host between Maundy Thursday and Easter Day.

Eaves: the underpart of a sloping roof overhanging a wall.

Entablature: all the horizontal members above a column (architrave, frieze and cornice).

Fan vault: see Vault.

Finial: the top of a canopy, gable or pinnacle.

Flamboyant: the last phase of French Gothic architecture, characterised by wavy or undulating window tracery.

Fleuron: a flower-like ornament.

Fluting: vertical channelling in the shaft of a column.

Foil: a lobe formed by cusping of a circle or arch; trefoil (3), quatrefoil (4), cinquefoil (5), sexfoil (6) etc. express the number of shapes so produced.

Foliated: decorated with leaf ornaments.

Frieze: the middle division of the entablature.

Gargoyle: a projecting spout from a roof-gutter, often grotesquely carved.

Geometrical: see Tracery.

Gothic: the style of architecture characterised by pointed arches, sub-divided into Early English, Decorated and Perpendicular; revived in the nineteenth century.

Gothick: a style of architecture of the second half of the eighteenth century, in which Gothic forms were imitated.

Green man: a human mask with foliage issuing from the mouth.

Griffin: a mythical beast with a lion's body and an eagle's beak and wings.

Grisaille: monochromatic patterns on clear glass, in grey, brown or yellow, used from the 13th century onwards.

Guilloche: an ornamental motif consisting of interlacing curved bands enclosing circles.

Hammer-beam: see Roof.

Head-stop: the stop of a drip-stone or hood-mould carved into a head.

Herefordshire window: a group of three stepped windows under a common arch, with the mullions flanking the middle light extending up to the arch above; frequently used in Herefordshire churches around 1200.

Herringbone masonry: in which the stones are laid diagonally, sloping in different directions in alternate rows to make a zigzag pattern; used in Anglo-Saxon or early Norman work (up to c.1125).

Hood-mould: projecting moulding over doors or windows to throw off rain-water.

Housel bench: long wooden stools with a flat table-top; used as communion rails.

Impost: the slab, usually moulded, on which the ends of an arch rest.

Ionic columns: one of the orders of classical architecture.

Jamb: the straight side of an archway, doorway or window.

Jesse window: in which Christ's descent from Jesse, father of King David, is depicted in stained glass.

King-post: see Roof.

Label: a drip-stone or hood-mould.

Lancet window; the tall narrow pointed window of the Early English period.

Light: a vertical division of a window.

Linenfold: panelling in which there is vertical patterning resembling parallel folds of linen, used in the 16th century.

Lintel: a horizontal stone over a doorway.

Lozenge: diamond-shaped.

Lucarne: a small opening to admit light.

Mandorla: an almond-shaped or oval panel.

Metope: in the Doric order, the space in the frieze between the triglyphs.

Misericord: a bracket on the underside of a hinged choir-stall, affording some support when standing, often intricately carved.

Mullions: vertical stone bars dividing a window into lights.

Nail-head: Early English ornamental motif, consisting of small pyramids repeated at intervals.

Narthex: a vestibule at the western end of a church.

Neo-Norman: the imitation of Norman architecture in the 19th century.

Nook-shaft: a shaft in the angle of the jamb of a window or doorway.

Norman architecture: the massive Romanesque style of building, from 1066 - 1200.

Ogee arch: a non-structural arch formed by two S-shaped curves, with the concave parts above coming to a point, typical of the 14th century.

Order: in classical building, a column, with base, shaft, capital and entablature; in Norman building, one of the successively recessed arches of an archway, or at the sides of a doorway, all the parts of a column (base, shaft and capital).

Parclose screen: a screen separating a chapel from the rest of the church.

Pediment: a low-pitched gable placed as a decorative feature above doorways, windows, etc.
 broken pediment: the central portion of the pediment is open.
 segmental pediment: part of the sloping sides is omitted.

Pellet: a Norman ornamental motif consisting of small balls regularly repeated.

Perpendicular: a historical division of English Gothic architecture, c.1350 - 1550.

Pier: a column of free-standing masonry supporting arches.

Pilaster: a shallow pier attached to a wall.

Piscina: a basin with drain in the wall to the south of the altar for washing the vessels used during Mass.

Plate tracery: see Tracery.

Poppy-head: a finial in wood at the end of a pew or bench, often carved.

Porphyry: a very hard rock, purple and white, used in sculpture.

Portico: a roof supported by columns at the entrance to a building.

Portland stone: an oolitic building-stone quarried in the Isle of Portland.

Pre-Raphaelites: a group of painters who, about 1848, sought to return to the style of painters before Raphael (Millais, Burne-Jones, Holman Hunt etc.).

Presbytery: the part of a monastic church east of the choir.

Principal rafter: see Roof.

Purbeck marble: an expensive shelly limestone from Purbeck, Dorset, often polished.

Purlin: see Roof.

Putto (pl. putti): a small boy or cherub.

Quatrefoil: an ornament divided by cusps into four lobes.

Queen-post: see Roof.

Quoins: dressed stones at the angles of a building.

Rebus: a pun, or play on words.

Recessed spire: a spire recessed within a parapet.

Rendering: plastering of an outer wall.

Reredos: a an ornamental screen or hanging on the wall behind the altar.

Respond: a half-pier carrying one end of an arch and bonded into a wall.

Reticulated tracery: see Tracery.

Retrochoir: an extension of a church to the east of the high altar.

Ridge-piece: see Roof.

Rococo: the last phase of the baroque style, prevalent on the continent c. 1720-1760.

Romanesque: another name for Norman architecture, defined by round arches and vaults.

Rood: a Cross bearing the body of Jesus, flanked by the Virgin Mary and St. John.

Rood-loft: a gallery on top of the rood-screen.

Rood-screen: a screen at the junction of nave and chancel bearing the Rood.

Roof: Arched brace: inclined curved timbers, strengthening collar- or hammer-beams.

    Collar-beam: a tie-beam applied higher up the slope of the roof.

    Common rafter: the roof-timbers sloping up from the wall-plate to the ridge.

    Double-framed: the use of longitudinal members (ridge-piece, purlins), the rafters then being divided into stronger principals and weaker subsidiaries.

    Hammer-beam: a horizontal beam projecting from the wall bearing arched braces.

    King-post: an upright timber connecting a tie- or collar-beam to the ridge-beam.

    Principal rafters: stronger rafters dividing the roof-structure into sections.

    Purlins: horizontal timbers parallel with the ridge of the roof.

    Queen-post: a pair of upright timbers placed symmetrically on a tie- or collar-beam connecting it with the rafters above.

    Ridge-piece: a longitudinal timber forming the ridge of the roof.

    Scissor-beam: a timber supporting the common rafters above the level of the collar-beams.

    Single-framed: a roof composed entirely of transverse members, not tied longitudinally.

    Tie-beam: a horizontal timber connecting the feet of the rafters.

    Trussed-rafters: a pair of common rafters pegged together at the ridge and stabilised by a linking collar-beam and bracing.

    Wagon roof: the appearance of the inside of a canvas over a wagon, obtained by closely set arched braces, the roof being panelled or plastered.

    Wall-plate: a timber laid longitudinally on the top of a wall.

    Wall-post: vertical posts placed against the side walls, supporting arched braces.

    Wind-braces: pairs of small arched braces joining the purlins and the wall-plate.

Rose window: a circular window with tracery radiating from the centre.

Rosette: a rose-shaped ornament.

Rustication: Large blocks of masonry separated by sunken or chamfered joints.

Sacristy: a room housing sacred vessels, treasures etc.

Saddleback: a tower roof with two gables.

Saltire cross: an equal-limbed diagonal cross.

Sanctuary: the area around the high altar.

Scagliola: an imitation marble, made of cement and colouring matter.

Scallop: decoration on the under surface of a Norman capital in which a series of truncated cones are elaborated.

Scissor-brace: see Roof.

Sedilia: recessed seats for priests in the south wall of the chancel.

Sexfoil: an ornament divided by cusps into six lobes.

Single-framed: see Roof.

Soffit: the ornamental underside of an arch, canopy, ceiling, etc.

Sounding-board: a canopy or tester over the pulpit.

Spandrel: the space between the curve of an arch and enclosing mouldings.

Squinch: a supporting arch displayed across an angle between two walls.

Squint: an oblique hole cut in a wall or pier to enable the altar to be seen from afar.

SS collar: a collar awarded to those in the service of John of Gaunt, Duke of Lancaster in the late 14th century.

Stiff-leaf: Early English type of foliage of many-lobed shapes, on capitals etc.

String-course: a projecting line of moulding running horizontally round the walls of the church or tower.

Stucco: plaster-work.

Sunken star: an early Norman ornamental motif .

Tester: a canopy or sounding-board over the pulpit.

Three-decker pulpit: a pulpit, with clerk's stall and reading-desk below.

Tie-beam: see Roof.

Tierceron: a secondary rib in a vault, springing from the intersection of two other ribs.

Tower arch: an arch usually at the west end of the nave opening into the ground floor of the tower.

Tracery: rib-work in the upper part of a window.

    Curvilinear: tracery consisting of curved lines.

    Geometrical: consisting of circles or foiled leaf-shaped circles.

    Intersecting: each mullion branches into two curved bars.

    Plate: an early form in which openings are cut through the stone in the head of the window, often producing a Y shape.

    Reticulated: in which circles are drawn at top and bottom into ogee shapes producing a net-like pattern.

Transept: transverse portion of a cross-shaped church.

Transitional: the style of building in which Gothic pointed arches exist alongside Norman architecture, typical of 1160 - 1200.

Transom: a horizontal bar across the opening of a window.

Tree of Jesse: in which the genealogy of Jesus is traced back to Jesse, father of King David.

Tree of Life: the motif of a tree sometimes found on Norman tympana.

Trefoil: an ornament divided by cusps into three lobes.

Triforium: an arcaded wall-passage or blind arcading facing the nave at the height of the roof of the aisle, and below the clerestory.

Triglyphs: blocks with vertical grooves in the Doric frieze.

Triptych: a set of three painted panels, hinged together.

Trumpet: a development of scalloped capitals in which each scallop assumes a concave or trumpet shape.

Trussed-rafters: see Roof.

Tufa: a limestone formed by spring-water laden with calcium carbonate bubbling through the rock.

Tuscan columns: one of the classical orders of architecture.

Tympanum: the space over the lintel of a doorway and below the arch above.

Undercroft: a vaulted room below a church.

Vault: an arched roof or ceiling.

    Fan-vault: in which all the ribs springing from their origin are of the same length and curvature and equidistant from each other.

Venetian window: a window with three openings, the central one arched and wider than the outer ones.

Vesica: an oval, with pointed head and foot.

Volute: a spiral scroll, found on Ionic capitals, and also on Norman capitals.

Voussoir: a wedge-shaped stone used in the construction of an arch.

Wagon roof: see Roof.

Wall-plate: see Roof.

Wall-post: see Roof.

Wimple: a veil folded round a woman's head, neck and cheeks.

Wind-braces: see Roof.

Y-tracery: see Tracery, plate.

Zigzag: Norman geometrical decoration found on arches etc.

Bibliography

TWNFC = Transactions of the Woolhope Naturalists' Field Club.

Allen, J.R. 1902 'Early inscribed cross-slab at Llanveynoe, Herefordshire'. *Archaeologia Cambrensis*, LXII, 239.

Annett, D.M. 1999 *Saints in Herefordshire*, Logaston Press, Herefordshire.

Bailey, B.A. 1962 'William Brydges and the rebuilding of Tyberton church', *TWNFC*, 210–221.

Blount 1675 *MS History of Herefordshire*, transcribed by R. and C. Botzum, ed. N.C. Reeves, Lapridge, Hereford.

Boase, T.S.R. 1953 *English Art 1100-1216*, Clarendon Press, Oxford.

Bond, F. 1908 *Fonts and Font Covers*, Oxford University Press.

The Book of Saints Sixth edition, 1989, Cassell.

Brooke, C.N.L. 1994 'The Diocese of Hereford 676–1200', *TWNFC*, 23–36.

Brooks, C. and Saint, A. 1995 *The Victorian Church*, Manchester University Press.

Cautley, H.M. 1937 *Suffolk Churches and Their Treasures*, Batsford, London.

Cave, C.J.P. 1948 *Roof Bosses in Medieval Churches*, Cambridge University Press.

Chatfield, M. 1979 *Churches the Victorians Forgot*, Moorland Publishing Co., Ashbourne, Derbyshire.

Clarke, B.F.L. 1969 *Church Builders of the Nineteenth Century*, David and Charles, Newton Abbot, Devonshire.

Clarke, W.E.H. 1919 'Notes on Bromyard Church', *TWNFC*, 156–158.

Clifton-Taylor, A. 1987 *The Pattern of English Building*, Faber and Faber, London.

Clifton-Taylor, A. 1989 *English Parish Churches as Works of Art*, Oxford University Press.

Coplestone-Crow, B. 1989 *Herefordshire Place-Names*, B.A.R., Oxford.

Cox, D.C. (ed.) 1997 *Sir Stephen Glynne's Church Notes for Shropshire*, University of Keele, Staffordshire.

Davies, W. 1979 *The Llandaff Charters*, The National Library of Wales, Aberystwyth.

Davies, W. 1982 *Wales in the Early Middle Ages*, Leicester University Press.

Day, E.H. 1927 'The preceptory of the Knights Hospitallers at Dinmore', *TWNFC*, 45–76.

Ekwall, E. 1960 *The Concise Oxford Dictionary of English Place-names*, Clarendon Press, Oxford.

Esdaile, K.A. 1946 *English Church Monuments 1510-1840*, Batsford, London.

Fenn, R.W.D. 1968 'Early Christian Heritage in Herefordshire', *TWNFC*, 333–347.

Foster, R. 1981 *Discovering English Churches*, British Broadcasting Corporation, London.

Gardner, A. 1940 *Alabaster Tombs of the Pre-Reformation Period in England*, Cambridge University Press.

Gelling, M. 1992 *The West Midlands in the Early Middle Ages*, Leicester University Press, Leicester.

Gethyn-Jones, E. 1979 *The Dymock School of Sculpture*, Phillimore, Chichester.

Glynne, Sir Stephen *Church Notes for Shropshire* – see Cox, D. C.

Glynne, Sir Stephen *Church Notes for Herefordshire* – to be published shortly.

Greenhill, F.A. 1976 *Incised Effigial Slabs*, Faber and Faber, London.

Grossinger, C. 1997 *The World Upside-down: English Misericords*, Harvey Miller, London.

Harbison, R. 1992 *The Shell Guide to English Parish Churches*, Andre Deutsch, London.

Hillaby, J. 1976 'The Origins of the Diocese of Hereford', *TWNFC*, 16–52.

Hillaby, J. 1993 *The Sculptured Capitals of Leominster Priory*, The Friends of Leominster Priory Church, Leominster.

Hillaby, J. 1997 in *A Definitive History of Dore Abbey* (eds. Shoesmith, R. and Richardson, R.), Logaston Press, Herefordshire.

Howell, P. 1989 in *The Faber Guide to Victorian Churches* (eds. Howell, P. and Sutton, I.), Faber and Faber, London.

Hutton, G. and Smith, E. 1957 *English Parish Churches*, Thames and Hudson, London.

Kemp, B. 1980 *English Church Monuments*, Batsford, London.

Keyser, C.E. 1904 *A List of Norman Tympana and Lintels*, Elliot Stock, London.

King, J.W. 1995 'Two Herefordshire Minsters', *TWNFC*, 282.

Kissack, K. 1996 *The Lordship, Parish and Borough of Monmouth*, Weidenfeld and Nicolson, London.

Knowles, D. and Hadcock, R.N. 1971 *Medieval Religious Houses in England and Wales*, Longman, London

Laing, L and Laing, J. 1996 *Early English Art and Architecture*, Sutton Publishing, Stroud.

Lewis, G.R. 1852 *The Ancient Church of Shobdon*, Pelham Richardson, London.

Lloyd, D. 1999 *The Concise History of Ludlow*, Merlin Unwin Books, Ludlow.

Marks, R. 1993 *Stained Glass in England during the Middle Ages*, Routledge, London.

Marshall, G. 1914 *TWNFC*, 52–53.

Marshall, G. 1918 'Remarks on a Norman tympanum and others in Herefordshire', *TWNFC*, 52–59.

Marshall, G. 1920 'Wooden Monumental Effigies in Herefordshire', *TWNFC*, 189–197.

Marshall, G. 1920 'The Church of Leintwardine', *TWNFC*, 223–231.

Marshall, G. 1924 'The Church of Edvin Ralph and some notes on Pardon Monuments', *TWNFC*, 40–55.

Marshall, G. 1927 'The Church of the Kinghts Templars at Garway, Herefordshire', *TWNFC*, 86-101.

Marshall, G. 1930 'Notes on Kingsland church', *TWNFC*, 21–28.

Marshall, G. 1930–32 'Croft Church, Herefordshire', *TWNFC*, 80–85.

Marshall, G. 1949–51 'Fonts in Herefordshire', *TWNFC*.

Miele, C. 1995 in Brooks and Saint, *op. cit.*

Millward, R. and Robinson, A. 1971 *Landscapes of Britain: The Welsh Marches*, Macmillan, London.

Morris, R. 1989 *Churches in the Landscape*, Dent, London.

Morris, R.K. 1977 'Pembridge and Mature Decorated Architecture in Herefordshire', *TWFNC*, 129–153.

Morris, R.K. 1982 'Late Decorated Architecture in northern Herefordshire', *TWNFC*, 36–58.

Morris, R.K. 1983 in *Studies in Medieval Sculpture* (ed. F.H. Thompson), The Society of Antiquaries, London.

Nash-Williams, V.E. 1950 *The Early Christian Monuments of Wales*, Cardiff.

Pevsner, N. 1963 *Herefordshire* in *The Buildings of England* series, Penguin, Harmondsworth.

Pevsner, N. 1968 W*orcestershire* in *The Buildings of England* series.

Phillott, H.W. 1888 *Diocesan Histories: Hereford*, S.P.C.K., London.

Platt, C. 1981 *The Parish Churches of Medieval England*, Secker and Warburg, London.

Platt. C. 1984 *The Abbeys and Priories of Medieval England*, Secker and Warburg, London

Platt, C. 1990 *The Architecture of Medieval Britain*, Yale University Press, London.

Powell, H.J. 1975 'Renaissance Churches of Herefordshire', *TWNFC*, 318–325.

Reeves, N.C. 1980 *The Leon Valley*, Phillimore, Chichester.

Robinson, J.M. 1995 *Treasures of the English Churches*, Sinclair-Stevenson, London

Rodwell, W. 1989 *Church Archaeology*, Batsford/English Heritage, London.

Royal Commission on Historical Monuments, England (RCHM)
    Herefordshire *Vol. I South-west*, 1931
                    Vol. II East 1932
                    Vol. III North-west, 1934 H.M.S.O. London.
Shoesmith, R. 1988 *Herefordshire Archaeological News*, No.50
Shoesmith, R. 1996 *Castles and Moated Sites in Herefordshire*, Logaston Press, Herefordshire.
Stanford, S.C. 1991 *The Archaeology of the Welsh Marches*, Stanford, Ludlow.
Sitwell, S. 1946 in Esdaile, K.A., *op.cit.*
Stone, L. 1955 *Sculpture in Britain: The Middle Ages*, Penguin, Harmondsworth.
Sylvester, D. 1969 *The Rural Landscape of the Welsh Borderland*, Macmillan, London.
Tasker, E.G. 1993 *Encyclopaedia of Medieval Church Art*, Batsford, London.
Taylor, H.M. and Taylor, J. 1965 *Anglo-Saxon Architecture*, Cambridge University Press, Cambridge.
Thurlby, M. 1980 'The Font at Hope-under-Dinmore', *TWNFC* xliii, 160–163.
Thurlby, M. 1999 *The Herefordshire School of Romanesque Sculpture*, Logaston Press, Herefordshire.
Tilbrook, R. and Roberts, C.V. 1997 *Norfolk's Churches Great and Small*, Jarrold, Norwich.
Tonkin, J.W. 1977 *Herefordshire*, Batsford, London.
Vallance, A. 1936 *English Church Screens*, Batsford, London.
Wade, G.W. and Wade, J.H. 1930 *Herefordshire*, Methuen, London.
West, J. and West, M. 1985 *A History of Herefordshire*, Phillimore, Chichester.
Whiffen, M. 1947–48 *Stuart and Georgian Churches Outside London*, Batsford, London.
Whinney, M. 1988 *Sculpture in Britain 1530–1830*, Penguin, Harmondsworth.
Wilson, D.M. 1984 *Anglo-Saxon Art*, Thames and Hudson, London.
Zarnecki, G. 1951 *English Romanesque Sculpture 1066–1140*, Tiranti, London.
Zarnecki, G. 1953 *Later English Romanesque Sculpture 1140–1210*, Tiranti, London.
Zarnecki, G. 1984 *English Romanesque Art 1066–1200*, Arts Council of Great Britain, Weidenfeld and Nicolson, London.
Zarnecki, G. 1994 *The Priory Church of Shobdon and its Founder* in *Studies in Medieval Art and Architecture*, eds. Buckton, D. and Heslop, T.A., Alan Sutton Publishing, Stroud.
Zarnecki, G. 1998 *The Romanesque sculpture of the Welsh marches in Medieval Art: recent perspectives* (eds. G. Owen-Crocker and T. Graham), Manchester University Press.

References

Origins
1. Fenn, 1968, 333
2. Davies, 1982, 144
3. Millward and Robinson, 1971, 46
4. The Book of Saints, 1989
5. Ekwall, 1960
6. Davies, 1982, 158
7. Gelling, 1982, 80
8. Millward and Robinson, 1971, 43
9. Bede's Ecclesiastical History, quoted by Hillaby, 1976, 17
10. Gelling, 1992, 159
11. Gelling, 1992, 70
12. Gelling, 1992, 160ff
13. West and West, 1985, 35
14. Thurlby, 1999, 42

Romanesque Carving
1. Nash-Williams, 1950
2. RCHM, 1931, 173
3. Allen, 1902, 239
4. Gethyn-Jones, 1979, 54
5. Zarnecki, 1998, 62ff
6. Gethyn-Jones, 1979, 22
7. Zarnecki, 1998, 69
8. Personal communication
9. Marshall, 1918, 56
10. Zarnecki, 1998, 68
11. Wilson, 1984, 155
12. Laing and Laing, 1996, 186
13. Zarnecki, 1994, 219
14. This description and what follows is largely taken from the RCHM, Vol III, 1934, 179
15. This description and what follows is much indebted to the work of Hillaby, 1993
16. Zarnecki, 1953, 11
17. Stone, 1955, 69
18. Allen, quoted by Keyser, 1904, 55
19. Zarnecki, 1953, 14
20. Thurlby, 1999, 90
21. Stone, 1955, 70
22. Zarnecki, 1953, 13
23. RCHM, Vol II, 1932, 27-9
24. Boase, 1953, 83
25. Gethyn-Jones, 1979, 46
26. Marshall, 1949, 18
27. Thurlby, 1999, 126
28. Zarnecki, 1984, 178
29. Thurlby, 2000, ADDED PAGE
30. Personal communication
31. Zarnecki, 1998, 72
32. Morris, 1983, 198
33. Thurlby, 1999, 99

Towers and Spires
1. Pevsner, 1963, 277

Porches
1. Cautley, 1937, 48

Fonts
1. Cautley, 1937, 54
2. Marshall, 1949, 5
3. Gethyn-Jones, 1979, 53
4. Marshall, 1950, 53
5. Marshall, 1950, 62
6. Thurlby, 1980, 87
7. Bond, 1908, 87

Memorials and Monuments
1. Kemp, 1980
2. Marshall, 1920, 189
3. Gardner, 1940, 2
4. Esdaile, 1946, 61
5. Lloyd, 1999, 100; West and West, 1985, 81
6. Whinney, 1988, 273
7. Whinney, 1988, 198
8. Whinney, 1988, 291f
9. Whinney, 1988, 313
10. Whinney, 1988, 337
11. Whinney, 1988, 344

Stained Glass
1. Marks, 1993, 128; Hillaby in Shoesmith and Richardson, 1997, 203
2. Marks, 1993, 76
3. Platt, 1981, 31
4. Marks, 1993, 164
5. Pevsner, 1963, 125
6. Church Guide
7. Hillaby, 1997, 192

Wall -paintings
1. Tilbrook and Roberts, 1997, 95
2. Tasker, 1993, 147
3. Pevsner, 1963, 251

Rood-screens and lofts
1. Vallance, 1936, 41
2. RCHM, Vol I, 1930, 8

Pulpits, Pews and Chancel Furnishings
1. Pevsner, 1963, 46
2. Grossinger, 1997, 42

Medieval styles
1. Clifton-Taylor, 1987, 99
2. Gethyn-Jones, 1979, 5
3. Pevsner, 1963, 29
4. Foster, 1981, 69

5. Morris, 1977, 129
6. Foster, 1981, 161

Monastic Foundations
1. Knowles and Hadcock, 1971, 69
2. Gelling, 1992, 160
3. Thurlby, 1999, 38
4. Knowles and Hadcock, 1971, 68
5. Platt, 1984, 28
6. Platt, 1984, 28
7. Knowles and Hadcock, 1971, 279
8. Pevsner, 1963, 22

Mortimer Country
1. Marshall, 1950, 51
2. Gelling, 1984, 212, 218
3. Marshall, 1914, 52
4. Vallance, 1936, 44
5. Marshall, 1930-32, 80
6. RCHM, Vol III, 1934, 59
7. Marshall, 1920, 227
8. Marshall, 1920, 229
9. West and West, 1985, 50
10. Morris, 1982, 37
11. Shoesmith, 1988, 38
12. Vallance, 1936, 71

Around Leominster
1. Gelling, 1984, 47
2. Marshall, 1951, 72
3. Day, 1927, 45
4. RCHM, Vol II, 1932, 67
5. Greenhill, 1976, 22
6. Glynne, 1870
7. Reeves, 1980, 4; Coplestone-Crow, 1989, 6
8. Marshall, 1930, 21
9. Morris, 1982, 53
10. Blount, 1675
11. Reeves, 1980, 7
12. Marshall, 1951, 71
13. Reeves, 1980, 9
14. Robinson, 1995, 223
15. RCHM, Vol III, 1934, 111
16. Tonkin, 1977, 180
17. Shoesmith, 1996, 162
18. Greenhill, 1976, 235
19. RCHM, Vol III, 1934, 148
20. RCHM, Vol III, 1934, 170; Pevsner, 1963, 273
21. Annett, 1999, 59
22. Pevsner, 1963, 294

Around Bromyard
1. Taylor and Taylor, 1965, 716
2. RCHM, Vol II, 1932, 36; Pevsner, 1963, 92
3. Clarke, 1919, 156
4. Gethyn-Jones, 1979, 53

5. Marshall, 1924, 40
6. Greenhill, 1976, 318
7. Gelling, 1984, 12
8. RCHM, Vol III, 1934, 79
9. Wade and Wade, 1930, 218
10. RCHM, Vol II, 1932, 146
11. Gelling, 1984, 4
12. Coplestone-Crow, 1989, 193
13. RCHM, Vol II, 1932, 191
14. Pevsner, 1963, 303

Black-and-White Villages
1. Ekwall, 1960
2. Pevsner, 1963, 111
3. Morris, 1989, 250
4. RCHM, Vol III, 1934, 50
5. Gelling, 1984, 104
6. Morris, 1977, 129

Upper Wye Valley
1. Greenhill, 1976, 14
2. Shoesmith, 1996, 64
3. Ekwall, 1960
4. Gelling, 1992, 118
5. Thurlby, 1999, 80
6. Pevsner, 1963, 96
7. Shoesmith, 1996, 77
8. RCHM, Vol II, 1932, 95
9. Phillott, 1888, 114
10. Ekwall, 1960
11. Gethyn-Jones, 1979, 5
12. Keyser, 1904, 37
13. RCHM, Vol I, 1930, 204
14. Marks, 1993, 164
15. Glynne

Hereford City and Environs
1. RCHM, Vol II, 1932, 28
2. Ekwall, 1960
3. Grossinger, 1997, 128
4. Stanford, 1991, 100
5. The Oxford Companion to English Literature, 1985
6. Gethyn-Jones, 1979, 68
7. RCHM, Vol II, 1932, 85
8. Grossinger, 1997, 42
9. Marshall, 1951, 94
10. Pevsner, 1963, 195
11. Pevsner, 1963, 207
12. Pevsner, 1963, 243; RCHM, Vol II, 1932, 123
13. Ekwall, 1984
14. Pevsner, 1963, 264
15. Gelling, 1984, 59
16. Pevsner, 1963, 295
17. Clifton-Taylor, 1989, 62
18. Greenhill, 1976, 218, 256
19. Marshall, 1951, 85

20. RCHM, Vol II, 1932, 182
21. Gethyn-Jones, 1979, 74
22. Pevsner, 1963, 298
23. Greenhill, 1976, 21
24. Pevsner, 1963, 323

Around Ledbury
1. RCHM, Vol II, 1932, 19
2. Tasker, 1993, 58-9
3. Sitwell in Esdaile, 1946, 13
4. Pevsner, 1963, 79
5. Whinney, 1988, 430
6. Esdaile, 1946, 59
7. Shoesmith, 1996, 76
8. Taylor and Taylor, 1965, 152
9. King, 1995, 282
10. Kemp, 1980, 22; Plant, 1990, 142
11. Whinney, 1988, 395
12. RCHM, Vol II, 1932, 141
13. Morris, 1989, 249
14. Shoesmith, 1996, 195
15. RCHM, Vol II, 1932, 154;
   Pevsner, 1963, 272

Ewyas and the Golden Valley
1. Pevsner, 1963, 59
2. Pevsner, 1963, 128
3. Shoesmith, 1996, 163
4. Ekwall, 1960
5. Marshall, 1950, 90
6. Annett, 1999, 11
7. Marshall, 1949, 9
8. Greenhill, 1976, 21

Archenfield
1. Ekwall, 1960
2. Marshall, 1927, 86
3. RCHM, Vol I, 1930, 69
4. Marshall, 1927, 86; Pevsner, 1963, 136
5. Shoesmith, 1996, 145
6. Gelling, 1992, 70
7. RCHM, Vol I, 1930, 157
8. Taylor and Taylor, 1965, 350; Thurlby, 1999, 42
9. Morris, 1989, 461
10. Thurlby, 1999, 41
11. Cave, 1948, 196
12. Pevsner, 1963, 238
13. Shoesmith, 1996, 182
14. Gethyn-Jones, 1979, 5
15. Pevsner, 1963, 258
16. The Book of Saints, 1989
17. Taylor and Taylor, 1965, 494
18. Shoesmith, 1996, 202
19. Gelling, 1992, 70; Ekwall, 1960

Around Ross-on-Wye
1. Gethyn-Jones, 1979, 17
2. Gelling, 1984, 113
3. Sylvester, 1969, 350
4. Marshall, 1951, 159, 176
5. Ekwall, 1960
6. Marshall, 1927, lxiii
7. Ekwall, 1960
8. Greenhill, 1976, 135
9. RCHM, Vol II, 1932, 193

Post-Reformation Churches
1. Powell, 1975, 321
2. Ekwall, 1960
3. Whiffen, 1947-48, 39; Bailey, 1962, 217
4. Bailey, 1962, 210; Marshall, 1951, 89
5. King, 1995, 282
6. Hutton and Smith, 1957, 66
7. Pevsner, 1963, 292
8. Whiffen, 1947-8, 44
9. Whiffen, 1947-8, 69
10. Harbison, 1992, 219
11. Gelling, 1984, 41; Ekwall, 1960
12. Shoesmith, 1996, 103
13. Howell, 1989, 41
14. Annett, D.M., pers. comm.
15. Gelling, 1984, 174
16. Davies, 1982, 145, 158; Annett, 1999, 60
17. Marshall, 1949, 4
18. Clarke, 1969, 261
19. Miele in Brooks and Saint, 1995, 162, 165
20. Pevsner, 1963, 97
21. Pevsner, 1963, 269
22. Marshall, 1951, 89
23. RCHM, Vol III, 1934, 52
24. RCHM, Vol I, 1931, 53; Pevsner, 1963, 110
25. Marshall, 1951, 65
26. Pevsner, 1963, 237
27. Howell, 1989, 94
28. Ekwall, 1960
29. RCHM, Vol II, 1932, 153
30. RCHM, Vol II, 1932, 156
31. Annett, 1999, 63

Index

Places are in Herefordshire unless stated otherwise
Bold figures indicate the main entry for each church
arch. = architect
mon. = monument

Also from Logaston Press

Churches of Worcestershire
by Tim Bridges   ISBN 1 873827 56 3   £12.95

Introductory chapters tell of the spread of Christianity across Worcestershire and detail the early development of churches. The major events that affected church building in the county—from new architectural fashions to political upheavals—are detailed to provide a background to the gazetteer that follows. Likewise a history of the changes in internal layout, and of the architects and craftsmen involved in furnishing, design, carving and stained glass is given.

The core of the book is a gazetteer to the Anglican churches of Worcestershire—some 270 in total—allowing this book to be used as a guide when exploring the county. Each entry places the church in its setting, describes the church, gives its building history and details the main decorations, monuments, glass and any notable external features such as lychgates and crosses. As such it is an invaluable aid to explaining what you are seeing—and for ensuring that you don't miss anything on your visit.

Tim Bridges lectures widely on church architecture and history and has gathered together a wealth of information in this book. He works as Collections Manager for Worcester City Museums and has lived in Worcestershire for many years. He also serves as a trustee for the Worcestershire and Dudley Historic Churches Trust, which will financially benefit from the sale of each copy of this book.

With over 140 illustrations.

In Our Dreaming and Singing
The Story of the Three Choirs Festival Chorus
by Barbara Young   ISBN 1 873827 31 8   £6.95

In this book, Barbara Young, for several years a member of the Three Choirs Festival Chorus, explores the origins of that chorus and how it changed to meet the demands of musical taste through three centuries.

This is not a 'dry' book, but a very personal account which will appeal to listeners and singers alike. The story is told from the inside by one who has enjoyed the challenge of learning the greatest works of the choral repertoire, has known the problems posed by new pieces, rehearsed under difficult conditions and felt the excitement and exhilaration of taking part in some memorable performances.

To help tell the tale, the author uses letters and anecdotes from chorus members past and present, and has included many engravings, drawings and photographs.

Also from Logaston Press

Radnorshire from Civil War to Restoration
A study of the county and its environs 1640-60 in a regional setting
by Keith Parker   ISBN 1 973827 86 5 (Pbk) £12.95   ISBN 1 873827 96 2 (Hbk) £18.95

Whilst this book is a record of the social, political, religious and military state of affairs in Radnorshire from before the Civil War to the Restoration, by its nature much reference is made to events in neighbouring counties and further afield. Many of those affecting the course of events in Radnorshire had a base elsewhere, and the military almost universally operated from outside the county.

Keith Parker has made much use of primary sources of information to confound the generally held view that Radnorshire was both a poor county at the time of the Civil War and essentially Royalist in outlook. A more confusing picture emerges of strongly held views by a few on each side, though most notably the pro-Parliamentarians, in a sea of neutrality, bewilderment and opportunism.

This is a story of Radnorshire gentry, farmers and clergymen caught up in an age of both danger and vibrant political and religious debate, when many had a rare chance to shape the future.

Keith Parker, a native of Kington and graduate of Birmingham and London Universities, lives in Presteigne where he was formerly deputy head of John Beddoes School. For many years he has lectured on local history for the Extra-mural Department of the University of Wales, Aberystwyth, and for the Workers' Educational Association. 1997 saw the publication of his popularly acclaimed *A History of Presteigne*, also published by Logaston Press.

The Gale of Life
Essays in the History and Archaeology of South-West Shropshire
ISBN 1 873827 36 9   £6.95

This book comprises twenty essays by a variety of authors with a shared enthusiasm for the history and archaeology of the area. The essays cover Iron Age hillforts, Saxon developments, Offa's Dyke, Roman settlements and roads, the arrival of the Normans, border unrest, vernacular architecture, the Civil War, transport, enclosure, the Community College and much besides.

Published by South-West Shropshire Historical and Archaeological Society in association with Logaston Press.

Also from Logaston Press

Ludlow Castle
Its History & Buildings
Edited by Ron Shoesmith & Andy Johnson   ISBN 1 873827 51 2   £14.95

Ludlow Castle has often played a pivotal role in the history of the Welsh Marches, indeed of the whole of the United Kingdom.

Commenced about 1075 to help control the Welsh border, it became the power base of the de Lacys whose importance escalated on the demise of the fitzOsbern earls of Hereford. The castle became the focus of much bickering for control in the Anarchy, leading to its capture by King Stephen. Subsequently it passed to the de Genevilles, staunch allies of both Edward I and II. When they died without male issue, the castle passed by marriage to the Mortimers. They had risen to prominence under Roger de Mortimer who ruled England as Regent with Edward II's widowed queen, Isabella. The Mortimer family's fortune ebbed and flowed thereafter, their caput being Wigmore Castle, a short distance to the south-west. On the death of Edmund Mortimer in 1425, the Mortimer inheritance passed to Richard, duke of York who was married to Edmund's sister. Ludlow became a favoured residence, and his eldest sons Edward and Edmund spent much their youth at Ludlow. Indeed, on the death of their father at the Battle of Wakefield in the Wars of the Roses, it was from Ludlow that Edward marched to victory at Mortimer's Cross, a few miles to the south, and then advanced on London where he claimed the throne as Edward IV. Ludlow and its castle flourished under its Royal lords. In later years this continued under the Council in the Marches of Wales which lasted from 1534 (when it gained added prestige under Bishop Rowland Lee) to 1689. It was one of the last Royalist garrisons to surrender in the Civil War, was on the point of being used as a PoW camp in the Napoleonic Wars, might have been about to be demolished to make way for a country house, and became a focus of the Picturesque. It still draws devotees.

The buildings themselves are complex, the keep most notably so, with the changes in the structure open to interpretation. Stone built from the beginning, what is now known as the keep started life as an unusual entrance tower. It has undergone extensions, contractions, additions and alterations, during which time the entrance was moved to an adjoining gateway. Towards the end of the 1200s the outer bailey was enclosed in stone, and a new entrance made to the castle which faced east, instead of south, to link directly with the expanding town on the crest of the hill, as opposed to the presumably earlier settlement of Dinham. As the castle's main function moved from that of a castle to that of a royal palace, so it was improved and modernised, and extensively so during the period of the the Council in the Marches of Wales, continuing in use when many of its contemporaries were starting to fall into disrepair.

This book aims to draw together the history of the buildings and its owners to provide a developing picture of the castle and its role in both border and national history and to interpret the changes that occurred in the buildings themselves.

With over 125 colour and black and white illustrations.

Also from Logaston Press

The Herefordshire School of Romanesque Sculpture
by Malcolm Thurlby ISBN 1 873827 60 1 £12.95

This highly illustrated book serves as both a Guide to the surviving work of the Herefordshire School, and provides a history of the school itself.

It compares the surviving work, both in stone and other materials, in Herefordshire, Gloucestershire, Worcestershire and beyond, with that of other styles both at home and abroad— Celtic motifs, Romano-British and Anglo-Saxon work, as well as sculpture in France and Spain.

The sources of inspiration are considered. Clearly the Bible provides some, but by no means all. *The Bestiary*, the Book of Beasts, provides others. Derived from Greek sources translated into Latin, this book described the nature and/or habits of many creatures, both real and fantastic, and reflected on the world of mankind in the realm of nature. The earliest surviving copy of this book is dated *c*.1120, and a copy appears to have used by the patrons of the Herefordshire School.

The book, therefore, also considers who the patrons were and their motives. It looks at the training of the sculptors and their role in the building work, and considers whose hands may have been at work on which sites.

The Herefordshire School of Romanesque Carving is an attempt to bring together the people behind the work, both patrons and carvers, with the architectural and sculptural styles in order to provide a comprehensive picture of the whole.

Contains over 240 illustrations.

Saints in Herefordshire
by D.M. Annett   ISBN 1 873827 26 1   £4.95

This book started as a supposedly simple task of listing all the dedications of Herefordshire churches, together with a note on the life of each saint. It proved to be much less straight forward than expected, as more and more churches were found to have had their dedications changed at some unspecified date. What has therefore emerged is a picture of dedications sometimes changing with ecclesiastical fashion, and sometimes through disuse and the often mistaken attempts of 18th-century antiquarians to recover them.

Herefordshire is peculiar amongst English counties, along with Cornwall, in having many churches dedicated to Celtic saints, and brief biographies of these, as well as of biblical and legendary saints, are included. The illustrations (with one exception) are taken from stained glass in churches in the diocese of Hereford.

It is hoped that this book can be enjoyed by anyone with an interest in Herefordshire's history and its churches, while a wealth of reference material has been provided for those who want to delve more deeply into the subject.